Another kind of space:
creating ecological dwellings and environments

Alan Dearling with Graham Meltzer

Another kind of space: creating ecological dwellings and environments

First published in 2003

Enabler Publications
3 Russell House
Lym Close
Lyme Regis
Dorset, UK DT7 3DE
01297 445024 (phone and fax)

Compiled by Alan Dearling with Graham Meltzer

ISBN: 0 9523316 5 9

Printed in the UK by Hobbs the Printers, Totton, Hampshire, on paper derived from sustainable sources

Cover design by Andy Wood with Alan Dearling. Front cover provided by Tony Wrench of the Brithdir Mawr roundhouse. Back cover illustration by Marianne Gibson, and photos provided by Graham Meltzer, Ezmerelda, Claudia Newman, Peter Cock and Bob Rich, David Renwick Grant, John Talbot, Alan Dearling and Jake Bowers-Burbridge. Photos in text include contributions from Selena Merrett, c/o 97 Westonfields, Bridgetown, Totnes, Devon TQ9 5UA. The photo by Alan Dearling used in the section title pages is of a part of the Sculpture garden at the Broomhill Art Hotel, near Barnstaple, North Devon, England.

Contents

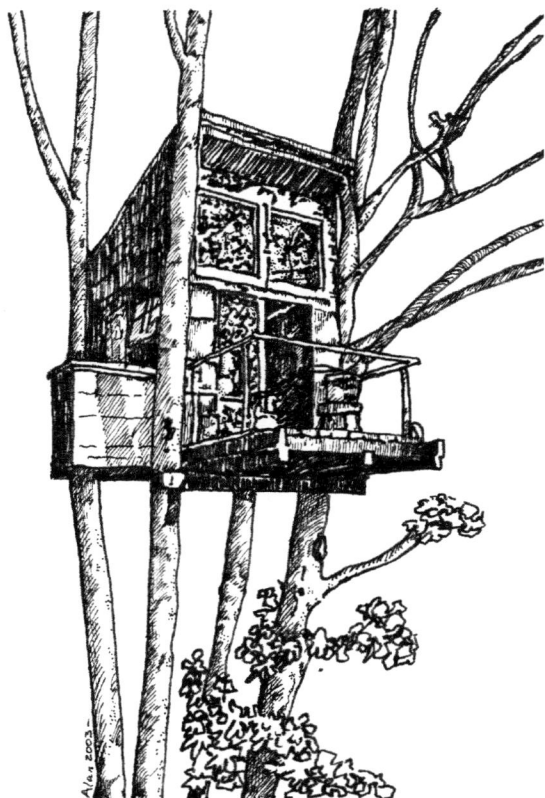

ii

Foreword

Thanks for sending me the material from this book, which I have read with a great deal of interest. I think it is a very good combination of the more adventurous and the more conventional approaches to new ways of sustainable living, and links in one book approaches that are normally treated very separately. For this reason it should appeal to a wide audience. It is interesting to see the likes of low impact villages rubbing shoulders with intentional communities, scrap rafts, eco-tourism, modern nomads and members of the international green community. We published a book on Housing and the Environment a few years ago, which proved to be one of our best sellers, so I see no reason why this shouldn't be equally popular given its broad appeal.

John

John Perry
Director of Policy
Chartered Institute of Housing
Octavia House
Westwood Way
Coventry, UK CV4 8JP

Acknowledgements

It was millennium Y2K. I was sitting sipping an ice cold drink on the verandah of Bill Metcalf's Queenslander, colonial-style wooden house, in the West End of Brisbane, Australia. Bill had been telling me about his recent experiences on visits to intentional communities around the world in his role as President of the International Communal Studies Association. In return, I'd been sharing 'tales from the edge' concerning alternative life-stylers of Europe, Australia, India and beyond. Different worlds, but frequently linked by people's desire to live more communally, more simply and more 'lightly' on the planet's surface. So to Bill – thanks for being there at the genesis of this book!

A book such as this is very much a co-operative effort. Thanks and respect are due to all the contributors for sharing their tales of eco-dwelling around the world. Especial thanks are due to Graham Meltzer for facilitating my stay in the School of Design and Built Environment at Queensland University of Technology. QUT, as it is known, kindly provided me with a base from where I began to make contact with potential contributors. Graham and myself also used this time to draw up the initial plans for the contents of the book, and Graham did his best to work with a less-academically inclined Pom!

Also in Australia, lots of hugs go to Liz and Kim Hall-Downs for reviving my sometimes flagging spirits at their personal woodland Utopia in southern Queensland. A part of me is still with you. Likewise, a variety of 'locals' in the New Farm area of Brisbane, and particularly in the Brunswick Hotel, befriended me and helped me to 'bounce' ideas off them about lifestyles and environments.

Back in the UK, David Fotheringham and John Perry, two of my colleagues at the Chartered Institute of Housing, 'kept the faith' and provided me with useful feedback on the book as it gradually evolved. Phil Bayliss, Julie Harvey, Andy (Ed) Wood and Dave Kelf were essential parts of my personal life-support system when I got a bit low and wanted a sympathetic ear or two!

Selena Merrett was kind enough to allow the use of some of her photos of eco-homes and Marianne Gibson painted the original design that forms part of the back cover. Finally, as ever, a word of thanks to my long-suffering partner, Christine – never live with a full-time writer/researcher, she'd warn...

And a quick note on spellings and the use of words: I've tried to adopt a 'light' touch with the editorial pen. English spellings and language vary around the world. I've left a fair amount of that cultural variety and richness in place.

Enjoy!

luv n' respect

Alan Dearling
February 2003, Lyme Regis, Dorset, UK

Introduction

Introduction
Alan Dearling and Graham Meltzer

At different levels, and for different audiences, this book offers a window into a better world. It contains a fascinating and inspirational selection of dwellings, living spaces and environments from around the globe, all of which are deliberately fashioned by individuals and communities seeking to live in greater harmony and awareness with each other and the natural world. Some of these dwellings provide shelter for nomadic travellers; some are situated on communes and intentional communities; others are in cohousing and organic settlements; some are sited in rainforests, caves and on floating structures; still more provide homes to rural and urban individuals, households and groups who are keen to find 'another way' of living.

Overall, the book provides an insight into some of the 'whys' and 'wherefores' of ecological dwellings – particularly focusing on the personal motivations and lifestyles of the people who have chosen to build and live in them. These initiatives have not taken place in isolation from the rest of urban, rural and global development. 'Big' issues such as population expansion,

Walter Segal timber framed self-build home (Selena Merrett)

environmental pollution, employment trends and transport developments are also parts of the wider canvas on which housing and lifestyle choices (or lack of them) are a part. Indeed, every new day supplies us with media coverage of local, national and international initiatives in environmental, economic and social arenas that have impact, both positive and negative, on all aspects of planetary life. It is frequently difficult to make sense, on the basis of these

commentaries and reportage, of the complex and contradictory developments taking place.

Unfortunately, and not a little confusingly, even the terms used: *'environment', 'sustainability', 'low-impact', 'green', 'alternative and intermediate technology'* and many more, are subject to widely varying interpretations. For conservationists and environmental activists 'low-impact' can mean protecting a piece of land from any development; whereas for nomadic people, it may mean living on the land in temporary dwellings which leave no lasting imprint. For 'green' architects a low-impact dwelling may mean building in a way that is sensitively integrated into the natural landscape, but for planners, it may mean building upwards to provide higher density accommodation.

You start to see the contradictions.

...personal views and alternative dwelling ...

This is a very personal book. It offers personal responses to divergent worldviews. It is also personal in the sense that we, the authors, believe passionately that its content is important, and personal in the sense that elements of our own lives have provided much of the rationale for the choices we've made about the contents. Without going into detail, the contents reflect the fact that Graham has been a longstanding member of intentional communities, an innovator in the cohousing movement and is now, a 'green' architect who teaches (socially and environmentally responsive) community design in Australia. Alan, as a youth and community worker, full time writer and university researcher of over 20 books, and contributor to the UK and European counter cultural and housing scene, brings to the book, a different set of experiences. Both have travelled extensively and actively use the Internet as an additional and powerful medium to communicate with people across the world.

Particularly since the early 1990s, questions about sustainability and the need for development with low environmental impact, have provided key challenges for planners, policy makers and housing professionals. Living holistically, in environmentally sensitive dwellings has become a focus for those striving to establish a lifestyle that reflects their social and environmental concerns. It is no longer just a part of an abstract, theoretical, semantic,

The prototype for Roger Dean's Willowater village in the UK (John Talbot)

academic or even utopian debate. In response, Part Two of this book offers divergent views and varied experiences of a range of 'alternatives'. These are personal accounts of the lives and lifestyles with which 'dwellings' are inextricably bound. They are also 'warts and all' in the sense that they include accounts of what goes wrong, practical limitations to 'greenness', as well as recounting the 'good times'. One of the messages at the heart of the book is that the relationship between people and their dwellings can be far more proactive and positive than previously imagined. How we build, use, and develop our dwelling spaces is a matter of lifestyle *choice*.

...there is 'another way'...

This book provides a wide range of contributions and examples that show that there is 'another way' – a number of ways, in fact. Across the globe, hundreds of thousands of people have

A local dwelling in Cavus, Turkey (Alan Dearling)

put extraordinary levels of thought and ingenuity into a diverse range of alternative types of homes and shelter. Some are based on the indigenous dwellings and lifestyles of tribal people. At the other end of the spectrum are

complex dwellings designed by a new wave of 'green' architects. Their commonality is frequently some kind of environmental ethos and aspiration. These dwellings are lifestyle statements – highly personal, frequently celebratory – shelters integral to other aspects of the occupants' lives. In a very real sense they are ecological, hence our choice of the term 'eco-dwellings', as a way of describing them in one, catch-all phase! Some are conceived and made a reality within a tribal, communal or cohousing social setting, the creative interactions contributing to the 'social

Eco-tourist tents at Byron Bay, Australia (Alan Dearling)

sustainability' of that community. Others are much more individualistic, even hedonistic, ranging from slightly eccentric living structures built in inaccessible spots in forests, mountains or underground, through to expensive, high-tech solutions to energy efficiency and sustainable living.

...inspiration, options and ideas...

To start with in Part One, we set the scene by offering our own contribution to the debate on issues such as environmentalism, design, energy efficiency, appropriate technology, sustainability, community and communality, nomadism and other development issues such as those identified in Agenda 21 of the 1992 Rio de Janeiro Earth Summit document. The examples presented in Part Two of *Another kind of space,* collectively offer a glimpse into the social realities and the personal stories lying behind the physical nature of ecological dwellings. At a time of increasing social alienation and dysfunction, we sincerely hope that the examples in the book can offer inspiration, options and ideas for people wishing to make an important and personally meaningful contribution to sustainable development.

Alan and Graham

This book belongs to, and is dedicated equally to, those who are already an active part of the eco-dwelling community and to those people who would like to learn a little more about their options and opportunities for developing more appropriate dwellings and living spaces for their own, and the planet's future.

A home in the intentional community at Bhodi Farm, New South Wales, Australia (Alan Dearling)

Part One

Kindred spirits and environmentalism

Graham Meltzer and Alan Dearling

"What we most need to do is to hear within ourselves the sounds of the Earth crying."
Thich Nhat Hanh

This section acts as a gateway to the book as a whole. It provides a preview of the contents to follow and, as its title suggests, two distinct routes into the subject matter.

...kindred spirits...

People who choose to live in ecological dwellings are often regarded, and/or regard themselves, as 'kindred spirits'. They are all seekers of some kind, pro-actively making lifestyle choices to reduce their personal 'ecological footprint'. Many see themselves working collaboratively and more co-operatively than others, beyond the confines of our predominantly individualistic, conventional society. Some of them live in communities, sharing their environmental aspirations with relatively like-minded members of a location-based group.

Cordwood House, built by Ben Law in Sussex, UK, but based on Hopi mandan lodge design with 99 per cent of the materials found in a half mile radius (Selena Merrett)

Others act autonomously (some are even reclusive) but still they see themselves as participants in a common project to 'save the planet'. Clearly this is not a homogeneous group. In fact, the attitudes and motivations represented are extremely diverse, even oppositional at times, as you'll see from the contributions! The dwelling types of these 'kindred spirits', and their lifestyle

intentions, are frequently a part of their 'spirituality' and invariably express their individuality.

Despite the diversity (some would say, because of it) these various participants together constitute a cohesive 'social movement'. Arguably, they strive for common ends and exhibit a collective consciousness. Their lifestyle choices invariably place them at odds with many of society's institutions. Deliberately or not, they openly oppose and combat the status quo, and it is the act of contestation rather than the different modes of action that characterises this particular social movement. Indeed, social movements generally, are said to be characterised by the contentious actions of *"people who lack regular access to institutions, act in the name of new or unaccepted claims, and behave in ways that fundamentally challenge others"* (Tarrow, 1994). This is a fitting description of almost all the contributors to this book, and supports our belief that the actions of ordinary people often speak louder than the words of intellectuals. As Hutton and Connors (1999) suggest,

> *"A scientist or a bureaucrat may share the movement's values and even contribute to the development of new cultural models and understandings but, unless they have engaged in contestation, they are not part of the movement."*

The range of kindred spirits actually encompass a disparate variety of lifestyles. These lifestyles include people engaging in organic farming and demonstration building projects; recycling and reclamation; intentional communities; and campaigning for environmental action and/or the right to choose a lifestyle, including being nomadic.

...environmentalism...

Concern in the West about damage to the environment has existed for longer than is usually acknowledged. In Britain, national conservation groups have existed since the middle of the nineteenth century. Since then, moments of heightened concern about environmental issues, during the 1890s, 1920s, late 1950s, early 1970s and mid-1990s have coincided with periods of high economic growth and material consumption when degradation of the immediate environment was at its most dramatic.

Historians suggest that the success of Rachael Carson's *Silent Spring* in the late 1960s, and/or *Earth Day* in 1970, marked the arrival of sustained and widespread public awareness of environmental degradation.

Environmentalism, as we have already suggested, is hard to pin down in a simple phrase. At various times over the last 30 years, and in different places, a range of problems have assumed ascendancy in popular consciousness. In the 1970s it was population growth and the supply of resources, whilst in the 1980s global warming and ozone depletion received more attention. In the 1990s habitat loss and species diversity dominated the debate and, currently globalisation and genetic modification of foods are predominant. In Europe, nuclear power, acid rain and water pollution have received most attention. In America, it's been air pollution, chemical toxicity and urban blight, whereas in Australia, loss of wilderness, mineral extraction and soil salinity have dominated the environmental debate. The range of issues is reflected in the diversity of environmentalist organisations representing a host of overlapping ideologies and cross-currents, such as Friends of the Earth, Earth First!, The Sierra Club, Greenpeace, Reclaim the Streets and Corporate Watch. It has also spawned a considerable selection of commentators and writers including the likes of David Bellamy, Jonathon Porritt, Arne Naess, John Seed, John Seymour and Herbert Giradet.

As a movement, environmentalism is both a gathering force for proponents, and a target for opponents. Compare, for example, a description by the US National Environmental Policy Institute of the 'new environmentalism' as, *"a consensus for change"* and that *"the future starts now…with collaboration, innovation and creativity"*, with that of the Ayn Rand Institute, which states that,

"environmentalism has become the gravest threat to human survival" because it is *"opposed to science, technology, and economic development."*

Surrounding the environmental debate there is a spectrum of 'green' political opinion ranging from a *technocentric* view of the environment as a valued resource which, on the basis of political negotiation, is available for the purposes of economic growth, through to an *ecocentric* one which perceives the environment not as a commodity, but non-negotiable and in need of active protection. Whilst this analysis incorporates economic and political theory that is not the domain of this book, it is worth mentioning as part of the wider context within which environmentally-orientated planning and development decisions are made in the industrialised countries of the world.

Allotments are one resource benefiting both the community and individuals (Alan Dearling)

…working for positive change…

As serious as each may be, singular environmental threats seem no longer to be the most pressing consideration. Separately, many of these threats are being addressed through conventional or other means. Rather, it is the confluence of so many different environmental problems that now appears to be the greater concern. Many active environmentalists – whether they are natural negotiators or confrontationists – now look to holistic, 'joined up thinking' as the optimal response. For many of the less politically motivated, lifestyle choice has become the means of expressing environmentalist aspirations. Accordingly, this book is concerned with how environmentalism can be translated into aspects of everyday life. This is not a prescriptive approach, rather, it embraces lateral thought and responsive action. For each individual and community this will be embodied in a range of choices about their:
- place of residence and the nature of their dwelling;

- energy consumption and mode of transportation;
- economic activity (employment) and recreational pursuits;
- partners, neighbours, friends and associates; and
- membership of social and political groups and organisations.

The kindred spirits represented in this book, work *pro-actively* for positive changes in the way humanity inter-relates with the environment. Their efforts include smaller and greater actions, rendered individually and collectively, to repair, maintain and improve nature's delicate balance. Our focus is mostly, though not entirely focused geographically, economically and socially on the so-called 'developed' world, particularly Western Europe, North America and Australasia. It is our world that is causing the greatest threats to the environment, and therefore it is from here that we have sought partial solutions and positive action at both the collective and individual level.

For many whose stories appear in Part Two, it is their lifestyle choices that offer a measure of their environmentalism. Their lifestyles are symbolic of their expressions of concern for the environment, and commitment to shades of 'greenness' – another spectrum of opinion. If we are deep green, then we expect (in the absence of extreme remedial action) some form of environmental apocalypse. A lighter shade of green presupposes that the Earth's ecosystems can be protected with minimal assistance from the people living on its surface. For many of the contributors to the book, their dwellings reflect their personal responses to these fundamental, often ideological issues which, in themselves, pose a raft of questions such as:

- *Land tenure.* Ownership or stewardship? Should we own land or keep it in trust for future generations? Is private ownership the best or preferred form of tenure? What other options exist?
- *Environmental footprint.* What is the impact of our dwelling and lifestyle on the environment? How could it be improved or modified?
- *Economic and social position.* To what extent is our dwelling a commodity and/or a status symbol? Can we afford to live in the dwelling and the location we would like? What other social and economic restraints do we face?
- *Collective versus individual action.* Are we, or should we be, seeking more collaborative or individualistic solutions? To what extent, and in

Demonstration garden at the Big Green Gathering (Alan Dearling)

what circumstances, is collaboration an advantage or a disadvantage?

- *Environmental activism versus negotiation.* Dwelling 'style' can represent very real lifestyle and political choices, relating to power, social inclusion or exclusion, enfranchisement and citizenship, and a wider commitment to either negotiated or confrontational environmental action.

...if we don't do our very best then we must take the blame...

This book offers examples of individual and collective responses to the above difficult and frequently divisive questions. These lifestyle options are very diverse, but they have something in common as well. It is worth remembering that while it is easy to be pessimistic and think that *'they'* are not going to do anything to halt the path of environmental destruction, *we* do so at our peril. Actually, 'we' are 'they', as Alan's mate, George Firsoff (1996), editor of *Greenleaf* magazine, explains, "*We can choose, we must choose, which of these ways we want, and act in accordance. As men and women of power...if we don't do our very best we [must] take the blame.*"

References
Firsoff, G. (1996), *Greenleaf* magazine. www.greenleaf.demon.co.uk
Hutton, D. and Connors, L. (1999) *A History of the Australian Environment Movement.* Cambridge University Press.
Lowe, P. and J. Goyder. (1983) *Environmental Groups in Politics.* George, Allen and Unwin.
Tarrow, S. (1994) *Power in Movement: Social Movements, Collective Action and Politics.* Cambridge University Press.

The agony of the long distance environmentalist
Graham Meltzer and Alan Dearling

...the problems are generally well-proven...

The severity and global scale of environmental degradation is now worryingly clear to most people. This process of degradation is linked with factors such as population growth, the reduction in scarce resources, and the disposal of wastes. Through the media we are constantly reminded of the effect of industrial and agricultural wastes in poisoning lakes, rivers and oceans. Climate change as a result of global warming and its potential for widespread destruction is now well established, if not fully understood, and is accepted by all but a few recalcitrants. The danger of chemical residues in food has long been proven, although the pros and cons of genetic modification are still hotly debated. There is undeniable evidence of farmland degradation due to soil salinity, topsoil erosion and the unrelenting encroachment of urban development. Our remaining rainforests and wilderness areas continue to be destroyed, resulting in further loss of species diversity, which in turn affects planetary health and stability (see for instance Porritt, 1990 and 1991).

A west London estate (Alan Dearling)

There is a different, but related, set of concerns about our quality of life. Extremes of noise, air, and visual pollution in our cities degrade the qualities of urban space and, therefore, social engagement and civic life. Indices of social dysfunction (e.g. depression, suicide and violent crime) continue to rise. Around the world, and for millions of people, there is a lack of choice and a very real sense of alienation from one's personal living environment. In developed countries, domestic life amounts to little more than 'making-do' with housing that is inappropriate to people's needs. Particularly for the economically prosperous, consumerism dominates contemporary life, resulting in many homemakers cramming an excessive quantity of material goods into ill-fitting, pre-packaged dwellings.

...and, we are aware of the problems...

In industrialised societies, concern about environmental problems is at an all-time high, and the same is increasingly true of developing countries. Most people know something of the nature and extent of these problems, and according to recent surveys, awareness is still rising. In North America, for instance, polls have consistently shown that around 80 to 90 per cent of the public are concerned about the state of the environment. Recent Australian surveys have shown similar results with both the Australian Bureau of Statistics and the Australian National Opinion Poll finding that about 75 per cent of people are deeply worried about environmental degradation. In the West, concern for the environment has become virtually a cultural condition and is now a permanent feature of public discussion and debate.

Levels of concern do not seem to vary much with demographic differences such as class, race, location and levels of affluence. Indeed *"improved environmental quality benefits the poor as much as, if not more, than it does the new middle classes – even if the latter...form the vanguard of the movement"* (Goodin, 1992). There is mounting evidence to suggest that 'the poor' are aware of this and are prepared to pay disproportionately more of their income in remedies. By one calculation, someone with an income just above the poverty level would be willing to spend (as a proportion of income) something like eight times as much on controlling water pollution, for example, as someone with a middle-level income (Goodin, *ibid.*).

...yet, we do little about it...

Most people are aware of the *causes* of environmental degradation. Human behaviour – high consumption lifestyles, in particular – in combination with continued population growth, are the generally recognised root causes. So the questions must be asked:

- Why isn't such widespread awareness and concern being converted into a wave of environmentalist activity at the household, neighbourhood and community level?
- Why are people generally not changing their (consumerist) behaviour to better accord with their beliefs?
- Why don't more people agitate for pro-environmental action at national and international levels?

Practical 'environmentalism' is often portrayed as either a middle-class pursuit or the battleground of direct action protestors. Both perceptions act as barriers to involvement for many. However, we believe that the principal reason is an absence of 'ownership' or 'stake-holding' of both the problems and the potential solutions, at a personal, local and grass roots level.

Despite general agreement about their causes, there is still considerable disagreement about what should be done to address environmental problems. An apparent lack of agreement amongst reported 'experts' contributes to the confusion. Polls have suggested that 20 to 30 per cent of people in the US believe that good progress has been made in dealing with environmental problems, but a further 40 to 50 per cent believe that ground is being lost. One source of the confusion may be the very enormity of the environmental literature, and its emphasis on the scale of environmental problems such global warming and the effects of carbon dioxide emissions. Probably because the scale of the problems seem so immense and the solutions so removed from our day-to-day lives, the majority of people feel disempowered and struggle to find strategies for

positive, individual and local, environmental action. Richards got to the heart of the matter when he said:

> *"Intellectuals, development agencies and governments have all pursued environmental management problems at too high a level of abstraction and generalisation. Many environmental problems are, in fact, localised and specific and require local, ecologically particular, responses"* (Richards, 1985).

...the grip of consumerism...

Another source of people's ambivalence seems to be the challenge (or threat) that environmentalist strategies may appear to present to many people's basic values. Of the generally recognised dual causes of environmental degradation, consumption and population growth, only the latter is openly acknowledged by governments and citizens alike. Consumption is almost universally portrayed in a positive light, as the essence of the 'American dream', the 'Australian dream' and, for that matter, the 'Western European dream'. As a part of economic growth and development, it is seen as a 'just reward' and a 'right' in democratic nations. Our lifestyles are embedded in a materialist view of the world – one which embraces conspicuous consumption, profligate car use, and the other trappings of 'success'. Continuous economic growth and accelerated consumerism goes unchallenged. Living with less, in a simpler way, is so contrary to deeply

With breathable walls and high insulation properties, straw bale dwellings such as this one built in Gloucestershire by Jim Wallis of the ABC Building Company can be very rustic in appearance with its turf roof (Selena Merrett)

ingrained values and aspirations (of material comfort and personal status) as to be difficult for most Westerners to comprehend, let alone enact.

Consumerism, defined in the Oxford Dictionary as, a *"preoccupation with consumer goods and their acquisition"* is derived from a basic principle of neo-classical economics, namely, the association of personal fulfilment and happiness with the possession and consumption of material goods. Over the last 150 years, human values have fundamentally shifted from *"the world of life and its productivity"* to *"the world of things and their amassment"* (Fromm, 1965). Basic human attributes of creativity and a sense of oneself as a useful member of society have slowly been supplanted with satisfactions of the market-place. Fulfilment of need has become associated with the consumption of commodities, entertainment, and substances, such as luxury foods, alcohol and drugs. A social and cultural void has developed, that is now filled with popular entertainment, recorded music, and prescribed radio and television infotainment. *"Consuming is essentially the satisfaction of artificially stimulated fantasies, a fantasy performance alienated from our concrete, real selves"* (Fromm, *ibid.*).

To make the necessary cultural shift toward environmental sustainability will require people to closely examine their own lives, lifestyles and the functioning of their neighbourhoods and communities. Ultimately, it will call for a very significant behavioural and lifestyle change in Western industrialised societies. For the deep ecologists, this will only be achieved when people fully discover their own intimate connection with the Earth and all living things. What John Seed refers to as *thinking like a mountain."* (1988)

...behavioural change, why is it so difficult...

There appears to be little association between people's professed concern for the environment and changes in their behaviour, let alone their lifestyle. Knowledge about environmental problems and responses present personal conflicts for many

people. Many are discouraged from getting involved in making their lifestyles and dwellings more environmentally 'friendly' by perfectly understandable fears. They are worried about the inconvenience involved, concerned about the disadvantages for them personally, and dubious about the effectiveness of conservationist and other green activities. Where they do adopt particular practices, inevitably there is often little consistency of approach. At best, people pick and choose between practices such as recycling, energy conservation and efficiency, car-pooling, cycling, tree-planting, organic growing, green consumerism and involvement in campaigning and direct action environmental organisations. Perhaps the 'marketing' of environmentalism is partly to blame. It is often branded as a righteous 'good cause' – its adoption providing a salve to the conscience. Instead, rather like with sport or music, perhaps it needs to be sold as 'enjoyable', 'healthy' and something we want to do. Green festivals and gatherings, demonstration centres for alternative technologies and even some forms of eco-tourism may help to provide a bridge into environmental lifestyles.

The connection between an individual's values and beliefs and their intentions and behaviour has been studied by behavioural psychologists for a long time, yet there is still little understanding of people's motivation for adopting particular activities that impact on the environment. The vast majority of research into the link between environmental attitudes and pro-environmental behaviour has been narrowly focused. There have been very few holistic studies that have related personal behaviour with social or political context, let alone, lifestyle. Yet, if a full understanding is to be sought, the social and lifestyle context of positive environmental behaviour is critical, for it can have substantial influence on motivation and effectiveness.

...beginning to make a difference...

How then, can we begin to create the sea change and cultural shift that is necessary? People's behaviour does not change overnight. And for those involved in trying to bring about a change in environmental consciousness, it is pragmatic to accept that attitudes and behaviour are only going

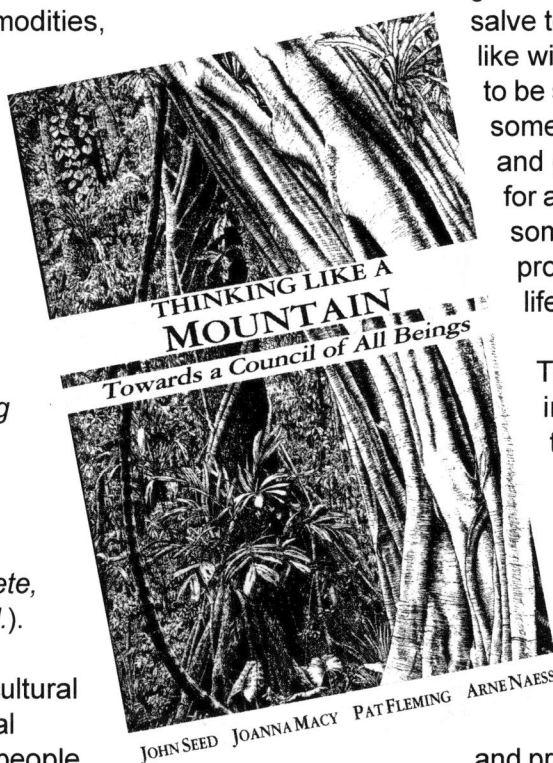

THINKING LIKE A MOUNTAIN
Towards a Council of All Beings

JOHN SEED   JOANNA MACY   PAT FLEMING   ARNE NAESS

Children playing simply at an eco-festival (Alan Dearling)

sketchy;
- green goods are generally more expensive; and perhaps most importantly,
- the problem of environmental degradation is exacerbated by *levels,* and not *forms* of consumption. A 'limits to growth' perspective demands reduced levels of consumption, not rearranged consumption patterns (Martell, 1994).

For radical environmentalists, the task is to generate enough public, popular stake-holding in a gradual rejection of high consumption lifestyles. This is, in part, dependent upon education through activism. For instance, in many parts of Europe, well ahead of the USA and Australia, a hard-hitting direct action campaign against the testing of genetically modified crops, coupled with high profile opposition (even from the UK's Prince Charles) has led to an almost complete ban on GM products on the shelves of many supermarkets. Similarly, radical green activists attracted media and popular support against the massive UK road-building programme in the 1990s. Prime Minister Margaret Thatcher had said that *"nothing can stop the great car economy",* The protestors helped to change public and political opinion, whilst their direct action tactics made the costs of road construction much higher for construction companies. By 1996, according to George Monbiot,

> *"...the road building budget had been cut to*

to be changed when there is the will to make the change. This pragmatism may translate, for instance, into the acceptance that 'green' consumerism' may have some part to play in this gradual continuum of change. For instance, in support of green consumerism, it might be argued that:
- not all forms of consumption are environmentally damaging;
- reduced consumption can not be reasonably or easily applied across the board, or fairly expected of third world countries;
- as a result of consumerist demand, more organically grown produce is now available in the market place;
- similarly, more people now consider vegetarianism and their dietary needs more carefully;
- green consumers wield a considerable amount of political clout;
- locally produced goods provide employment and reduce transport costs;
- fair trade agreements with developing countries can provide ethically produced goods available to the industrialised markets; and
- green consumerism can be a first step to a deeper understanding and commitment.

However, a more radical analysis would argue that:
- any kind of consumerism reinforces material acquisitiveness;
- consumerism locks people into a cycle of working – to consume – to having to work – so as to *never* enjoy the benefits;
- information on which goods are genuinely environmentally benign is

Fairmile road protest site (Greta Gunnarsson)

just £6 billion, saving the taxpayer £17 billion, and the fabric of the nation some of the most monstrous abominations ever proposed…It's a remarkable victory, one of the few genuine triumphs that people power has ever enjoyed" (in the Introduction to Evans, 1998).

This book argues that *social* and *lifestyle* satisfaction can more than substitute for material acquisition. The somewhat shallow satisfaction provided by consumption needs to be replaced by satisfaction of a less material kind. We believe that such satisfaction is most likely to occur if it is an intrinsic part of one's lifestyle rather than incidental to it.

We mentioned *social dysfunction* earlier. One way of helping to counteract it is through people actively making their choice of dwelling as an integral part of their lifestyle choice.

Hundertwasser haus in Vienna – a creative mix of art and environmentalism (Claudia Newman)

Aesthetics are a part of this too. Living in an austere box may be ecologically defensible on the grounds that is energy efficient, low impact and sustainable – but homes must also allow for, and reflect, artistic preferences. The creations of a number of the environmental architects and designers featured in this book, such as Hundertwasser, Dean, the Vales, Bender and Manrique exemplify this point. Affordable homes are vital, but so too are homes worth living in. Many of Hundertwasser's housing designs featured grass roofs and trees as central elements of their structures. Hundertwasser said that dwellings are 'a work of art in progress' (in Restany, 2001).

In the following section, we continue this discussion of the potential for the integration of environmentalist aspirations with lifestyle choice.

References

Evans, K. (1998) *Copse: a cartoon book of tree protesting.* Orange Dog Productions.

Fromm, E. (1965) *The Sane Society.* Routledge & Kegan Paul.

Goodin, R. E. (1992) *Green Political Theory.* Polity Press.

Martell, L. (1994) *Ecology and Society.* Polity Press.

Porritt, J. (1990) *Where on Earth are we Going?* BBC Books.

Porritt, J. (1991) *Save the Earth.* Dorling Kindersley.

Restany, P. (2001) *Hundertwasser: the painter-king with five skins.* Taschen.

Richards, P. (1985) *Indigenous Agricultural Revolution.* Hutchinson.

Seed, J. *et al.* (1988) *Thinking like a mountain: towards a council of all beings.* New Society Publishers.

Integrating dwelling AND lifestyle WITH environmentalism
Alan Dearling with contributions from Graham Meltzer

'Phew', we thought, as we revisited the title of the section, 'a pretty tall order'!

In fact, this is what *was* historically achieved in many countries of the world, in the creation of totally appropriate local dwellings, suited to the setting and lifestyles of the local people. Rudofsky (1964) characterises these as *"undesigned shelters."* One example is the conical stone cassellas and trullos in Apulia in Italy. Such designs were achieved with respect for the natural environment in which they were constructed. They are indigenous architecture – buildings which have shaped people – as well as being buildings shaped by people. As one of the most famous architects of recent times said towards the end of his life, *"You know; it is always life that is right and the architect who is wrong"* (in Wines, 2000). These buildings combined simple functionality with grace. Now, they are being replaced as Edward Allen (1969) has said, by, *"flat-topped rectangular boxes"* in the 20th century's 'superstone' – concrete. It has produced what Allen calls, *"towns without souls".*

This is the challenge that many if not all of the contributors to this book have faced in their choices of dwelling spaces. The struggle continues and together with many of our contributors, we've been there ourselves, as you'll see later in the personal stories in Part Two of this book.

Greek vernacular architecture

...and so, on to sustainability...

As you read through the individual stories in Part Two of this book, it will become increasingly clear that underpinning the cultural, social and economically diverse range of eco-dwellers, their homes and lifestyles, are the key concepts of sustainability and environmental impact. The range of dwellings include very low impact nomadic dwellings through to high technology Smart houses, and the settings for these dwellings in different parts of the world are a mix of both urban and rural.

Once again we're faced with problems of definition. Politicians, policy-makers, architects, planners, surveyors, housing managers, community development workers and other professionals all hold strong views on what sustainable development actually means in terms of housing. But then, so do scientists and environmentalists, farmers, commuters, tourists, the list goes on and on – in fact just about everyone on the planet!

Without turning this into a separate book, we've assembled some of the disparate views on the subject. It provides a backdrop for much that follows and like a snake, it is a theme that slithers, hard to grab hold of, throughout the text.

...the need to do something, and soon...

We wouldn't be writing this book unless we felt passionately that everyone can, through considering their lifestyle in relation to their dwelling and their environment, make some positive choices which impact on their own lives and the environment. We agree with Gro Harlem Bruntland who, as head of the World Commission on Environment and Development said:

> *"Humanity has the ability to make development sustainable – to ensure that it meets the needs of the present without compromising the ability of future generations to meet their own needs."*

At the Sustainability 2000 Earth conference in Mexico, Michael Meacher, representing the UK government, outlined sustainable development as being a recipe for a better quality of life. He said there were four objectives:

- *social progress which recognises the needs of everyone;*
- *effective protection of the environment;*

- *prudent use of natural resources;*
- *maintenance of high and stable levels of economic growth and employment.*

Debate continues about whether the current (and growing in some cases) levels of economic growth can be sustained across the industrialised countries without compromising future generations and the developing nations particularly in the Southern hemisphere, but it does at least show that many national governments are at very least paying lip-service to the need for sustainable growth. However, even the positive sounding words of government ministers fall short of providing a clear idea as to how this quest for sustainability can be organised and monitored effectively.

Environmentalism is not just concerned with the protection of the natural world. It is equally concerned with people's cultural, economic and social activities, and in developing an understanding of the nation, world and universe which they inhabit. The environment also includes 'us' – the way we live, issues such as commuting, the built environment, poverty and illiteracy, as well as global problems in the world 'out there', which can often be too abstract for many people to comprehend. For instance, while countries such as the U.S. Canada and Australia create the largest quantities of un-recyclable waste, a country such as India recycles 90 per cent of its rubbish (Chapman *et al.*, 1997).

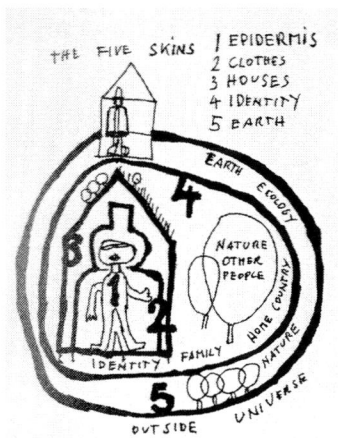

One model for seeing ourselves as part of the environment perhaps helps to make this inter-connectedness between us, our dwellings, lifestyles and the environment a bit clearer. The artist and eco-dwellings designer, Friedensreich Hundertwasser claimed that all his works and life were in harmony with nature (Restany, 2001). From 1950s onwards, until his death in 2000, Hundertwasser developed a pictorial metaphor to describe every person's power over, and relationship with, the other essential elements in the environment. He called these our five skins, and maintained that each person has a responsibility to show ecological

commitment in the way that they 'wear' them. This picture of each individual as a person who is an active participant in choosing their own identity through their body, their clothes, their dwelling, their friends and people with whom they inter-relate, and their inter-action with the global environment provides us with a model depicting the 'five skins' of environmentalism.

...sustainability in housing terms...

In a later section in Part One, we develop the theme of appropriate technology and dwellings. For now, suffice it to say that whilst not all eco-dwellings fit all the following categories in housing terms, it seems to us that fully sustainable dwellings, whether sited in rural or urban settings should seek to:

- make a smaller footprint on the landscape;
- be constructed from more natural materials (that are sustainably produced);
- be built in a manner to blend in with the natural environment;
- offer a healthy environment for their occupants;
- provide energy efficient spaces using renewable energy sources, including water supply;
- incorporate a range of recycling of waste and food producing opportunities
- more contentiously, they should introduce something which is aesthetically pleasing into the environment, even make you smile!

Eco-dwellings at this point in time also probably need to sell themselves as examples of what can be done without opting wholly outside the normal built environment. This is why it is so important that larger scale developments which have elements of an ecological-focus do take place, especially when they are part of social housing (rented or subsidised accommodation provided by the state or through not-for-profit organisations).

Coin Street Community Builders, London:
In London, nearby Waterloo station, and a mere stone's throw from the prestigious South Bank with its London Eye Millennium wheel, is one of the more interesting inner urban regeneration developments. In the 1970s there were only about 4,000 residents left in the Waterloo area of London. The world famous architect, Richard Rogers was involved in designing a 16 storey office block for the Coin Street site, but this was

blocked in the 1980s public inquiry by a concerted local campaign that eventually had the backing of Lambeth Council. The group of local activists, led by Iain Tuckett formed the Coin Street Co-Op which evolved into the Community Builders. These Coin Street builders initiated a number of local developments including, at the end of 2001, the establishment of 59 high density dwellings forming the Iroko Housing Co-op.

It was the tenacity and dogged determination of the local residents and businesses to fight for a *local regeneration* which was developed along environmentally sound grounds that won the day. The Iroko flats and houses are in some ways similar to co-housing, built to a very high density, with low-energy recovery systems, high specification insulation, passive and active solar power, and some shared communal land. Located along one side of the heavily used public space on London's South Bank, they offer imaginative dwellings in one of the city's busiest locations. Potential residents all face a

mandatory 27 hour induction course on aspects of self-management and living in the co-op. The aim is to ensure that the scheme is available to key workers and people deemed to be in 'housing need'.

Romolenpolder in Haarlem, the Netherlands: With about 1,000 residents in 384 residences (286 for rental and 98 privately owned), Romolenpolder was a radical development both in terms of ecological and social principles, particularly community management. About 80 per cent of the future residents (Brakkee, 1996) were involved in the planning and development process. This high percentage occurred because they were amongst the locals who had opposed the earlier Haarlem City development plans for this green belt land.

Romolenpolder offers an extraordinary mix of dwellings and residents. It includes sites for twelve residential caravans, self-build houses, communal housing, housing for geriatric patients and units for one, two person and family groups as well as workshops and businesses, including people working from home. It is self-managed even down to refuse collection and maintenance of open spaces – the Romolenpolder Management Foundation (RMF) receives substantial funds from the local authority to

employ residents to undertake and manage gardening and street cleaning (Schmitz-Günther, 1999 and Bakkee, *ibid.*).

In terms of ecology, the family homes incorporate grass roofs, there is a heavy emphasis on recycling, and composting is subsidised. The Klaus Novy Institut from Köln served as consultants on the establishment of neighbourhood management, and their shared agenda determined that the management should be based upon:

- *respect for the people and the environment; integration of management tasks;*

16

- *a decentralised office based in the neighbourhood;*
- *residents' involvement in neighbourhood management; aimed at the average resident, not depending on the highly motivated environmentalists.*

Perhaps what defines an 'eco-dwelling' has more to do with the adoption of some sort 'eco-lifestyle'. To place this in a wider context, one also needs to examine the impact that the developments in some countries have on other less economically advantaged countries, and to look at the social and community aspects of 'sustainability'. Friends of the Earth (FOE), in their book *Tomorrow's World: Britain's share in a sustainable future* contend that current development is not sustainable. Whilst this is a UK-centric point of view, it would hold equally or even more true of countries such as the United States and Australia. They argue that,

> *"Despite increasing average incomes and lifespans it (current development) is failing us in three critical ways:*
>
> *1. It is reliant on excessive use of environmental resources – thus breaching global environmental limits and causing impacts such as climate change (this is 'cheating on our children' because they will inherit a world less able to support human life)*
>
> *2. The benefits are inequitably distributed. Inequality is growing, both globally and within the UK (this is 'cheating on our neighbours' because most of us in Britain are relative beneficiaries).*
>
> *3. This development and excessive resource use is not increasing quality of life for those that receive its material benefits (this is 'cheating on ourselves' because we all play along with the game of consuming more)."*

We particularly nodded our agreement with FOE when they said,

> *"…quality of life is not directly dependent upon material consumption."*

And it is eminently obvious that our dwellings for a sustainable future need to be constructed within the context of other aspects of planning and land use to reduce the use of non-public transport; to encourage people to walk and cycle; share more resources among

Built from whiskey barrels at Findhorn community in Scotland, these homes have been constructed to strict ecological guidelines with high levels of insulation, passive solar orientation and active solar panels for water heating (Selena Merrett)

communities; and to reduce the distances between employment, leisure, educational, shopping and residential locations. Home-working, amidst the technological and information revolution, may gradually help in this area.

…not just for the hippies!…

One of the problems frequently encountered is the view that environmentalism is for the 'loony-Greenies and hippies'. Perhaps this view is impossible to avoid since some of the most active people in the movement have decided to live their 'green' lives more outside of mainstream society than in it. This is illustrated in an example from one of the loose-knit organisational groups which is working for more sustainable housing around the world: the Global Ecovillage Network (GEN). Following their 2000 bi-annual conference in Spain, Tony Gosling wrote a report of the proceedings. Here are a few challenging word-bites from that report (even if we don't fully endorse its slightly separatist stance):

> *"One thing became clear during these presentations. No-one really knew what an eco-village is! There are two main elements it seems. The first is a degree*

of communalism, i.e. shared space and resources/money, and the other is non-dependence on the outside world, providing eco-alternatives to energy, water, food, waste etc."

"Strangely for the host nation, the Spanish ecovillage movement was almost entirely absent over the four days. A large part of the programme was taken up with 'New-Age' singing and circle-dancing. Something I didn't want to take part in and was accused from the top of being 'anti-social'. One of the Lakabe residents explained that they didn't see GEN as the best forum to meet like-minded people. Was this why? Being force fed spirituality, is for me, a problem with GEN" (from *Eco-Village news*, August 2000).

As you read in Part Two about the examples we have collected together, the links between lifestyle and dwelling need to be carefully considered. The intentional communities movement across the world carries the same baggage: how do you live in a more ecological dwelling if you don't want to 'join' a group or 'community'? No simple answers to that one! Our own view is that it is the rich variety on the 'eco-dwelling' menu,

FOR THOSE THAT UNDERSTAND
DO NOT. NONE IS POSSIBLE
THE MYSTERY, NO EXPLANATION
IS NECESSARY. FOR THOSE WHO

Illustration by Marianne Gibson

offering options for housing and lifestyles and their relationship with the environment, that make the future of 'eco-dwellings' a hopefully bright one.

...the debate continues...

However, a word or two of warning. There is a sizeable scientific body of opinion which claims that there is no environmental problem in the world today and that resources are not under threat. They are much more powerful and vocal than you might think, especially in universities and corporations. Simply surfing the World Wide Web uncovers as many sites which are techno-focused, as enviro-focused. Typical of their viewpoint is Paul Treanor, writing from the Netherlands under the title *'Why sustainability is wrong'*:

"...(sustainability is) a desperate search for every possible argument against change in the existing political, social, economic and technological order...the ideology is...a radical conservatism...to change to a change avoiding order" (www.inter.nl/users/Paul.Traeanor/sustainability.html).

Provocative stuff.

In their different ways, the contributors to the book are all descendants of the seventeenth century Diggers and Levellers, described by Gerrard Winstanley in the following way:

"The work we are going about is this, to dig up George's Hill and the waste ground thereabouts, and to sow corn and to eat our bread together by the sweat of our brows. And the first reason is this, that we may work in righteousness, and lay the foundation of measuring the Earth a Common Treasury for all, both Rich and Poor, that everyone that is born in the land, may be fed by the Earth his Mother that brought him forth, according to the Reason that rules in Creation."

As in the England of the Civil War, all environmental solutions include elements that are social, economic and political. Again, quoting Winstanley,

"Was the Earth made to preserve a few covetous, proud men to live at ease, and for them to bag and barn up the treasures of the Earth from others that those may beg or starve in a fruitful land; or was it made to preserve all her children?"

(The New Law of Righteousness, 1649).

Everything changes – nothing changes. Much more recently, Art Ludwig has said in *Design for Living*,

> "…the obstacles to widespread adoption of the practices of living with nature are primarily cultural, not technical or economic."

For many environmentalists, especially those of 'deep green' persuasion even this is not at the heart of the matter. They point to what the Dalai Lama called the ethical responsibility of mankind to examine what we have inherited, what we are responsible for, and what we will pass on (in Porritt, 1991). This emphasises our role as guardians and custodians of the land. However, while many people continue to view the planet (and often even its people) as a commodity that can be owned, used, sold and destroyed, then environmentalism remains an empty slogan. Maneka Gandhi, as Minister of State for Environment and Forests in India, recently quoted Chief Seattle of the Suquamish in Washington State, who spoke in 1854:

> "How can you buy or sell the sky, the warmth and the land? The idea seems strange to us. If we do not own the freshness of the air and the sparkle of the water, how can you buy them? We are part of the Earth, and it is part of us…"

> "We know the white man does not understand our ways. One portion of land is the same to him as the next – for he is a stranger who comes in the night and takes from the land whatever he needs."

References

Allen, E. (1969) *Stone Shelters.* Massachusetts Institute of Technology.

Brakkee, G. (1996) *Romolenpolder, Haarlem – Ecological neighbourhood selfmanagement.* Klaus Novy Institut, Köln.

Chapman, G., Kumar, K., Fraser, C. and Gaber, I. (1997) *Environmentalism and the Mass Media.* Routledge.

Friends of the Earth (1998) *Tomorrow's World: Britain's share in a sustainable future.* Earthscan for Friends of the Earth.

Ludwig, A. (1989) *Design for Living.* Oasis Design.

Porritt, J. (1991) *Save the Earth.* Dorling Kindersley.

Restany, P. (2001) *Hundertwasser: the painter-king with the five skins.* Taschen.

Seattle, Chief, as written by Henry Smith, *Scraps from a Diary – Chief Seattle – A Gentleman by Instinct – His Native Eloquence,* The Seattle Sunday Star, 29.10.1857.

Rudofsky, B. (1964) *Architecture without architects.* Doubleday/New York Museum of Modern Art.

Schmitz-Günther, T. (English edition, 1999) *Living Spaces – Sustainable Building and Design.* Köneman.

Wines, J. (2000) *Green Architecture.* Taschen.

Winstanley, G. (1649) *The True Leveller's Standard Advanced, 1649,* Giles Calvert.

A relatively unspoilt beach in India (Alan Dearling)

Nomadic living: by tradition and by choice
Alan Dearling

This is a book ostensibly about dwellings – about the spaces we live in. There is, for many people, an automatic assumption that a dwelling is a static structure. It is perceived as being anchored to a place and probably to a community/neighbourhood/country, with a whole array of cultural, societal and economic implications.

Whilst Graham's predominant interest and involvement has (I think) been with communities and their dwellings, mine has frequently been with certain groups of modern day nomads. Some are bound by their ethnicity to a rich

Romanies from Eastern Europe have been seeking asylum

nomadic heritage – Romanies of England and Europe, Irish and Scottish Travellers – all with many generations of their own cultural histories. Then there are modern day Travellers, who have chosen, or been forced by economic and/or social circumstances, to leave their sedentary lives behind, either on a full-time basis, or for part of their lives.

In this section, I have tried to provide some background information, some history, some vibrant 'colour', which may help readers to make more sense of 'nomadism'. In Part Two of the book are a number of personal stories from modern nomads. Most of these people have made some level of conscious decision to live as Travellers. Their dwellings are an integral part of their lifestyle,

whether by tradition, choice or necessity.

This section offers a brief introduction to some of their antecedents. Additionally, there are other environmental and spiritual themes that link indigenous nomads with both the world's newer nomads and eco-dwelling builders in many parts of the world. But this area is at times contentious, on the real or potential grounds that there can be tribal, cultural and spiritual vandalism and theft. More on that a little later!

The personal accounts of people living nomadically in Part Two offer a sometimes conflictual set of messages about lifestyle, dwelling and the impact on the environment. The rest of this section is not focused on eco-dwellings, but on nomadism.

The countries in which people live nomadically, define, at least to some extent, the nature of the dwelling they choose. Though having said that, I have a friend, Rachael, who lived for three years in a traditional Native American tipi in the border region of Scotland. She endured and coped with the snow and wind swept valley at Traquair! Social relationships, especially extended family groupings and the historic role of the woman as the home-maker in many nomadic cultures, have also played a major part in determining the design and nature of particular forms of nomadic dwelling space. For instance, the Masai of East Africa traditionally lived in simple and easily dismantled mud daubed huts, shaped like a loaf of bread. Known as 'barracks', women actually built them, and provided the food for their warrior husbands and children. (Huckaby, in the

Gypsies in the early 20th century often lived in benders alongside their waggons

20

Shelter publication, 1973). Nomadic Gypsies used their vardo (waggon) for travelling and as a social space, but often actually slept in portable benders built alongside at each stopping place.

Nomads, whether indigenous like the Tuareg, traditionally of Mali and other parts of the Sahara, the Penan of Borneo, Evenki of Siberia, Aborigines of Australia, native Americans, Gypsies/Roma of Europe; or the nomads of choice, such as the new Travellers of the UK and the international travelling posse of performers, artists, eco-activists, would-be-shamen, do appear to share some interesting features (as well as equally varied differences, of course!).

...the journey itself is the ritual...

Without stretching the argument too far, viewed from the 'outside', where sedentarism is the norm, all nomadic people are seen as emblems of the 'otherness', exotic and threatening. Their appearance, lifestyles, burgeoning folklore and media representation all add to their folk-devil, or occasionally romanticised status. And from the inside of these cultural and ethnic groups, there are some fascinating similarities in terms of both motivation and belief structure. The differences are often ones more of degree and social and cultural context, especially in relation to the different groups' degree of rejection of Western materialism.

Amongst indigenous nomads, theirs is a resistance to conform to other people's and society's beliefs and lifestyle. They are often the last representatives of their own tribal culture. For nomads of choice, theirs is often a proactive rejection of their

Modern day tipis at an eco festival in the UK

particular society's sedentary lifestyle and values. Later we will see some of the same diversity of lifestyle and dwelling choices within the people who have chosen to live in sedentary dwelling spaces. Perhaps this is one of the connections between the diverse people who are in some way 'eco-dwellers'?

I think that anyone who has travelled for an extended length of time would identify with the concept that: *"In the nomadic mind, the tent is not tied to a territory, but to an itinerary. The journey itself is the ritual."*

I spotted that in a book attributed to someone called Berman. I don't know who they are or were, but it rings true. Especially so, when considered in terms of people who are, to some extent, making lifestyle choices about how and where they want to live.

...conscious disconnection...

On the margins of our supposedly developed/civilised world there still lives an ever diminishing number of nomadic tribes. The Penan in Borneo are one, but they are on the edge of seeing their environment and with it their culture finally annihilated. In 1993 in the book *Nomads of the Dawn* the old headman, Wé Salau lamented,

> *"Surely we live here peacefully, and they have no cause for destroying our forest, they have no cause for destroying our land. They have no cause for making our rivers muddy. They never told us, 'Now we are going to demolish your sago, now we are going to destroy your rivers, your hills, your land, your home. Now we are going to obliterate your rattan, and all the other things you get from the forest. All the fruit trees. The place where you Penan live.' They never spoke to us thus. Instead they acted without warning, straightaway they destroyed everything"* (Davies, Mackenzie and Kennedy, 1995).

At a time when 'globalisation' is being used as a buzzword for the corporate and governmental restructuring and management of world resources, fewer and fewer indigenous people are still untouched by Western influence. From Mali in Africa, Stephen Buckley, reported in the *Washington Post Foreign Service*, Sunday, December 8, 1996:

> *"Sididi Ag Inaka has never used a television, toilet or telephone. He has never read a newspaper. He has never heard of a facsimile machine. He has*

never seen an American dollar.

He is entirely disconnected from the global economy and its ever-rippling waves. And he does not care.

'My father was a nomad, his father was a nomad, I am a nomad, my children will be nomads,' said Inaka, who was not sure of his age but looked to be in his fifties. 'This is the life of my ancestors. This is the life that we know. We like it.'

Thousands of nomads pepper this western tip of the Sahara desert and most share Inaka's perspective. For centuries, they have subjected themselves to the oft-bitter whims of nature, without real connections to society. They have lived off their camels, goats and sheep, depending upon them for everything from food to transportation. And they have survived.

But they have paid a price for their conscious disconnection from the modern world. They are among the world's poorest people, unable to educate and provide health care for their children, continually scratching to make it through one more day, always one drought away from seeing their animals and families wiped out.

In many ways, their lives mirror those of Africans who live in the villages, towns and cities of the world's poorest continent. The difference is that many of those Africans long for an economic escape from a torturous existence. Most nomads say they do not."

For Romany Gypsies, Irish Travellers and many others who for centuries lived nomadically, assimilation and integrationist policies have

The Aboriginal heartland of Australia, north of Alice Springs

made a travelling lifestyle virtually unsustainable.

...cultural landscapes...

The practical and symbolic significance of the land we live upon – our natural environment, is a major recurring theme in this book. The World Heritage Committee of UNESCO coined the phrase 'cultural landscapes' to describe (my paraphrasing):

- A landscape which displays evidence of previous civilisations.
- Landscapes which continue to have an active social role in modern societies.

Cultural practices can serve as a powerful means of protecting environments. Nomadic people feel especially strongly about their relationship with land, the elements and the environment. Indeed, it is the basis of the spirituality behind many cultures, not least the tribes and clans of the Aborigines and the Native Americans.

W.E.H. Stanner said:
"There are no English words good enough to give a sense of the links between an Aboriginal group and its homeland. Our word 'home', warm and suggestive though it be, does not match the Aboriginal word that may mean 'camp', 'hearth', 'country', 'everlasting home', 'totem place', 'life source', 'spirit center' and much else all in one. Our word 'land' is too sparse and meager. We can scarcely use it except with economic overtures unless we happen to be poets. The Aboriginal would speak of 'earth' and use the word in a richly symbolic way to mean his 'shoulder' or his 'side'. I have seen an Aboriginal embrace the earth he walked on. To put our words 'home' and 'land' together in 'homeland' is a little better but not much. A different tradition leaves us tongueless and earless towards this other world of meaning and significance." (quoted in Libesman, 1995)

And the Aboriginal sense of connection to the earth was honed very much out of nomadism. Their appreciation of what land means to them is measured in 'dreamings' – their oneness with the land and all that lives or grows on it. It is also connected with their personal travels – to be born by a goanna, is to become one with the goanna. As Broome (1982) suggests, *"...when the great ancestors had roamed the earth, they were human, animal and bird at one and the same time: all natural things were in unity."* In their culture, dreamtime began at the time of the land's creation by a series of superhuman creatures. These spirit creatures were believed to have 'become' the features of the landscape after they had created the living creatures on it. These are the sacred, special places for the Aborigines, inextricably linked with their personal songlines. All things, rocks, animals, birds, fish are for them part human. Therefore, when land was denied to them, many believe that they lost their connection with their dreaming, and began to part with some of their 'human-ness'.

Amongst the nomadic people of India, 'animism' is central to their daily life. As Randhawa has stated, *"A pantheon of nature spirits is believed to inhabit jungles, rivers, wells, animals, totems, the sun and the moon"* (1996). In India, nomads suffered under British colonial rule and many were branded criminals under the Criminal Tribes Act. However, in more recent times, Randhawa suggests that forms of enforced 'integration' are changing the lives of India's nomads, but some of the rural, pastoral nomadic tribes are just using government allocations of land and subsidies for building a hut as a *"base camp and education for their children"* (ibid.).

...everybody wants to be an Indian now...

Alongside the loss of traditional cultures around the world, there is also a growing concern that 'sedentary' people, academics and media folk in particular, are debasing, commercialising and misappropriating the remaining tribal and nomadic cultures. I have shared this worry on occasions, for instance, when visiting yet another sweat lodge for a medicine wheel session, employing the traditional talking stick – yes, you guessed it, in a farmer's field in Pilton, Somerset, UK, at the time of the annual Glastonbury Festival!

Across the world, a number of us who are active in Traveller and Gypsy issues, share our own discussion and news group. Fairly typical of the depth of feeling about this process of 'misappropriation' is a recent communication from Kent Hellman, who said, *"I agree on what you call a 'Gypsy industry'. It's very important for us to preserve our language and cultural heritage, but I'm a bit critical to outsiders trying to 'earn money' on my people, and my ancestors who passed away long time ago – that is disgusting. But in the same time, of course, we appreciate the many nice non-Travellers who understands us, write good books about us etc. etc."*

By coincidence, if there is such a thing, I've just finished reading Melanie McGrath's book, *Motel Nirvana – Dreaming of the New Age in the American Desert* (1995). In it she recounts her own travels through America's Navajo lands. As she moved into the Taos area, a friend had sent her an article from *The European* newspaper. Briefly, it concerned a stagehand from Paris, who had reinvented himself as Cheval Debout. He'd gone feral and set himself up in a leather tipi in Le Var forest. He found forestry work and very soon had been joined by a small community of Parisian tipi dwellers. The reporter asked Cheval why he had decided to become an Indian, and he replied, *'Everybody wants to be an Indian now'."* Obviously, he retained the option to stop being a native American as well!

In my own compilation, *Alternative Australia – celebrating cultural diversity*, Tatiana wrote,

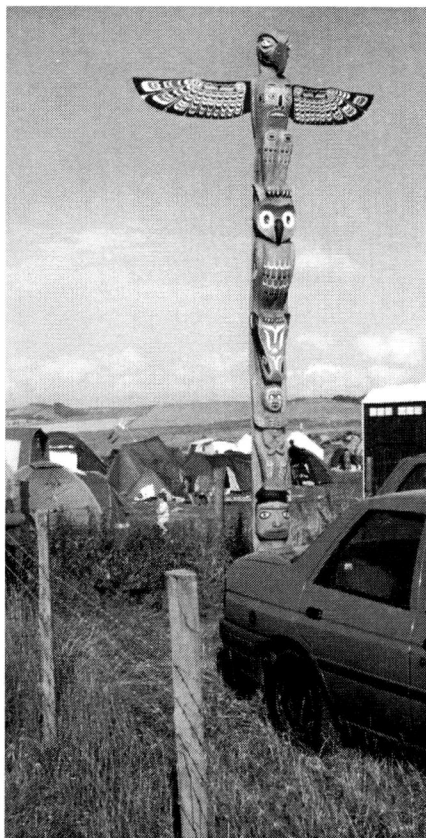

A native American-style totem in Salisbury Plain in England

"Some Australians ignore the culture of the Aborigines, but believe in the way of the American Indians" (Dearling with Hanley, 2000). This does seem to be more than a little worrying when tribal beliefs and practices are co-opted in a roughshod, piecemeal and culturally insensitive way. But at the same time, it seems positive that possibly more people then ever around the world are trying to learn more about environmentally spiritual belief systems. Perhaps there are culturally sensitive ways to navigate a way through this problematic area. Just possibly, it may be the

23

people who are developing sustainable, communal, more spiritual and low-impact dwellings who build the necessary cultural bridges.

The root of the problem actually relates to a rather complex process. Roughly speaking, what occurs is that the general public and the media see those people they dub 'New Agers' and others involving themselves with some sort of tribal cocktail of rituals borrowed in a pick-and-mix and probably inaccurate way from the indigenous cultures of the world. The rituals themselves can through this process become devalued, regarded as slightly ludicrous, or at very least culturally dislocated. Centrally, it is a question about authenticity, and where rituals are practised entirely out of context, this can still further denigrate the rituals in the view of many people. In turn it may make it harder for the surviving indigenous people to gain the rightful respect for their traditions.

...a story of reindeer...

The far north of Siberia is the traditional home of nomadic tribes such as the Tungus and Evenki. From the 1920s onwards, the Communist government regarded these hunters, fishers and reindeer herders as a problem. An official communication from about 1929 stated:
"...nomadism as a way of life represents a major obstacle in the building of Communism in the north."
Throughout the 1930s, the Evenki pursued a relatively successful campaign of avoidance – they moved north into the tundra – and they provided fierce resistance. The Communist regime continued with its dual policy towards these nomads differentiating between nomadism *as a way of life,* which they wanted to end, and nomadism *as a way of production,* which out of economic necessity, they needed to continue.

Bizarrely, the attack on their particular nomadic lifestyle has failed because as Evenki were forced to settle (even though they continued to live in tents), and corral the reindeer, this non-nomadic form of herding drastically degraded the pastures and the health of the herd. Subsequently, the number of domestic reindeer dropped from 64,000 in 1965 to just 8,700 in 1996. And now the present government is trying to persuade the young Evenki to return to nomadic reindeer herding. Perhaps we may even eventually see governments such as the USA, Australia and some of the African states offering incentives to native indigenous populations to return to their nomadic roots!

...So, who are the modern day nomads of the world?...

I've posed the question, but I'm only going to offer a partial answer. That answer also relates specifically to some of the people who have made contributions to this book. The answer would also need to reflect the tremendous diversity of the people who are, or become, nomadic. Some are nomadic all their life, some switch in and out of nomadism. Some travel for part of each year, but keep a settled, sedentary base. If you think about it, you can see that answering the question as to whether you 'chose to be nomadic or not' can quickly become problematic!

Another question brings us back to authenticity, in terms of, for instance, of who is a 'real' Gypsy? This question has worried me and some other writers in this area, since it poses a problem akin to the ethnic cleansing or exclusion of those who are not pure or real – hardly a desirable consequence! Helen O'Nions indeed comments on the category of pure Romany (her spelling) (1995): *"In fact after five hundred years of co-existence with the dominant population, such categories are meaningless."* However, for a group such as the Romanies, many who are impassioned about their ethnic identity, it is certainly not meaningless! Consider for instance, Prince Nathaniel Petulengro Lee, interviewed by Jeremy Sandford in his book, *Gypsies* who said:
"My mother was a true Romany Rackley and my father was an Espanolo Gitano.

My Mum was a cushti duckerer and her great grandmother was burned as a witch...There are various types of Gypsies. There's true-blooded Romany Chal, the blackberry Gypsy. Then there's the Tinker, which is from Ireland. And then there's the Didicoi, which is very rare, a Tinker girl marrying a Romany Chal, and you get the Pikie which are Tinker and Romany mixed blood" (1973).

However, nomadism, with its long history is arguably more important as a 'personal freedom', as is suggested in Thomas Acton's report (1998) on a major joint UK wide initiative on Travellers' rights, where he states: *"Any Bill of Rights should reflect a human right to travel, rather than a special position for an odd legal definition of 'gypsies'."*

Some of the realities of modern-day nomadism include that:

- Relatively few of the population of traditionally nomadic cultures such as Gypsies actually travel any more. For example, the official statistics for 1997 in England, Wales and Scotland suggest that there were only about 14,000 traveller families on sites, despite there being an estimated 120,000 Travellers on the island. (based on figures in Kenrick and Clark, 2000)
- Many people who would call themselves 'Travellers' or 'Gypsies' are only semi-nomadic, travelling occasionally, or for only part of each year. Others live in some form of mobile dwelling, but have that sited on a legal, tolerated or illegal site/encampment, from which they rarely or never move.
- Many people are nomadic for a part of their lives because of negative economic and social circumstances, including the break-up of families and relationships, homelessness, psychiatric, drink and drug problems, and leaving 'institutions' which range from prisons and children's homes through to the armed forces.
- Much travel for today's nomads in the Western industrialised nations and beyond is in pursuit of work and economic gain, which is in the time-honoured tradition of 'wayfarers'. There is also a blurring of the edges around this focus, with many people travelling, at least for some of the time, for its own sake; as a learning process about places, people and cultures; social interaction; and more intangibly, for the 'buzz', the inherent 'right' to be able to travel and to celebrate a nomadic existence.
- Modern nomads' choices of dwelling will usually be influenced by and often restricted by knowledge, finance, opportunities and tradition. Partly as result of this, their environmental impact can range from acting as a negative force, through to being a very positive catalyst for environmental protection.
- For quite a few of these nomads, their dwellings and their lifestyle are constantly in transition. As you will see later in the book, some of them have aspirations to ownership or stewardship of land, floating structures, low-impact farms and an array of alternative technological options.

...continuing a Travelling tradition...

Because of their campaign to achieve legal recognition as an ethnic group or race, many Romanies have focused their efforts in seeking recognition of the Romani 'separateness' and identity. In Europe there are between 8 and 10 million Roma/Gypsies (Council of Europe Web site). In some Eastern European countries they represent over 5 per cent of some country's populations. However, they have faced discrimination and persecution throughout their existence including the Nazi's attempts to exterminate them along with the Jews during the second world war. Since that time, through a range of legislative and state organised actions the majority have ceased to be nomadic, though their culture remains rich with its travelling heritage.

At a very personal level I was struck with the harsh reality of life for the Roma in the Czech Republic when I was invited there to run a workshop at a conference aimed at supporting

Czech Roma frequently face serious intimidation and harassment

ethnic minorities in Europe. Because of my work in the UK with a variety of Travellers, and some experience of meeting with nomadic Roma in France and Spain, I hadn't realised that not only had living in a vardo (traditional Gypsy caravan) been illegal since the 1930s under the

Communist regime, but so had any sort of nomadism. This has left many of Europe's Roma bereft of much of their own culture and any personal experience of a positive nomadic life. Their only experience of being 'on the drom (road)' has far too frequently been as refugees, as part of Europe's diaspora. For those Roma left in many of the towns and cities of the Czech Republic and Slovakia, they remain a despised, discriminated-against and ghettoised underclass.

Putting this into the context of this book, the ethnicity issue is of less direct relevance than the continuing practice of nomadism amongst Romani and other Travellers. To quote Colin Clark (1999), in the context of the UK where there are considerable threats to the last vestiges of nomadism:

> "A nomadic way of life – sometimes romanticised, almost always demonised – is a criminal offence in Britain (thanks mainly to various clauses in the 1994 Criminal Justice and Public Order Act). Gypsies and Travellers who follow a nomadic way of life – usually because it suits their preferred mode of economic activity – have very few legal options available to them now. If they don't 'park-up' permanently and move into a house then they risk facing heavy fines, prison sentences and even losing their caravans (that is, their homes). Such draconian measures as this – forcing an ethnic group (and, according to the 1976 Race Relations Act, Gypsies are an ethnic group) to give up its long-standing and proud traditions and heritage – is almost akin to a form of cultural genocide. I do not say this flippantly or lightly; nomadism is that important to some of the Gypsies and Travellers I know who still travel."

...and the new world nomads...

You only have to check out the Internet to witness how the word 'nomad' has been adopted for use in a remarkable number of circumstances. The University of Kentucky (2000) advertised its Brazilian artshow as being by *"a large tribe of electronic nomads."* And this association is not restricted to virtual reality. My own work with new Travellers and related members of the world's counter cultural collectives of sound systems, musicians, crafts-

people, eco-warriors and performance artists has opened my eyes to the vast numbers of people who are constantly travelling around the world, as they might say, 'celebrating diversity'.

In this book we've included some examples of their dwellings and lifestyles and explored their environmental activity from protest sites through to semi-permanent nomadic arts centres. My own book, (Dearling, 1998) *No Boundaries: new Travellers on the road (outside of England)*

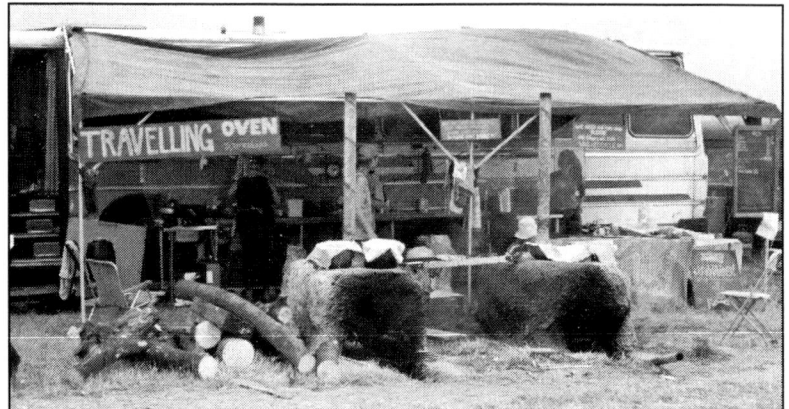

The economy of the road – a bakery run by Travellers

chronicled the lives of a number of these modern nomads, but in it there was no specific focus on the dwellings they lived in, so hopefully this book redresses the balance.

Their lifestyles can, at least at first glance, be at some variance with a 'green consciousness'. For instance, Lizzie Bean told of some of her adventures on the road:

> "We make pay parties and free parties in the area (of Lisbon and Sintra in Portugal) for several months...the techno-machine cranking up high and above on the clifftops and the waves of the Atlantic crashing down below...I think we know something. We definitely feel something. Children of the ley-lines or children of the aliens. Ley-line aliens. Can you feel the force? The Portugese punters can. They love it and lap it up. Smiling from behind their mirror shades. They've never had anything like it and don't want us to leave. We wash wind-screens so we can stay. Sometimes dressed as chickens to liven it up" (Dearling, 1998).

The lifestyle significance of the mobile dwelling is central for many of these new nomads, whether it is a quickly assembled bender or dome, or the comfort of a bus or a converted horse-box. Alan Lodge, better known as Tash, has a major web site entitled *One eye on the road,* which he uses as rich repository for information, photos and 'rants' from travellers and counter-cultural activists. Here's one poem which explains its writer's feeling for her nomadic dwelling:

"I love this bus
That I call my home
I dig this coach
That allows me to roam
My little space
That can take me any place
My sanctuary
No matter where I be
And when I know that she's ready to go
And a time to travel's dawning
Reaching, to start her heart
She turns, she breaths, she fires, she vibrates gently
We move into the morning
Wondering whence we do depart
Knowing that there's nothing wrong with where I am
Some folk simply do not understand."

Perhaps it is fitting to end with a quote from Bruce Chatwin, one the 20th century's most perceptive travel writers. He reminds us that nomadism has a very old place on the earth, and does not belong to just Australia's Aborigines:

> *"Perpetual movement was their creed, not simply to avert the bad consequences of sitting still, but as an end in itself. In their eyes man was born a migrant, settlement the perversion of degenerates, and cutting the soil to grow crops, murder."* (Chatwin, 1989)

References

Acton, T. (1998) *Land, People and Freedom.* National Council for Voluntary Organisations.
Broome, R. (1982) *Aboriginal Australians.* George Allen & Unwin.
Chatwin, B. (1989) *What am I doing here?* Cape Books.
Clark, C. (1999) *Britain and Human Rights: should Travellers be allowed to retain their way of life?* Patrin Web www.geocities.com/paris/5121/britain-rights.htm
Davies, W., Mackenzie, I. and Kennedy, S. (1995) *Nomads of the Dawn.* Pomegranate Books.
Dearling, A. (1998) *No Boundaries: new Travellers on the road outside of England.* Enabler Publications.
Dearling, A., with Hanley, B. (2000) *Alternative Australia: celebrating cultural diversity.* Enabler Publications.
Kenrick, D. and Clark, C. (2000) *Moving On: The Gypsies and Travellers of Britain.* University of Hertfordshire Press.
Libesman, T. (1995) *Indigenous people and the law in Australia.* Butterworths.
Lodge, A. (Tash) *One eye on the road* website at www.gn.apc.org/tash/
McGrath, M. (1995) *Motel Nirvana: dreaming of the New Age in the American Desert.* Harper Collins.
O'Nions, H. (1995) *The marginalisation of Gypsies* in the Web journal of current legal issues. Blackstone.
Randhawa, T. (1996) *The Last Wanderers: Nomads and Gypsies of India.* Mapin Publishing.
Shelter Publications. (1973 and 1990) *Shelter.* Shelter Publications.
Sandford, J. (1973) *Gypsies.* Secker and Warburg.
Stanner, W.E.H. (1979) *White Man Got No Dreaming: Essays 1938-1973.* Australian National University Press.

A travelling home with built-in humour!

Community participation and empowerment
Alan Dearling and Graham Meltzer

It is striking that so many green visionaries (such as E.F. Schumacher, Theodore Roszak, Bernard Shaw and Kirkpatrick Sale) focused their attentions on the nature of a future sustainable society. Their visions were often very rural, what Marsh (1982) has called, *"the cult of the countryside."* As early as the 1840s, the Chartists built nearly 300 cottages in five settlements, with the focus on becoming independent small-holders – a form of radical peasantry. Sometimes referred to as a Nature-Priest, Richard Jefferies (1879), was one of the communitarians who continually emphasised the links between mankind and nature:

> *"Let us always be out of doors among trees and grass, and rain and wind and sun…A something the Ancients called divine can be found and felt there still."*

…community and communality…

The early experiments in planning and building various forms of Utopian community, evolved from a diverse range of political and social perspectives. That history is one of both organised 'communities' and 'communality'. Dregger (2000) in the *Eurotopia* handbook states that all communities *"try to find their way between vision and reality."* Of communality, Darling (1984) argues that there are many *"different degrees and interpretations of communality: the aspects of one's life that one shares."* What is not in question is that forms of communal living can be traced back to at least biblical times.

The first kibbutzim was established in 1909 at Deganya in Palestine. *Encyclopaedia Britannica* (1999) says,
> *"…others were created in the following years, and by the late 20th century there were more than 200 kibbutzim in Israel, having a total population of more than 100,000. The early kibbutzim in Palestine were actually kevuzot; these were relatively small collectives that gradually evolved into the larger and more extended collective community known as the kibbutz."*

Indeed, by the early 1970s the highly organised kibbutzim were producing 28 per cent of Israel's farm output (Rosenfield, 1977). The kibbutz, according to Rosenfield, provided, *"…a collective way of life (that) does require the individual to put the good of the community first."* At its heart, the kibbutz system established forms of communal child-rearing (Bettelheim, 1971), which brought with it a close sense of community and belonging. After military service many 'children of the dream' returned as full adult members of the kibbutz.

Many different social experiments have taken place in the period since the nineteenth century. For instance, planned communities such as W H Lever's model garden village, were based on the principle of social reform, or enlightened capitalism. Lever saw Port Sunlight, built in 1888 near Birkenhead for his employees and their families, as, *"…a village, green and spacious, self-contained yet open and tranquil, quite cut off from the industrial world surrounding it"* (quoted in Marsh, 1982). It even included a Men's Club and the Lady Lever Art Gallery for its 3,000 residents.

Communal living has been seen as an antidote to the perceived loss of community caused by urbanisation, and increasing individualism in

· A · GARLAND · FOR · MAY · DAY · 1895 ·

society following the advent of liberalism and spread of capitalism. It has even been the seed bed of Tolstoy-type socialism in such settings as the early Whiteway community in the Cotswolds of England. But that group, like many since, suffered a rift in 1883, leading Bernard Shaw to rather rudely comment that the two groups went off, *"...one to sit among the dandelions, the other to organise the docks."* Other communal living and planned community experiments include the Cadbury family's Quaker model village of Bournville (1906), outside of Birmingham, which included the Ruskin Hall, adult education centre. This, like the later *Garden Cities of Tomorrow,* envisaged by Ebenezer Howard was founded on the notion that an 'ideal' community would be based on an allotment and garden-tending, yet urbanised community, of up to about 30,000 people. Assessed alongside a host of other communal and community experiments world-wide, the popular jury has long been undecided whether these social experimenters were, cranks, pioneers, innovators, or terminally deluded!

Arctic domes (Graham Meltzer)

Since the 1960s, communal living has appeared to many to be an effective means of escape from the unacceptable excesses of modern society. Increasing levels of alienation and stress are often successfully countered in smaller groups, where social relationships can become more authentic and the group more supportive than in societies based on cities and the nuclear family. Houriet (1971) estimated that there were more than 2,000 communal groups in the United States between 1965 and 1970. Yet, it is now more obvious than ever, that the 'alternative society' was not an invention of the 1960s – it has a much longer history. However, it now seems increasingly unlikely that the green vision of a society comprised of decentralised communes or intentional communities will arrive soon enough, or be sufficiently widespread to bring about a sustainable future.

A humane and ecologically sane future for society will more likely come about through the spread of communitarian attitudes and lifestyles in more ordinary ways and circumstances. This is already happening through processes of community participation and empowerment in the cities and suburbs. Girardet in *The Gaia Atlas of Cities* (1996) has stressed that the priority for sustainable developments across the world should be focused on the five per cent of urban land that is derelict, and on prioritising building homes that are energy efficient and serve to limit the distance between home and work. Before we explore this and other possibilities any further, it's necessary (once again) to consider definitions and meanings.

...definitions of 'community'...

The concept 'community' has been discussed, either directly or indirectly, by almost everyone who has ever written about human groups. 'Communico' is the base Latin word which means literally, 'to share'. However, theories of community have always been problematic and, to this day, the concept remains elusive. In reality, there are incredibly diverse types of community, making them difficult to define. Consequently, there's a lack of consistency amongst the variety of definitions, although there are common threads. Definitions commonly include three important attributes:

- social interaction
- shared ties, and
- a common geographical location.

This is the classical definition of community, which often, incorporates other characteristics such as clear boundaries, a human-scale, a sense of identity and belonging, mutual obligation etc. There is a danger that such a definition can, all too easily, lead to an idealised or romanticised view of community. Care must also be taken with the role of territory or location in this definition. Sociologist Herbert Gans found strong community ties existed amongst Italian Americans living in Boston in the 1960s. He discovered, however that their 'sense of community' was not rooted in physical place at all (that is, the neighbourhood) but rather, the

29

institutions (church, schools, pubs etc.) that were located there. Bill Metcalf (1999) in *Diggers and Dreamers 2000/2001* states that, *"...sustainable community has two dimensions: social/cultural sustainability, and environmental/economic sustainability. One without the other is of little use."*

For Metcalf, the degree of communality is of the utmost importance. Indeed he is critical of anything less than fully fledged intentional communities, saying of eco-villages and co-housing initiatives, *"...co-housing and eco-villages have the greatest popular appeal, yet have the least impact on environmental sustainability."*

Unlike us, he argues that they are the *"least radical forms"* and are *"pretending that they are part of a sustainable communities movement."* We would beg to differ, and feel that it is in the impressive diversity of dwellings, communities and lifestyles, including the likes of co-housing, eco-villages and permaculture collectives, that the seed-bed for lasting communities and sustainability will be born.

Contemporary definitions of community have broadened to include association in 'communities of interest', such as the scientific community, the gay community and even the community of environmentalists. Increased mobility and the influence of the Internet have caused a similar broadening of the concept. Participants in an Internet discussion group may consider themselves a 'virtual community', yet they share no territory or location other than cyberspace (Rheingold, 1993). In this process of updating the concept, 'community' has more popularly become characterised by the first two of the three attributes noted above, that is, the quality of the social interaction between members and their shared ties or bonds. As well as being 'seekers', many members of alternative communities are also 'questioners'. Brig Oubridge , from Tipi Valley in Wales (Hoult, 1991) suggests: *"If you live by habit and not by question, you are making no progress."*

...the decline of community...

Across the world, it appears that there are contradictory lifestyle trends. We hear of examples of both more and less materialism, increasing and deteriorating environmental awareness and activity. In a newspaper article entitled *Anti-social disease is spreading: Welcome to Lonely Street,* Lindsay Tanner, an Australian parliamentarian, wrote:

> *"Contemporary Australian society seems overwhelmed by social problems. At a time of apparent economic prosperity, community anxiety about family breakdown, drug abuse, gambling, youth suicide, violence and home invasion continues to mount. ... These social problems broadly reflect steadily increasing loneliness, alienation and social exclusion. Since the late 1960s our society has seen the collapse or erosion of many of the social structures around which people built relationships, personal worth and belonging"* (Tanner, 1999).

Tanner suggests that until the 1960s, material well-being was the 'guiding story' of our society. Since then, personal growth and individual expression has emerged as another guiding story. It has now become clear, he argues, that simplistic notions of individual or household well-being or comfort, no longer provide answers to contemporary social problems. A new guiding story is required, one with *social* objectives that ensure a 'sense of belonging' through participation in community life and in society. Tanner advocates *"building a new community framework to counter alienation, social exclusion and loneliness."* He calls for a halt to the progressive dismantling of community-based structures (in the current climate of economic rationalism) such as sports clubs, neighbourhood centres, playgroups, residents' associations and community health

Poundbury estate in Dorset, England – a 'community' designed for Prince Charles (Alan Dearling)

centres. Further, Tanner demands that strategies be established for *boosting* community participation in urban and suburban areas. Essentially these are all components of all regeneration strategies.

In terms of some communities in Australia, Tanner's point of view has some resonance, but in other locations, in Australia and elsewhere, the last twenty years has seen an increased awareness of participation, empowerment and community involvement. We offer some examples in the following sections.

...the importance of a sense of community...

"Beyond their social and democratic merits, community and participation are seen as conducive to people making publicly minded decisions and feeling involved in carrying them through, both of which are important ingredients in the agency and transition of radical green change" (Martell, 1994).

Community empowerment is said to be the process by which participation is encouraged and sustained. It is characterised by voluntary co-operation, self-help, and mutual aid between and among residents of a particular location, and has the potential to improve the physical, social, and economic conditions of the community. Importantly, the stronger their sense of community, the more control participants will feel they have over their immediate environment (Chavis and Wandersman, 1990).

Community life can also lend cultural and spiritual dimensions to human existence, making it much richer than that available in more individualistic scenarios. If differences are valued and respected, then the diversity of practices and traditions available within a diverse community vastly enriches the lives of individual members. Art, music, literature and drama become ways in which members experience and express both their personal and collective identity. Hagmaier and Stengel (Eurotopia, 2000) say of intentional communities that they,
*"- regard themselves and their togetherness as a community
- demonstrate this awareness by living together*

- *share things such as world views, possessions, money, business, self-help etc."*

Thus, community development and cultural life become fused and a sense of community is built. Activities that bring members together (for instance at festivals, celebrations and rituals)

Woodford Festival Forum, Queensland, Australia
(Alan Dearling)

deepen their sense of community identity and unify them. Tom Davies, a child brought up on an intentional community, puts it rather well: *"One of the best things about growing up in a community is the amount of contact that a child gets with people from outside of the 'conventional' family set up"* (in Diggers and Dreamers, 2000).

Hoult (1991) made a cycle journey around the UK visiting communes and intentional communities. At Tipi Valley, he recounted that,

"Brig described the valley as a university of outdoor living, peopled by researchers, postgraduates, undergraduates and freshers...All sought the answer to living in harmony with the environment on a basis of minimum consumption. Live simply so others simply live."

...participatory process and community design...

An essential part of any practical strategy to boost community participation needs to place far more emphasis on listening to people's views and involving them at the local neighbourhood and community level. It is through this sort of grassroots participation that empowerment involving environmental activities actually takes place. Often, the opinions of experts will need to be considered, but in moving toward ecological outcomes, communities must make their own decisions about how much change they wish to make, and at what pace. The participatory process is based on the following assumptions:

- There are no 'best' solutions to social and environmental problems, since each problem has a number of alternative solutions.
- Imported expert opinion should only be used in collaboration with those affected. All involved should participate; be able to state their opinions and contribute their expertise.
- The process is continuous and ever changing, since the process must be re-evaluated and adapted to changing needs.

Thankfully, there are some practical, useful processes that people and communities can now adopt. 'Planning for Real', in the UK, has evolved a set of hands-on techniques to sort out, at a local level, *"What needs to be done to improve (their) surroundings?"* (Shell, 2000). These involve local people in the building of three-dimensional models of their community. This gives the participants a bird's eye view of their surroundings and can help them to look at community facilities, derelict spaces, traffic problems, anti-social behaviour – in fact a whole range of problems and possibilities. It engages people in looking critically at their area and assessing what is good and bad about it. From its roots in community development in Scotland during the 1970s, the technique has become a major tool for rural and urban regeneration. For instance, thousands of schoolchildren and adults have been involved in workshops assessing facilities in the region around Exmoor National Park in Southwest England. The model is simple, accessible, and allows everyone to contribute their ideas. As the model evolves it can be used to 'test out' the location of new facilities and develop local action plans. It effectively levels the playing field between the professionals, planners and anyone else taking part in the exercise. The process is non-threatening, frequently 'fun', and provides a high level of community participation.

Variations of this process have included elaborate Internet based 'Planning for Real' exercises, such as the Web based public participation project run by the University of Leeds in the West Yorkshire village of Slaithwaite (Carver *et al.,* 1999). This made extensive use of the Web based Geographical Information System (GIS) maps, which allowed participants from the community to examine their community's structure in extreme detail and accuracy. Two particular community environmental issues were tackled as a result of the exercise: nuclear waste disposal and woodland planting.

The research community has also made a contribution to the furtherance of community participation in environmental improvements. This has developed through the evolution of participatory action research (PAR), which itself developed from participatory rural appraisals (PRA), many of which have taken place in developing countries. The techniques mark a move away from the process whereby experts are brought in to study and solve local problems, toward a collaborative framework where any member of the community can participate in the research, planning and evaluation process. It is applicable to very diverse issues whether it be the selection of crops to be grown in Nigeria, or situating a Travellers' site near Hull. It has been found to be particularly effective in giving a voice to those not usually heard, such as people with disabilities, ethnic minorities, homeless people, children, women and older people (see for instance Kontinnen, 1995). As we've already suggested, effective change occurs best when it is part of an empowerment process and organised *from the bottom up.* This also seems to be the most likely route through which fundamental environmental lifestyle changes can be brought about.

Finally, community participation can be aided by adopting empowering 'processes', such as the one known as 'Social Action' (Centre for Social Action, 1999). The process puts the stress on 'ownership' of actions by participants. Originating from a proactive youth work approach, workers act as facilitators, not as leaders. One easily adaptable version of this, which is appropriate in a variety of community settings, takes a group through various stages of reflection and involvement:
- What's good and what's wrong with your community?
- Why is it like this?
- How can you change things?
- Planning and taking action.
- Reflection on what has been achieved and what next?

...from community participation to community development ...

In the book, *Community Development,* Jim Ife (1997) suggests a number of 'grassroots' participatory strategies and outcomes for the Australian suburbs. Local communities, he says, should have the authority and responsibility to initiate and manage services that *they* decide they need, in a way that best suits them. Problems should be dealt with in their community context, rather than in a removed and artificial environment. Even the justice system could, to some extent, become community-controlled rather than operated only through the formal mechanisms of remote

At a more practical level, community facilities (such as schools, clinics, offices, halls etc.) could be shared rather than be used by a single interest. There could be community or group ownership of items such as garden and woodworking tools, washing machines, lawn mowers, books, recreational equipment, games, bicycles, computers and so on. In many existing communities the local library is a prime example of a community-focused resource. Others could be the convenient central location of a computer room, a workshop, a community laundry, or a community vegetable garden. Another possibility is for a particular person or family to take responsibility on behalf of the community for the storage, care and maintenance of a particular item. This not only establishes community ownership and responsibility, but also creates a role for a person in the community, perhaps someone with little other purpose who might otherwise feel marginalised.

All these measures, Ife argues, help people move away from the dominant forms of private ownership and consumerism, which present the main obstacle to collaborative alternatives. Yet, their implementation

Street commons: amalgamated back yards (top left), community vegetable garden (top right), common house kitchen (bottom left) and shared workshop (bottom right)

courts. For instance, this has already occurred in Scotland with the establishment of the Children's Hearing System. Dependent people should be seen as the community's responsibility, rather than the family's or the State's, and the community itself would determine how best their needs might be met. Where people need practical or emotional support they would be able to seek it locally from people or services with which they are familiar. Ife contends that problems of poverty would be seen as the community's responsibility, as long as the community was in control of its local economy, and the distribution of its own resources (Ife, 1997).

is essential if we are to move towards lower levels of material consumption without a corresponding loss of quality of life. Ife notes the importance of due and fair process in the management of community resources, suggesting that, participation will only be encouraged if communities redefine traditional decision-making processes and formal meeting procedures. He suggests that conventional procedures can be very alienating and notes that more recent consensus-based decision-making processes can overcome these obstacles to participation.

Some of these possibilities have already been demonstrated by N-Street Cohousing, the so-called *retro-fit* cohousing project in Davis, California, that started when two neighbours decided to remove the fence between them and garden their lots collaboratively. Over time, more and more neighbours who saw the value of greater sharing and collaboration joined the group simply by removing perimeter fences and making the necessary commitment to contribute to community life. Each household was required to house a facility they shared with community members, such as a workshop, laundry, sauna etc. The ground floor of one building became a dedicated neighbourhood centre.

An Australian example of a genuine, grass-roots community initiative has been described by Baird (1984) in a section of his book entitled, *Pull down the fences and rip up the roads.* Baird reports that four families living in Thornbury, Victoria, decided to demolish their fences and establish a community with the following features:

- a 'luxurious' shared vegetable garden and compost/mulcher;
- a large play space for the family's children;
- the sharing of 1 lawnmower, 2 washing machines, 1 set of tools, 1 dog, 1 cat and 1 rabbit between 4 families;
- the conversion of garages into a food store, a tool shed, a workroom and a rumpus room for the kids; and
- monthly shopping for bulk food items.

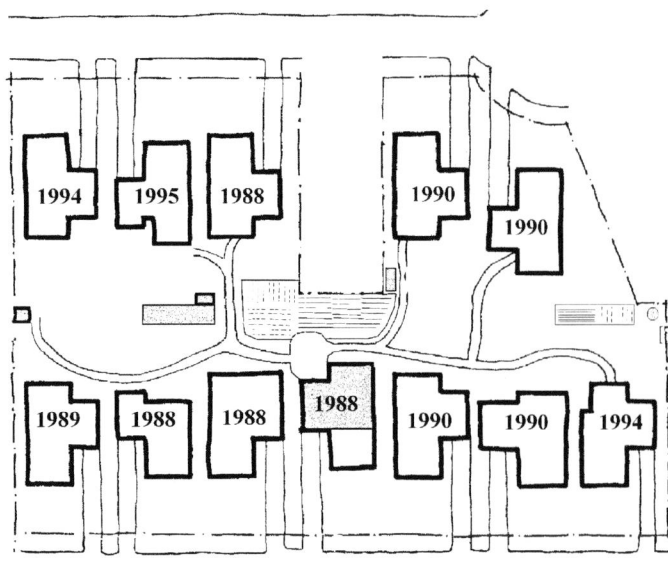

N-Street site plan with date of each household's admission

The people involved became close, supportive friends. The operation of their small cooperative helped build a sense of community and provided members with the time and facilities for satisfying, non-domestic pursuits. It is our understanding that the community still existed (in 2000) and has grown to include 6 households.

Ultimately, people need to be encouraged to assess their own preferences with regard to the level of communality they wish to engage in. These preferences include decisions concerning:

- personal space
- shared ownership/use of property and belongings
- child rearing and education
- personal income
- communal work
- meal preparation and eating.

Cohousing offers some positive opportunities to move towards a more communal lifestyle, as do a variety of other forms of collective organisation – many of which feature in the personal contributions in Part Two of this book.

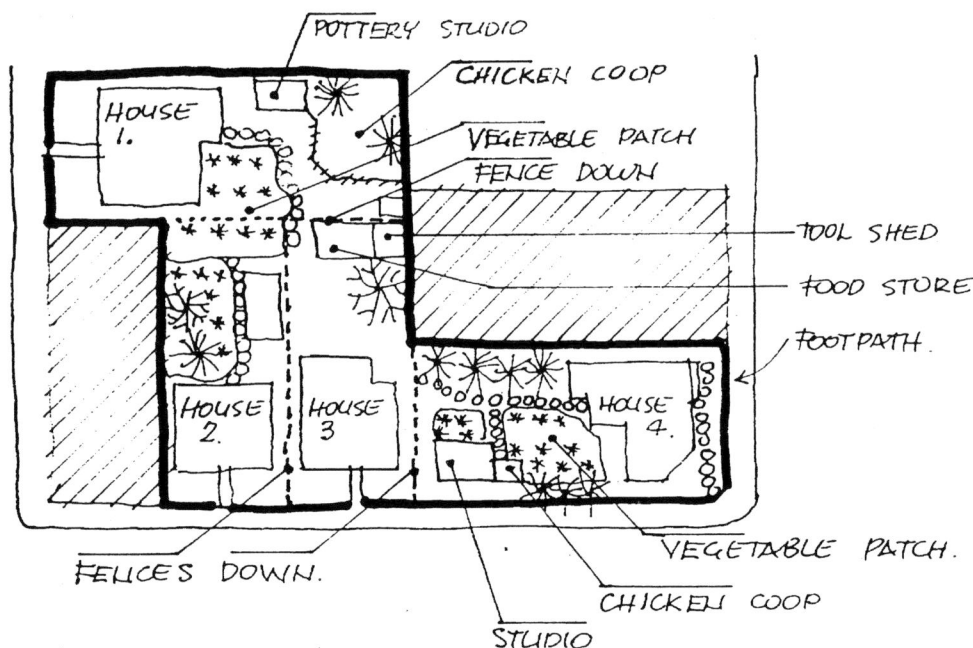

An example of *retro-fit* cooperative housing (after Baird 1984:20)

...a quality of life...

Clark (1995) reminds us of the community-focused social norms of indigenous communities. Such peoples might be considered 'poor' from a conventional Western perspective, yet they have much to teach us about social and community relations.

> *"Their material throughput is small, but their security within the group is high. Ideas, information, stories, songs, humour, grief, listening and talking – the human aspects of living – are abundant and readily shared"* (Clark, 1995).

Can community involvement alone turn round run down estates?
(Alan Dearling)

Marsh (1982) has pointed out that the *"disregard"* of the nineteenth and twentieth century *"cluster of back-to-nature and Simple Life ideas was almost total"*, but it did contribute to, *"...the loose popular belief that primitive and peasant communities possess a quality now lost to frenetic, modern, alienated and genocidal mankind."*

Once we begin to believe that humans might prefer to be pro-social, through sharing, collaborating, and participating in the activities of a socially cohesive group, then there are many social institutions we might choose to redefine, some of which we have already mentioned in relation to Ife's work. Interestingly, aspects of this are already occurring in the mainstream of housing and social welfare planning. Cole *et al* (1998), building on the work of David Page (1993 and 1994), suggest that, *"A more fruitful approach may rest on enhancing social diversity at neighbourhood level."*

In social housing, provided by or through the State apparatus, the need for community involvement in planning has become a major debating point. In the UK, this is characterised by an almost obsessive move towards viewing social housing as being one of the last bastions of the Welfare State – with a strong social engineering aspect. The emphasis is now on providing housing that is affordable, and provided as a part of the Housing Plus/enabling function of local and national government. Within this scenario, 'communities' are seen as needing to be carefully constructed entities, planned and built to reflect a social balance, based on class, housing tenure, ethnicity and

age. Mumford and Power (2002) add that, *"there is an urgent new emphasis on urban regrowth."*

Dearling (forthcoming) points to the level of 'anomie' and dislocation being felt by many people living in large housing estates. He states that there is *"a mix of optimism and pessimism about community involvement"* and how far it can provide an answer to the problems of every day street crime, alienation and severe deprivation.

We hope that some alternatives are offered in Part Two of this book, where our contributors offer a rich variety of personal stories reflecting their own quests for dwellings, communities and lifestyles that are, in different ways, a contribution to alternative, more ecological ways of living. As you will quickly realise, communities of interest, as well as geographical communities and communes feature quite strongly. But a common thread is that almost all of these contributors feel that society as a whole needs to achieve a 'cultural shift'. Various forms of communality, sharing, and a move towards more tolerance, inclusion and less competitiveness are all parts of this mosaic (we won't dare to call it a blueprint!). The changes to our value system will be profound but ultimately, suggests Clark (1995), it will evolve a culture far more satisfying of our basic human needs. Bertrand Russell was prophetic when he identified the single biggest block to cultural change – it is: *"...the preoccupation with possessions more than anything else that prevents man from living freely and nobly."*

References

Baird, J. (1984). *By Design: Changing Australian Housing.* AE Press.

Bettelheim, B. (1971) *The Children of the Dream.* Paladin.

Carver, S. *et al.* (1999) *Virtual Slaithwaite: A Web based public participation* at www.geog.leeds.ac.uk/research/papers/99-8

Centre for Social Action (1999) *Youthagenda.* Centre for Social Action, De Montfort University.

Chavis, D. M. and Wandersman, A (1990). 'Sense of Community in the Urban Environment: A Catalyst for Participation and Community Development'. *American Journal of Community Psychology* 18(1): 55-81.

Cole, I. *et al.* (1998) *Creating communities, or Welfare housing?* Chartered Institute of Housing.

Clark, M. E. (1995). 'Changes in Euro-American Values Needed for Sustainability'. *Journal of Social Issues* 51(4): 63-82.

Darling, P and Fulcher, S. (1984) 'Searching' in *The Rural Resettlement Handbook.* Prism Alpha.

Dearling, A. and Newburn, T. (forthcoming, 2003) *Real Lives: talking to residents on one estate during regeneration.* Joseph Rowntree Foundation.

Dregger, L. (2000) 'Aspects of community life. *Eurotopia.* Eurotopia collective.

Fromm, E. (1965) *The Sane Society.* Routledge & Kegan Paul.

Hagamaier, S. and Stengel, M. eds. (2000) *Eurotopia.* Eurotopia.

Hoult, C. (1991) *Living Green.* Green Books.

Houriet, R. (1971) *Getting Back Together.* Sphere.

Ife, J. (1997). *Community Development: Creating Community Alternatives - Vision, Analysis and Practice.* Longman.

Jefferies, R. (1879) *The Amateur Poacher.*

Kontinnen, P. (1995) *Solar cookers for use in Namibia.* Helsinki University of Technology.

Marsh, J. (1982) *Back to the Land.* Quartet.

Martell, L. (1994). *Ecology and Society.* Polity Press.

Metcalf, B. (2000) 'Sustainable communal living around the globe'. *Diggers and Dreamers 2000/2001.* Diggers and Dreamers.

Metcalf, B. (2000) 'Where do you come from, my lovely?' *Eurotopia.* Eurotopia collective.

Mumford, K. and Power, A. (2002) *Boom or Abandonment?* Chartered Institute of Housing.

Neighbourhood Initiatives Foundation (n.d.) *Planning for Real.* Neighbourhood Initiatives Foundation.

Page, D. (1993) *Building for Communities.* Joseph Rowntree Foundation.

Page, D. (1994) *Developing Communities.* Joseph Rowntree Foundation.

Rheingold, H. (1993). *The Virtual Community: Homesteading on the Electronic Frontier.* Addison-Wesley.

Rosenfield, H. *et al.* (1973) *The Kibbutz.* Sadan Publishing.

Roszak, T. (1979) *Person/Planet: The Creative Disintegration of Industrial Society.* Victor Gollancz.

Sale, K. (1991) *Dwellers in the Land: The Bioregional Vision.* New Society.

Schumacher, E. F. (1973) *Small is Beautiful.* Abacus Books.

Tanner, L. (1999). 'Anti-social disease is spreading: Welcome to Lonely Street, Australia'. *The Australian.* Brisbane: 13.

Technology of an appropriate kind and making 'spaces'
Alan Dearling, with contributions from Graham Meltzer

As you will realise by now, this isn't a technical-manual type of book, so in this section we are not attempting to provide a guide to alternative power sources and technologies. Rather, we are trying to describe the context in which people choose their dwellings to reflect their lifestyle relationship with the environment. These options and choices are not absolute and are part of complex relationships with our families, friends, work, ambitions and ideology. Satish Kumar, visionary behind the UK's *Resurgence* magazine and many other eco-oriented projects, once summed it up saying that we have 'no destination'. Instead we are, or should be, forever on a journey.

A major part of this journey requires us to start 'unlearning' involvement in the rampant consumerism that has become the underlying obsession of Westernised humanity. But 'treading lightly' (in technological and environmental terms) takes some learning as well; it is as much an art as a science, and a move in that direction will require a cultural shift for many people. Part of the art is embedded in a search for wholeness and holistic thinking in tackling local and global problems.

As much as anything, it is about re-learning our relationship with nature. And that has a lot to do with our lifestyles – what goes on inside our buildings and its relationship with the surrounding habitats. A few years ago, a regular 'urbanite' called Peter Mortimer embarked on a personal journey of discovery walking from the southern coast of England up across the borders into Scotland – without any money in his pockets. He was ill-prepared for the journey, both physically and mentally, but his learning curve related to the central theme of 're-discovering our place'. At the end of the trip he recounted that:

> *"I discovered startlingly simple truths, prominent among which (for a townie) was the fact that everything we make or manu-*

facture, we eventually tire of. What's made or created by nature, on the other hand, never worries us."

Bernard Rudofsky was one of the first to urge the architectural profession to look back over its collective shoulder in search of answers in 'vernacular architecture' based on locally available forms and materials. He said that,

> *"The untutored builders in space and time...demonstrate an admirable talent for fitting their buildings into natural surroundings"* and added that, *"vernacular architecture does not go through fashion cycles. It is nearly immutable, indeed unimprovable"* (Rudofsky, 1964).

He added that: *"...the philosophy and know-how of the anonymous builders presents the largest untapped source of architectural inspiration for industrial man."*

With new scientific knowledge and understanding of appropriate technology in terms of energy efficiency, passive and active alternative power sources and recycling through composting and grey water systems, these original 'spaces' are obviously improvable, but the forms themselves remain much closer to nature than most 21st century urban dwellers might be comfortable with.

Organic field with windturbine (Graham Meltzer)

We believe that just perhaps, the last thirty or forty years of re-discovery of environmentalism, 'nature' if you like, and in parts communalism, may help to evolve this new fabric into a form for a more caring and eco-focused society. Once referred disparagingly to as the 'Aquarian Conspiracy' there does seem to be a new groundswell of concern for truly ecological 'solutions'.

...towards a new satoyama...

In Japan, *satoyama* means literally, the precious landscape, which can be a mountainside, a forest, a river or whatever. More recently, the Japanese have started talking about the 'new satoyama', which is being used to describe the delicate relationship between technology and nature. We cannot disregard technology, but we can look towards finding technology that is appropriate to our needs and to the location/environment we live in. As we have tried to explain elsewhere in this first part of the book, and through the personal

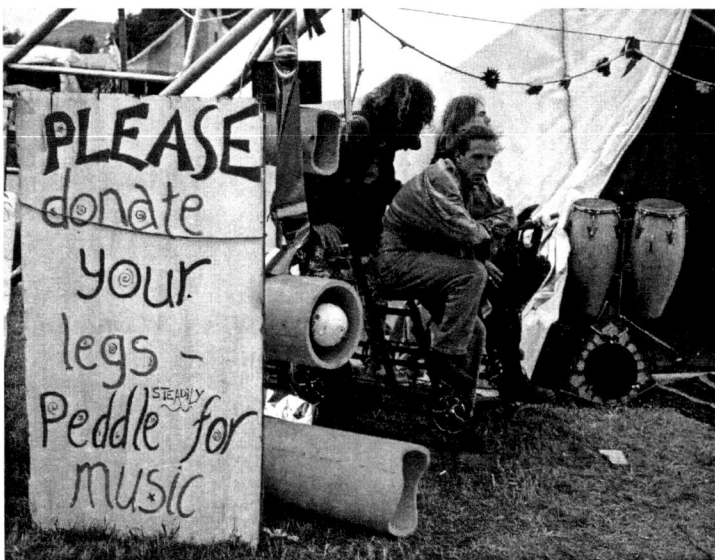

Pedal for Power! (Alan Dearling)

'stories' of the dwellings and lifestyles that we have included in Part Two, our dwellings are extremely indicative of our diverse range of responses to:

- environmental sustainability,
- the level of impact they make on the environment,
- the making of lifestyle choices about how and where we live,
- social sustainability, and for some
- economic sustainability.

The 'technologies' we are referring to are also a mixed list:

- solar, wind, hydro and other forms of renewable power sources,

- use of locally available, recycled and low embodied energy materials,
- effective, localised waste management,
- the use of building systems and materials that enable high levels of energy efficiency

Running parallel to this list are the appropriate technological and social changes that need to be occurring alongside changes in building types, design and construction, and choices of dwellings including:

- available and sustainable employment, education, leisure and health opportunities in the local area,
- new and extended public transport systems, coupled with pollution and hazard free networks for walkers and cyclists,
- participation and involvement of local people in decisions affecting their homes, lives and lifestyles,
- proactive partnerships between architects, planners, builders and current or prospective residents concerning the designs for and structuring of new and regenerated living spaces,
- a move towards greater communality.

As you will read in Part Two, a number of our contributors feel that their current dwellings and their lifestyles involve considerable compromise in terms of the above criteria. This may be particularly true for some of the younger writers who are still at transitional stages in their own personal lives. And for others, their more permanent choice of dwelling, lifestyle and community may be further down a personal road

Straw bale house (Graham Meltzer)

toward their utopian ideal. Inevitably, personal choices and options are often severely restricted not just by finances, but also by the social norms and cultures of the countries and societies that they are living in, and the commitment and willingness of would-be eco-dwellers to challenge commonly held assumptions about 'acceptable behaviour'.

...what is appropriate?...

We used the phrase 'technology of an appropriate kind' as part of the title for this section, yet appropriateness is obviously a very personal and subjective criteria. Clearly, it is important to respond intelligently and sensitively to climate, topography, landscape and existing vegetation. However, one of the greatest challenges is to ensure that dwellings are as appropriate as possible for a range of human societies and cultures.

Underground passive solar house (Graham Meltzer)

Too often the designs for eco-dwellings have been seen as remote from 'normal' communities. They are 'remote' in at least two senses. At one extreme, there are designer homes and Smart houses, filled with high cost solutions to energy efficiency. At the other end of the spectrum, there are the proponents of some kind of 'back to nature' solution. Perhaps predictably, this divide exists in this book as well. Many of the people and communities represented in Part Two of this publication are characterised by making lower cost, lower impact choices in rural settings for their dwellings. But this does not *necessarily* mean that they represent an environmentally sustainable lifestyle, nor offer blue-prints of any kind for mass-housing.

Whilst two-thirds of the world's population live in

rural areas, the vast majority of the people in post-industrialised nations live in towns and cities. Sadly, their beliefs and aspirations are more attuned to the hard sell of the media, than the proselylitising of environmentalists. Their world remains a quantum leap away from those who have been at the forefront of championing an alternative philosophy for living, such as Gerard Morgan-Grenville. He was the founder in the early 1970s of Europe's foremost showcase for alternative technology at the Centre for Alternative Technology in Wales and has no self-doubts, saying:

> "Alternative Technology provides for communal self-sufficiency, without sacrificing comfort, without waste, without depleting non-renewable sources and without harming the environment" (quoted in Osmond and Graham, 1984).

Many people have grappled with this conundrum, amongst them, delegates to the Rio de Janeiro Earth Summit in 1992. Agenda 21, which was published following that conference, was designed as an environmental action plan for the 21st century. Two quotes from Chapter 7 of the Agenda may help to clarify the issues:

> "All countries should...strengthen the indigenous building materials industry, based, as much as possible, on inputs of locally available natural resources...promote the increased use of energy efficient designs and technologies and sustainable use of natural esources...promote the use of labour-intensive construction methods...develop policies and practices to reach the informal sector and self-help builders...discourage the use of construction materials and products that create pollution during their life cycle.

> All countries should, as appropriate, support the shelter efforts of the urban and rural poor by adopting and/or adapting existing codes and regulations to facilitate their access to land, finance and low cost building materials."

Interestingly and importantly, the second quotation

39

makes the link between housing need and supply, which sometimes gets forgotten, especially in texts for builders, architects and planners. It begins to make 'real' the 'mission statements' of politicians and statesmen around the world. It also underlines how crucial a supportive planning system is to the adoption of the plethora of alternative technologies. In reality, while the political support for sustainable technology and dwellings appears to be in place, the eco-dweller is often forced to operate outside of, or on the fringes of planning legislation. Some of this comes down to the 'visibility' of the dwelling and the people involved; the reaction of neighbours and the general public, and the personal attitudes of the officials involved in the planning process. To challenge, inform and bring about positive change in that process is a major factor in the necessary 'learning revolution', and it is the focus of many lobbying and campaigning groups worldwide (for instance, Friends of the Earth; Earth First!; Reclaim the Streets; Greenpeace; The Land is Ours and Chapter 7). We would guess that many of the contributors to Part Two of this book would also identify themselves as a part of that groundswell and revolution.

...making spaces...

The contributions and interactions of different people are very important if our impact on the environment is to become more benign. Making our own living space can be a solitary activity, but it is likely to offer more opportunities through co-operation and sharing both of information about technology and in the activity of construction. This is true for the person who lives in a scrap raft, a tipi or an energy-efficient straw bale house. It is true whether one opts for learning through doing and a hand-made approach to building, or using professionals in partnerships. It is about knowledge, choice and empowerment at least as much as it is about technology. Two of the main groups who potential 'consumers' of eco-dwellings may need to learn more from are what we've called environmental technologists and architects. Particularly in urban settings and where refurbishment and renovation of buildings are concerned, their involvement may be imperative. Books and manuals can offer some of the information, but as we've already discussed, taking the eco-dwellings 'journey' is usually greatly enhanced where it is co-operative activity!

Environmental technologists: are not one group of people, but include environmentalists, alternative technologists, green activists and campaigners and more. Their motivations can be complex and conflicting as was often the case with the people who established and then developed the Centre for Alternative Technology. From their account of their progress, *The CAT Story: Crazy Idealists,* they saw themselves as people with *"first class brains and hands, giving up promising careers and generous salaries to throw in their lot with a mixed bag of human greenery."* There was internal conflict about whether their efforts were in order that they could *"raise a drawbridge"* and live at the cutting edge of alternative technology, or were geared to providing a *"service to the public"* (CAT, 1995). The roles and knowledge base of the CAT community are perhaps typical of the range of environmental technologists, and can include being educators and even prophets regarding:

- construction materials

- the range of possible dwellings

- energy consumption and conservation

- passive and active power sources and types of power storage and converters

- solar orientation of dwellings

- recycling

- self-build and co-operative building

- low maintenance and high durability systems

- ventilation and insulation methods

- composting and grey water systems

Alternative power demonstration at the Centre for Alternative Technology in Wales (Alan Dearling)

- organic and permaculture cultivation

Architects: have traditionally tended to value monumental architecture above the everyday vernacular of living spaces. Some of the more famous and publicised architects have perceived themselves as artists and as being hierarchically, the 'Master Builder'. However, the majority of architects have always focused their attentions, away from the spotlight, on designs for private and public buildings. More recently, that has begun to be augmented with some new options for their profession. As Joseph Wines (2000) has suggested, *"...the profession is being compelled to force a radical re-evaluation of its priorities."* Indeed a number of architects have been the trailblazers in evolving a new tradition of green or ecological architecture. Their new roles include:

- offering an antidote to man's alienation from nature;

- pioneering green architecture which offers both aesthetic design appeal and utilises the essentials of sustainable building practices and technologies;

- helping to reflect nature in designs and stressing the inter-dependence of natural and built environments;

- working in partnerships with residents in decision-making to carry out community or social architecture, and achieve what Ted Cullinan claims is to *"...produce something which is visually beautiful and socially useful"* (Wates and Knevitt, 1987);

- considering use of a whole range of locally sourced and as far as possible, renewable, building materials and techniques including wood framed dwellings, rammed earth, mud-brick, earth covered structures, kit houses, straw-bale, stone, troglodyte-structures – the list is almost endless and takes us beyond the scope of this publication;

- looking at ways in which design can help to create community, and considering the use of more communal spaces and co-operation planning, design and building schemes;

- offering housing design options which are in harmony with nature, and as architect

David Lea suggests, make them *"...have a resonance which quickens our spirits"* (in Wines, 2000) and takes a building beyond being just a structure and towards becoming 'art' as Hundertwasser also suggested;

- ultimately to evolve a Taoist architecture where architecture and landscape can become a single blended entity.

...housing facilitation...

The need for socially appropriate, affordable housing is, and will increasingly become, a major factor in the development of sustainable urban communities. Yet there are few, if any areas, where the contrast between conventional (consumerist) approaches and sustainable alternatives is as great. Ted Trainer, author of *What is to be done – Now?* (1999) remains pessimistic about the transition to a 'simpler way', as he calls it.

"Our best hope is that as consumer society increasingly fails to provide for people that they will be able to see around them

Papier mâché house (Graham Meltzer)

settlements in which people are living with a 'high quality of life', in sustainable and just ways."

It may also be that negative pressures such as the volume of traffic, crime and disorder, vandalism and pollution will become so insufferable that individuals, communities and planners will look for new housing options and ways of regenerating both buildings and geographic areas.

Access to and ownership and tenure of accommodation and land are the keys to more participative forms of housing facilitation. The provision of

41

Ecologically sustainable sewage plant (Graham Meltzer)

In terms of eco-regeneration one suggestion is to support the provision of a local building resource centre. This type of facility can become a gateway for the community to share information and resources with different professionals and sources of expertise. At Lea View House in a run-down part of Hackney, Hunt Thompson architects moved three of their team into a flat on the estate. They said afterwards that their,

> "...search for a meaningful and lasting solution was the tenant community itself, available at first hand and with detailed and highly critical knowledge and opinions about every single aspect of their own environment...the process of regeneration of the estate has also regenerated the community spirit." (Wates and Knevitt, 1987)

Ultimately, it may be possible to establish centres which offer everything from experienced advice and a wide range of information on design and planning, architects and builders, technology engineers and the provision of recycled construction materials, solar, water and wind power. This base could support real partnership schemes incorporating environmentally-friendly approaches to a whole range of building and renovation projects. Some people might build for themselves, more would contract out the difficult initial stages of set-out, foundations and work up to floor level. Others might wish to work with contractors until the shell is secured and carry out later modifications themselves. Such a local resource could also support the establishment of new agencies and associations, born out of need. In this scenario, genuine community architecture could be nurtured from within communities.

housing through forms of community tenure, co-operatives, co-housing, housing associations and intentional communities can all be seen as steps forward towards more participation. However, much more thought needs to be given to the eco-renovation of existing buildings and communities. There are no simple solutions, and without employment opportunities in particular locations, regeneration is almost bound to founder.

An ecological perspective is fairly obviously concerned with preventing waste. Therefore, tired, older buildings and buildings whose use has changed should be used as the focus for evolving, creative and reparative activity. Design can become an ongoing activity that integrates with user control. Construction and assembly can be augmented by adaptation, extension and upgrading. In fact, housing *facilitation* is central to this process of adaptation and evolution. A process that can more readily respond to the changing needs and visions of the occupants. Wellesly-Miller is amongst the proponents of this facilitation/adaptation approach:

> "A 'start-up' structure is built and moved into immediately. Over time the structure is extended and added to, new systems are incorporated, and the older ones integrated or sold. After some time a relatively stable state is reached, and the mature dwelling enters a long cycle of tuning, upgrading and adaption" (Wellesly-Miller, 1972).

At the level of community development, some communities have begun to develop self-help responses. This often arises from positive community work by a housing co-operative or housing association; sometimes as a result of a strong local residents' association. Money alone is usually not the answer.

References

CAT. (1995) *The CAT Story: Crazy Idealists.* Centre for Alternative Technology.
Mortimore, P. (1999) *Broke through Britain.* Mainstream Publishing.
Osmond, J and Graham, A. (1984) *Alternatives.* Thorsons.
Trainer, T. (1999) *What is to be done – now?*
Rudofsky, B. (1964) *Architecture without Architects.* Doubleday/Museum of Modern Art, New York.
Wates, N. and Knevitt, C. (1987) *Community Architecture.* Penguin.
Wellesly-Miller, S. (1972). 'Work Notes on the Need for a New Building Technology'. *The Responsive House.* E. Allen. MIT Press.
Wines, J. (2000) *Green Architecture.* Taschen.

Part Two:
Pioneers, innovators, artists and crafts people

Brithdir Mawr – the secret village
Alan Dearling

It was in 1998 that a pilot surveying the Pembrokeshire coast in Wales spotted the reflection of a solar panel near the farm-house at Brithdir Mawr. His find led to the be-lated 'discovery' of a secret eco-village lo-cated in the Pembrokeshire Coast

The dome house

National Park. It had already existed for over four years. It is home to 22 residents, who had quietly developed a sustainable intentional community with its own wind generator, water turbine, solar panels, water and fuel sources, organic gardens, horses for work-duties and goats for milk and cheese. The National Park had originally given permission for the renovation of the dilapidated farmhouse, but had been unaware of the development of the other eco-buildings, including a geodesic dome meeting house, a roundhouse with a turf roof, and a straw-bale barn.

In March 1999, the park authority planning officers allowed the villagers to stay on but ordered the removal of the three most ecologically sustainable buildings. At the time, Paul Wimbush, one of the villagers, was reported in the *Daily Telegraph* (26/3/99) saying: *"People are beginning to realise that there must be a better way of living than in noisy, crowded cities. There has been a definite change in attitude towards communities like ours who wish to live a sustainable existence."* However, despite this limited 'success', the villagers have had to fight against a tide of bureaucracy, based it seems on fear of setting a precedent for environmentally sustainable building. Subsequently, the community have gained a range of planning permissions for all except the roundhouse. At the time of putting this piece together, the fight continues. Their website includes an update: www.thatroundhouse.info

They are not alone

Simon Fairlie in the *Big Issue* (12-18/3/01) wrote,

"Self-building is far cheaper than renting or buying a conventional house…local materials such as stabilised earth, timber and straw bales cost very little and labour is free…It is not just affordability that self-builders are looking for. Many are disillu-sioned with conventional housing and want to live

sustainably without contributing to global warming or excessively using the world's dwindling re-sources."

Simon lives what he preaches. He helped establish Tinkers' Bubble, a 40 acre, low-impact village, complete with an orchard and about a dozen permanent residents, near Stoke-sub-Hamdon in Somerset. He is also the co-ordinator of Chapter 7, a campaigning arm of The Land is Ours which publishes an informative newsletter on low-impact developments and offers planning advice at

Building with straw bales

The outside of the roundhouse

(www.oneworld.org/tlio/chapter7/). Like Brithdir Mawr, the King's Hill bender collective (also in Somerset), Tipi Valley in Wales and Caroline Barry's straw-bale smallholding near Glastonbury, Tinkers' Bubble has had to fight for its right to remain on land they purchased for £50,000 in 1994 by selling 25 shares at £2,000 each. Some of the tricks of the eco-building trade, are to persuade the planning authorities that the buildings are 'temporary' and do not intrude on the landscape, so as Nicole Veash reported on Tinker's Bubble in the *Observer* (17/1/99),

"One of the local authority stipulations was that the community should be hidden from sight...Next to the orchard, Simon and Chris are hammering pieces of corrugated iron into a half-built barn. The council won't let them build a permanent structure, so they've bound it together with string."

Because planning permission for low-impact dwellings in rural areas is so hard to obtain despite national policy commitment to sustainable developments, many self-builders have moved on to the land first and fought for planning permission later on. In England and Wales, it seems easiest to persuade planners of the need for a low-impact dwelling if the land use surrounding the dwelling can generate at least a part time income. So, permaculture and organic farming, chicken farms, woodlands and orchards are among the typical developments practised by would-be eco-dwellers.

And back at Brithdir Mawr – the roundhouse

For the preparation of this piece, Tony Wrench who lives at Brithdir Mawr, kindly sent me a selection of wonderful photos taken by himself and Spike Watson of their community and in particular the roundhouse. He said,

"I'm struggling with the permanent feeling of being gutted by the planning inspector's decision that this roundhouse must be demolished before July 2002. I put so much of what I believe into this place, and I can increasingly see what a threat such a harmless abode is to the established wisdom. No mortgage, no bills, no car, no cement – what if everybody tried to live like this?"

Olwyn, a neighbour, wrote about roundhouse,

"It is an experimental structure built into a south-facing bank at the head of a small valley. The bracken covered slope was dug out using a JCB, and the building was set into the semi-circular excavation. Visually it blends in well – it's nearly invisible from a distance."

It even incorporates its own miniature fruit farm,

The roundhouse

with strawberries growing on the roof, four grape-vines, fruit bushes and tayberries around the base of the building. Power comes from a Siemens 50 watt photovoltaic cell, which charges two old 6 volt British Telecom batteries for lighting and radio. Behind the roundhouse are yellow flag and bullrush reed beds which clean grey water outfall and nearby is a composting toilet. Cold water is piped from a spring into a recycled cistern, which acts as a header tank. This in turn feeds water to a wooden whiskey barrel, where it can be heated by either a solar panel or a wood stove. Tony has written up a detailed account of how the round-house was constructed by himself, his partner, Jane Faith and their friends in *Building a low impact roundhouse* (Permanent Publications, 2001).

Jane says, *"We are appealing to the Welsh Assembly to listen to our case, especially as it has been doing a study on low impact settlements and sustainability."*

A supporter of the roundhouse and the community is the Very Reverend Canon James Cunnane of Cardigan. He eloquently sums up the situation:

"It was hard to believe my eyes when reading the inspector's reasons for refusing consent: '…a harmful effect on the natural beauty of the national park if it was allowed to remain.'

I went to see it and was almost upon it before spotting it. Has the inspector forgotten it was only discovered from the air, and then only because the spotter plane 'caught the reflection from a solar panel'?

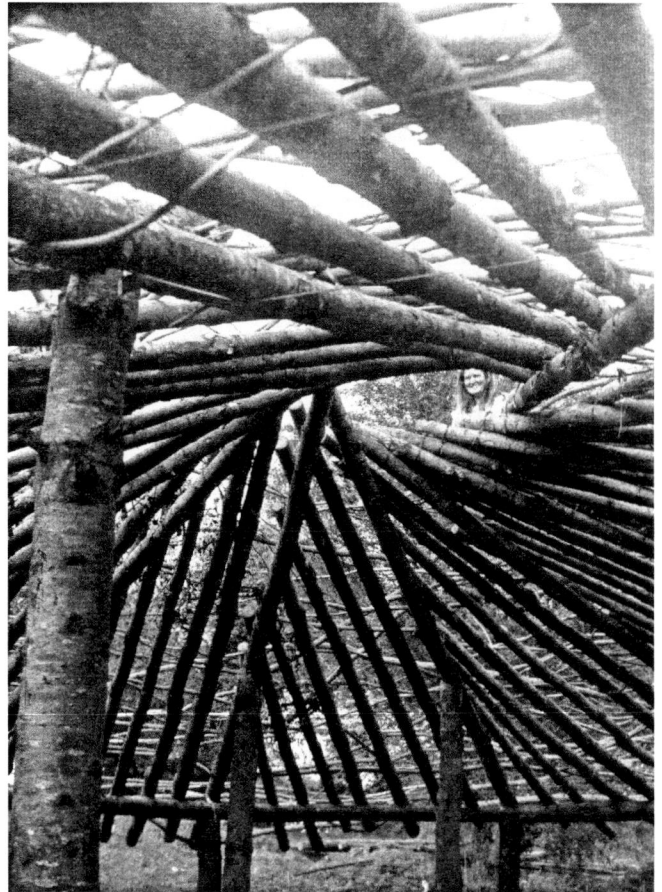

The roof of the roundhouse

The fact that neither I nor, I suspect, most of us would want to live like Tony Wrench is irrelevant. His house is ingenious, unique and the product of deep thought. I admire it. Contrasted with those that the rest of us live in, its impact on the environment is tiny. Let it be!"

Life at Brithdir Mawr

Tony Wrench told me that among the most important aspects of Brithdir Mawr is, *"…the synergy possible in living on a community like this with others of a like mind."*

Each family or single person has their own living space, and the four teenagers have a personal 'quarter' – a bedroom and a loft area to themselves. The members all arrived at the community in an organic way. The community handout reflects this, saying,

"Paul and Erica arrived from Devon in a horse-drawn Gypsy wagon whilst Tony and Jane arrived on a

The reed bed system

46

The Brithdir Mawr farmhouse

who are encouraged to be as involved as possible. Preparing food around the table is one great opportunity for conversation and exchange of ideas. Although a constant stream of new faces can be challenging at times, each new perspective that they bring serves to prevent our own view becoming jaded."

The old farmhouse, built in about the 1850s of Preseli stone, is the hub of the community. Since 1993 the community have largely completed the restoration of the building and eventually hope to rebuild the stable and even the barn water-wheel.

Community living is described by them:

"We eat together four or five times a week – with everyone here (22 of us in total). It's a cosy

milk float from their permaculture holding 20 miles away."

The primary purpose of the community is the *care of the land.* The land is managed through an Environmentally Sensitive Area (ESA) scheme which requires the care of woodland and wetland and the restoration of features such as hedges, green lanes, earth-banks etc. Over 6,000 trees have been planted, hay meadows enhanced and ponds restored. The land has also provided the community with a source of income through the selling of hay, baskets, furniture and wood crafts, and the use of coppice wood for wood turning and charcoal burning. This supplements the income received from guests in their low-cost hostel accommodation in a converted barn. In 1997 this won a prestigious Prince of Wales Award for being an outstanding example of renewable energy in practice. The electricity for the hostel is all generated from the sun, wind and water. Heating depends upon keeping wood in the stove. The community also welcomes camping. Bring your own sleeping bags and other bedding. (Telephone: 01239 820164 or e-mail: brithdir@brithdirmawr.freeserve.co.uk)

Brithdir Mawr means Great Speckled Land in the Welsh language, a striking and apt image for this 165 acres of mixed farmland. The community which was formed in 1993, includes in its aims: *"...to demonstrate experimental building techniques using locally-sourced and natural materials."* Inviting visitors to share in this experiment is central to this mission. The residents say,

"We have a constant flux of visitors and volunteers

Inside the roundhouse

47

squeeze around the substantial home-grown table, but always a lively occasion. Nearly all the ingredients will come from the garden even in the winter and extra points are awarded for inventive and delicious ways to eat through the surplus gherkins!

The community shares responsibility for the land, the gardens and the maintenance on the basis of a single shared workday a week and each person from the age of 11 up being allocated a part in

Putting in the tarp membrane

everyday tasks, according to their skills and desires: these tasks include looking after the hostel, kitchen, teenage loft etc., firewood, gardening, maintenance of machinery and buildings and child care. Community decisions are made by consensus.

There is a tendency towards home education, although Agnes (14) has chosen to go to school for a term in Brittany. When she is home the weekly school day will resume where two other out of school children will come for lessons in maths, history, French, Spanish and English. The younger children are taught on a less formal basis and the teenagers have opted to do vocational courses at local colleges.

As part of the cycle of life we find it nourishing to celebrate the changing seasons. Equinoxes, solstices and cross-quarter days are marked by simple ceremonies that help us to focus on the greater world around us and affirm our place in that world."

A model for the future

Brithdir Mawr is one of three case studies being investigated for a report commissioned by the Welsh Assembly. Hopefully, if that report gives it a favourable recommendation, Tony and Jane will be able to live their dream a little longer by receiving permission to retain the roundhouse. Its continued existence would also give the rest of us some optimism for a more sustainable future.

As Simon Fairlie says,

"Don't despair – most eco-builders win in the end. If you can't face the planners, the other option is to follow the Geoff (from Wiltshire's) example – build your house underground and hope that no-one notices."

There is a little known section of the 1948 Town and Country Planning Act that most planners according to Tony Wrench, *"...don't want us to know about. If you construct a dwelling and live in it for more than four years without receiving an enforcement order, you can prove that you are entitled to a Certificate of Lawful use. Our dome, like Geoff's underground home, has now got one too!"*

Making charcoal

48

Autonomous living
Brenda and Robert Vale

The one thing an architectural education teaches is arrogance, the arrogance to believe that you can do something that runs against norms and conventions; that you can do something that other people have found too difficult to try; and that you can do something that has not been done before. The autonomous house really began with this attitude, though some 20 years were to lapse between the student project, the first autonomous house design, that was published in the 1975 book of the same name[1], and the house that was actually completed in Southwell, Nottinghamshire, in 1993. It did, indeed, take that time to pull together the financial resources to build a detached house with a building loan from the bank, as the aim was to do undertake this project, as anyone else would have to do, with real money in the real world. Research is useful, but if people are to be convinced that it is necessary to change the way we make and live in buildings, then these have to be real buildings for real people made with real money[2]. Research projects alone will not be convincing.

To tell the story of autonomous living, therefore, it is necessary to understand something of the 22 year journey between idea and reality and the story begins, as so many stories in this field do, with the heady days of the late sixties and early seventies. This was the generation that was not just convinced that it could change the world – nothing different there – but that it could change the world quite simply through building a new one of a different shape. This was a generation of architectural determinists who thought that if the buildings were the right ones, then somehow the rest of society and its economic machinery would be transformed into a utopia of environmental respect and concern. Architects were naturally concerned with buildings, but the same attitude can be found throughout this time. It was a time of eating the right food, educating children in the right way, wearing the right hand spun clothing, riding the right bicycle and trailer; a goat in every backyard and a copy of the Whole Earth Catalogue[3] in every piano stool.....

...theories become realities...

What this meant was that theories had to become realties as soon as possible, so our first home was a small holding of one and three-quarter acres with several goats, a cow, sheep, pigs, chickens and various weedy vegetable plots, together with a house insulated to reduce 80 per cent of its energy use[4] and with a 5 kilowatt aerogenerator in the backyard that was, probably illegally, connected into the national grid. In fact the authorities knew about the windmill, well it is hard to conceal something that is five storeys high, but could not think of anything really to do about it. So it unwound the meter when the wind blew and we turned it back the other way when it was not blowing, and so invented net-billing before the Germans had thought of their first solar roof

Small-holding with Mulberry tree

programme. Having a wind generator in the backyard, carefully positioned so that if the tower fell over it would miss the house, is a commitment. It has to be regularly serviced, and this is like servicing a motor bike standing on one leg at the top of a five storey tower. The number of spanners that fell into the blackcurrant bushes below are probably equivalent to the number of times we had to carry (one at each end) a rather recalcitrant goat called Saso, up into the field to graze. Always ready to walk back to the stabling at night, her reluctance to go to proper goat employment became legendary, but you just never give up. If the goat won't walk, then carry it. We even made one goat into a rug but the world is probably not yet ready for publication of *The Misdemeanours of Marigold*!

...moving to Sheffield...

The Vale story should really have ended at that point, the aim being to perfect this self-sufficient life-style in rural Cambridgeshire, and then to live it. However, the need to earn the money to pay off the mortgage on the house and land was interrupted by redundancy, and so we moved to Sheffield in the north of England and found ourselves living in the central city, walking to work at the University and bumping into students over the frozen peas at the local supermarket. Not that small holding was

Passive solar small-holding

totally abandoned, as we had the decency to move the cats and the children with us, but we had to start all over again and dig up the tarmac in the backyard in order to plant a small vegetable and fruit garden. There is something gratifying in being able to mark out a garden plan at 1:1 in chalk on tarmac before any digging starts. Nor was the wish to be self-sufficient in terms of the operation of the house entirely abandoned. The Victorian stone house that we occupied was given a new superinsulated roof. Whilst helping to install this, 100 years of the soot of industrial England was discovered when the old ceiling was removed, and most of it followed gravity downwards. It takes several baths to make any inroads on such greasy soot. We also double glazed windows and insulated under a raised floor and, although we made provision to insulate the stone wall externally, this was never completed before we moved again.

It was during the time that we lived in Sheffield doing up first the house described above, and then a much more modern house which was also

insulated by us in walls, roof, floor and windows to a standard above that normally found, that we acted as architects for a series of medical buildings that achieved high levels of energy reduction in use, typically 80 per cent of normal energy use, at no extra cost[5]. It is one thing to try these techniques out on your own house, but it takes another level of arrogance to assume that you can do them in the real world with other people's money, and using a contractor who may never have heard of a vapour barrier before. Our experience with contractors, however, is that they are all made of the right stuff. If they are asked to do something not encountered before, the response is always one of interest and a desire to know how to do the job properly. When we transferred the same approach of making very energy efficient buildings at no extra cost to social housing, the first job involved a contractor who, putting in his first ever vapour barrier, produced a job of lapping and taping that was straight from the pages of the best Swedish textbook on the subject. It was a superb job and all completely hidden once the building was finished. This was the same job on which a complete set of scaffolding was stolen during the night, and nobody reported hearing any strange noises – but then, it was a very rough neighbourhood. Certainly the UK building industry, as found in the north of the country, was no barrier to making excellently crafted buildings. We just hoped that they all made some sort of profit on these jobs.

...making the autonomous house...

This experience was an important part of making the autonomous house in Southwell, Nottinghamshire[6]. To show that on a number of occasions it was possible to achieve 80 per cent energy reduction, and to measure this in use, somehow seemed too easy. It was necessary to set a higher goal, but for a long while it was hard to see this. Only after attending a conference in Vienna did we realise that what we were doing, which had once seemed outrageous, was now becoming a norm in Europe. So we revised the goals and set out to make a house with zero carbon dioxide emissions, which meant that all its energy would have to come from renewables, and which was to be autonomous for water supply and disposal and sewage treatment as well. This again set a goal such that we had no idea of whether or not it could be achieved, but then it is always good to live dangerously.

In some ways the autonomous house was a really easy thing to design, and did not take very long, as it built upon a lot of work that had gone before. As usual we took the drawings along at an early stage to discuss what we intended to do with the planners and building inspectors. We recall talking nervously to a local building inspector, saying first that we wanted to make a house with lots of insulation so that it would not need any space heating, and after a bit of thought he could see some merit in that. Next we tentatively suggested that we would install enough photovoltaic panels so that we could make all the electricity we needed from the sun, to which he murmured a tentative acquiescence. Lastly we presented the idea that we thought we would not connect to the water or sewerage systems but would undertake these services for ourselves and put a large tank in the basement and a composting toilet. He looked a bit pale at this point and we could not quite catch what he said. Later we learned from the council chief architect, who had being trying to make his local housing stock more energy efficient for years, that the drawings had been brought up to his office and the question asked, *"are these people for real or are they having us on?"* It was probably extremely fortunate for the whole venture that the chief architect knew what he was doing and understood our intentions immediately. We have never lost touch with him since. We also had very little trouble with the planners and building inspectors, and the chief building inspector later used to bring all the lads out to watch the progress of the house as he told them this was the future of building and this was what they would be dealing with on a daily basis.

When it came to building this environmentally friendly house it soon became evident how destructive building really is. Having bought a very expensive piece of land in the middle of England, we then dug a very large hole in it in order to make the basement foundation for the house, since it

was necessary to put the water storage tanks in a place where they could not freeze. One cannot, after all, drink only gin and ice. At this stage the rumour going round the village was that someone was going to build an ice rink on the corner site. Fortunately, the builder, who had been recruited through the normal tender situation, was very sympathetic to the idea of making low impact buildings and located a hole in a field that someone wanted filled, so the excavated spoil went to a good, and local, home. We think the topsoil also found its way to the builder's father's garden, and very good topsoil it was, as the garden adjoined a spot where a local butcher had been slaughtering animals for many years, so there was no need to add any blood and bone meal to it.

Autonomous house, photo-voltaics and the veggie patch

It is great fun building a house, as anyone who recalls the *Honeywood File*[7], might agree. It is also fraught with minor problems that have to be borne with in order to keep the major goal in mind. A nice lady from the Water Company arrived on site one day and asked why there had been no application for a water connection since it was obvious that a new house was being built. The builder carefully brought out the drawings and explained that there was no need for a connection since we were going to install some twenty second-hand orange juice containers from Israel, that he was busy steam cleaning back at the workshop. (In fact the water supply only tasted faintly of citrus for about a month). The next day a very irate man from the Water Company arrived on site and began ranting on about how he would not have his junior employees wound up in this disgraceful way. So the builder had to get all the drawings out again

51

and go through the same explanation all over again, at which point the guy visibly calmed down and began to muse about whether he could do the same thing on the new bungalow he was building nearby. Then there was the time when the builders downed tools for a month in order to go off and surf for the UK (not as good an excuse as the site we ran once where the builders went off for three weeks to do an anti-nuclear live theatre presentation in Amsterdam). At that point the

Autonomous house conservatory

rumour ran round the village that the people building the strange house had run out of money.

Living very close to a building site can also bring other problems. The triple glazed windows with specialist coatings that were used in the autonomous house were factory made, glazed and finished in Sweden. Independent calculations showed that, despite making such a long journey, they had saved the energy of transport in the first two weeks of operation, but then one does have to worry about such things. Such complete windows are, however, very heavy, and this is where the problem came. The windows arrived when the on-site personnel amounted to one builder and two architects, so architects suddenly become jobbing builders and the 1.75 tonnes of windows were duly unloaded and carted into the house. This is

something that those 'running the project' lectures never really warn you about.

Once completed the family moved into the new house at the end of November, which is not a good time of year to inform your children that they are moving to a house with no heating and, worse, no mains drainage. In fact we lived in daily fear of the children being taken into care for being forced to drink rainwater and living above a tank of shit in the cellar. Our daughter kept her legs crossed for long into the first day of the move but eventually had to go and found the composting experience a lot less worse in reality than in imagination, which is true of so many people who are faced with change. In fact the loo, because it had two very small bathrooms back-to-back, with the loos falling into the one composter proved to be rather a chatty place as the connection through the composter carried the sound well, so you could sit back to back and hold a private privy conversation. The biggest coup with the children came, however, when the house appeared in a mock national examination question in the fifth form at school. Our daughter and all the children who had visited the house were able to give very complete answers to the questions as set.

In fact the presence of the house meant that no-one could say that it was not possible to build and live in a much more sustainable way. Demonstration is a very powerful motivator, and some further five autonomous houses have now been built in the next village of Hockerton to some designs by us[8] . The local authority are committed to an expanding programme of zero space heating and autonomous dwellings centred on the Sherwood Energy Village[9], and even the Minister of the Environment came on a visit, but this is digressing from the family story.

...domestic sustainability in New Zealand...

To bring the story to date, the family have grown up and children and parents have now left home, the latter finishing up in New Zealand. The move has given the chance to produce a comfortable zero heated house for Auckland[10], a much easier climate to tackle than that of the UK, and electric transport is now part of the family experience, in the form of a converted Diahatsu Mira purchased from the local power board, which was then privatised. For a tenth the cost per kilometre, it is possible to trundle around home, going fast downhill and taking it carefully on the up. If Newton had had an electric car he would have discovered gravity without having to wait for autumn. However,

Super insulated construction in Auckland

Untreated timber cladding in New Zealand

range is always limited, and the complete set of eight traction batteries in the car only amount to the equivalent energy storage of a litre of petrol, so light-footedness is essential. The car also has some curious design quirks, such as an interconnection between the lighting battery and the traction batteries, the idea being that the car won't go if there is no light. Great in theory but difficult when the lighting battery fails on the way home on a winter's evening – and Waiheke Island, where we live, is not known for its street lighting. The car eventually came home very slowly with the indicator light being used to track the edge of the road.

In many ways this brief history has tackled the three main areas of domestic sustainability – the need to reduce the energy found in food, the energy used in running the house and household and the energy for household transport. An analysis will show that food is the largest energy flow through any household[6] because of the energy bound up in growing, transporting, processing and retailing it. The other two quantities are normally equivalent for an average household. Strange then, that the first project we ever tackled was to do with self-sufficiency in food in ignorance of an analysis that we carried out many years later, but then perhaps first thoughts are often the best. Maybe we should start looking around for a few chooks (chickens) to keep in the backyard.....

References

1   Vale, B. and Vale, R. (1975) *The Autonomous House: design and planning for self-sufficiency*, Thames and Hudson, London.

2   Vale, B. and Vale, R. (1991) *Green Architecture: design for a sustainable future*, Thames and Hudson, London – the premise of this book was to try and refer to real buildings that were attempting to achieve aspects of green architecture.

3   Brand, S. (ed.) (1970) *The Whole Earth Catalogue* Spring edition, Potola Institute Inc., Menlo Park, California. This was the third WEC issued and the first we bought.

4   Vale, R. (1977) 'Low cost thermal upgrading of an existing house' *Environment and Planning* Vol. 4 pp 173-184.

5   Vale B and Vale R (1987) 'A superinsulated masonry health centre within cost yardsticks' *Proceedings of the Conference on Superinsulation* International Solar Energy Society, London, March 26. pp 43-52.

6   Vale, B. and Vale, R. (2000) *The New Autonomous House*, Thames and Hudson.

7   Cresswell, B. (1929) *The Honeywood File*, Faber and Faber.

8   Vale, B. and Vale, R. (1999) 'Gone to Earth: in search of cheap interseasonal thermal storage for low cost zero energy houses' *Proceedings of the PLEA '99 International Conference,* Brisbane, 22-24 Sept Vol 1 pp 275-282.

9   Department of the Environment (1998) GENERAL INFORMATION REPORT 53: *Building a sustainable future*, Department of Environment, Transport and the Regions' Energy Efficiency Best Practice Programme, Crown Copyright, UK .

10   Vale, B. and Vale, R. (2001) 'Thermal performance of superinsulated light-weight residential construction in the Auckland climate' Paper NOV09 in *CD-ROM Performance in Product and Practice: Proceedings: CIB World Building Conference* Wellington, 2 -6 Apr. 9 pp.

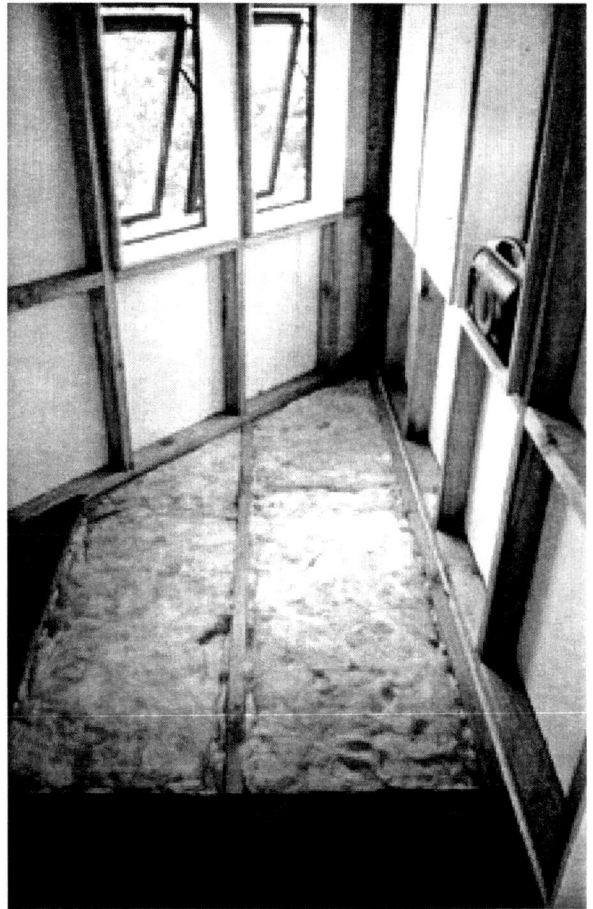

Underfloor insulation

Euphoric at 'Euphoria' or, Who needs cows when you can have koalas?

Liz Hall-Downs and Kim Downs, Queensland, Australia

Here's a personal tale of would-be environmentalists in Australia bucking their national trend of city-dwelling. Follow them on their search for a piece of 'land for wildlife' and what happened next. It's definitely a story with a beginning, a middle, and an end which is still taking place!

Looking for land

We're five weeks into the great loan hunt. We've been on the phone to banks, mortgage brokers and credit unions for weeks, but our acceptability to the powers-that-be as people worthy of a housing loan, even with a guarantor, has left us despairing. On a whim, Kim calls a local real estate agent to inquire about a rural property listing, and has agreed we'll go out to look at property we probably don't stand a snowball's chance in hell of purchasing anyway.

The agent is a big, jovial man who looks like John Candy; he uses the typical ploy of first showing us a very exposed 3 acre block that's been cleared, leaving only a few miserable-looking ironbarks. It's on a crossroad of what will clearly soon be a busy street in a burgeoning suburb, and is $30,000 more than we intend to pay. We know he's showing us this to contrast with the private, treed place we've told him we have in mind, but still the block feels exposed and depressing.

What John Candy doesn't know is that we already have a list of requirements that differ from those of most rural property buyers. Both of us have moved around a lot and are of an age and state of health where we are feeling a need for more security. In addition, we're both pissed off with paying off the mortgages of landlords. We are writers, performers, and community artsworkers. Kim is also a musician, sculptor and technician. We are looking for a quiet haven from which we can produce our best work.

We are both interested in permaculture principles and have longed for the opportunity to put these ideas into practice on our own land.

We practice positive manifestation techniques such as making lists of what we are trying to acquire or achieve. Here are the features on our 'must-have manifestation list' for the perfect block that we were seeking:

- The presence of wildlife – resident kookaburra absolutely essential;
- Established trees, as many as possible;
- Acreage, not a house block;
- Forest floor, not lawn;
- Privacy (proven by the ability of the male of the household to pee off the verandah during the night without being seen by the neighbours);
- Commuting distance between Brisbane and northern New South Wales;
- Access to electricity to run computers and tools.

John Candy drives us through the district. We watch the passing scenery – the rural feedstore, the local school, and the huge expanse of land, dotted with cabins, that is the Greenbank military camp. A herd of kangaroos lounge on the grass, under a stand of bluegums. We pass a sign, 'You are now entering the Spring Mountain to Greenbank Wildlife Corridor'. This looks promising.

We cross a bridge, and turn east. A few more turns, then onto a long driveway. John Candy stops the car before the double iron gates, and Kim gets out to open them. We drive through the gates and over a bridge that crosses a fern-studded dry creek bed below. The estate agent stops the car, we get out, and immediately a blue-winged kookaburra lands on the black wattle just a few feet away from us.

In the wildscape of Euphoria

The property is 9.3 acres of dry, schlerrophyl forest 40 minutes south west of Brisbane. It's been 'selectively cleared' (which means the whole understorey has been burnt) some time ago, and only a few of the oldest trees remain. But there are abundant other trees, most 50-100 years old, and some regenerating understorey. A track cuts right down the centre of the block, parallel with the creek. Even with her gammy leg, Liz can walk it easier than John Candy. It's a hot day and he's wheezing and coughing; sweat stains appear on his white business shirt. We worry he's going to have a heart attack if we push him too hard. So we stop and turn back, only quickly glimpsing the house-sized, volcanic rocks on the northern edge, and the lomandra-studded track winding down to the creek bed on the south side. On the way back to the car, a native frog jumps out in front of us and we bend to look at it.

LAND
FOR
WILDLIFE
QUEENSLAND

How you can help wildlife on private and community assisted land

Back at John Candy's office, we stand firm that we won't decide on anything today, and climb back into our station wagon. As we reach the highway at Browns Plains, it starts to lightly rain and we notice a huge rainbow traversing the wet road. How many signs and wonders do we need?

The move to custodianship
It took months to sort out the details of the loan, (and the banks tried to screw over our guarantor in the process). But finally, on April 7, 2000, we became the proud custodians of 'Euphoria'. Now all we had to do was...everything! At the time of writing (February 2001) we've made it through the bureaucratic maze to obtain building approval, have connected power and phone (solar would have been nice, but work life must go on), and are about to start building a very simple, small, steel-framed prefab kit home on 8 ft high posts. We plan to use the underneath space as an office, and showroom for Kim's timber sculptures. Future building projects will include a small studio each for writing and artmaking, and a permanent teepee for visitors. We decided to mark out 2 acres for our own housing and food production needs, and have signed an agreement with *Land for Wildlife* to preserve and improve the ecological values of the remaining 7 acres (*Land for Wildlife* literature describes the scheme as 'a voluntary nature conservation program which aims to support the maintenance and enhancement of native habitat on 'private' and community owned land'). In our opinion, one of the greatest (and increasingly rare,) privileges, in this polluted and degraded world, is to be able to live harmoniously *within a working ecosystem*, and to feel that our choice of lifestyle can help to preserve and enhance that ecosystem for future generations.

Liz and feathered friends

This privilege means living on the coal face of the existing ecosystem's struggle to retain its legacy of 'biodiversity'. This much bandied term – due to the very complexity of what it denotes – is not an easy idea to sell. We search endlessly to find a simple metaphor for 'biodiversity' which most people can grasp without a lengthy explanation. So far, the best one that we can come up with is what is termed 'hybrid vigour' in breeding circles. Think of the planet as a mongrel dog, with the genes of a thousand harlots in its blood. The dog is

The temporary home

nearly bullet proof from viral infections and common diseases. Contrast this with a 'pureblood' line with its inbred throwbacks and disease-prone offspring. Our planet was once a glorious thriving mongrel dog with endless genetic variety coursing through its veins. Now, with the plague of humans spreading over the surface abetting monocultures (think corn, potatoes, rice, lawns, cotton, cattle, sheep) and simultaneously destroying biodiversity, our mongrel dog is slowly transforming into a disease-prone, immuno-suppressed organism, waiting for the next systemic disease to tip it into total collapse.

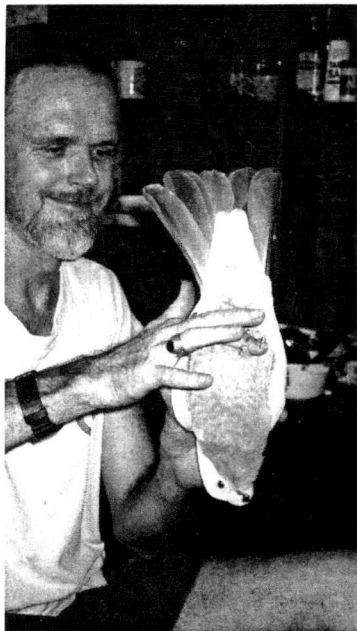

Kim organising the acrobatics

Preservation and experimentation

We truly believe that actively preserving biodiversity is of fundamental importance to any presumed future. Unfortunately, even those with the best intentions must grapple with hard choices and irony every step of the way. We want to be able to live on our block in order to preserve it. To do this we had to make the choice to claim a small portion large enough to accommodate a house, garden, and driveway. The upshot was that we had to fell some ten trees to create a house site. Sewerage was another obvious problem. Our property borders a creek bed which is usually dry, but flows strongly after several days of rain. As we are not serviced by either town water or sewer mains, we opted for a dry composting toilet and rainwater tanks. We've also created several small dams which fill readily with decent rain. We're planting a small permaculture garden with a grove of fruit and nut bearing trees in the area immediately surrounding the house. We agonized about whether to stay entirely native with our garden or introduce 'foreigners' like lemon trees, grapefruit trees, apple trees and the like. We decided to go with the trees we loved *and* experiment with native equivalents. These are the sorts of choices over which sundry purists would throw buns and blows at each other.

The habitat as a natural resource

We feel that it is essential to educate ourselves as much as possible about the native species of

plants, animals, insects, and birds which abound on this property. The most obvious invasion/eradication problems we quickly discovered here, were lantana, groundsel, assorted invasive grasses and the dreaded cane toads. (Catch 'em in a plastic bag and chuck 'em in the freezer.) But that's only the beginning. We watch bemused as cherry tomato plants spring up in open passages – the seeds digested, passed through, and dropped by currawongs raiding the surrounding Vietnamese market gardens. We hiss and shriek like stick-wielding banshees chasing wandering pet cats and dogs from our boundaries. Our aim is to aid and abet everything that we know for certain should be here while discouraging all interlopers.

Let's talk about *impact* on biodiversity. On a tiny segment, some 20 metres in diameter, we have on our block three large trees. Two blue gums and one stringybark form the apexes of a rough triangle, each tree probably 300 years old, boasting 4 ft diameter girth boles at ground level, with many large broken limbs in which hollows have formed. These hollows only form in trees which are over a hundred years old. Many species of wildlife nest in these ancient hollows and to remove the hollow is to destroy for eternity a nesting spot.

In the first ten months that we have been here, we've seen king parrots, kooka-burras, galahs, possums, and native ducks produce young from the hollows of the three trees in question. This is only what we've noticed. But hollows such as these are also the exclusive nesting spots for countless nocturnal

The garden

mammals, (which are seldom seen) like sugar gliders, bats, tuans, small marsupials; not to mention hundreds of varieties of birds from wrens to owls. In addition, each hollow is usually serially occupied by a succession of birds and small mammals every spring. It would not be stretching it

57

to say that our three trees produce in the order of sixty to a hundred clutches of diverse offspring every year. Telescope these figures over a hundred years and the sums become staggering. Cut these three trees down and the cascade effect over a hundred years is equally staggering.

The flow-on effects of human activity on the environment are nearly impossible to grasp. Who stops to consider what even gentle landclearing does? Eradicate the native flowering ground covers and replace the space with grass – as do most of our neighbours –– and frogs, tiny lizards, and many insect species never return to forage. This impacts on countless larger insects, small lizards, and birds which depend on those insects and tiny lizards as a food source. With the insect eating species in decline, birds like kookaburras, owls, eagles, falcons, currawongs, kingfishers, magpies, and crows find it harder to survive. The larger carnivorous snakes do well, though, with their predators gone and abundant small mammals about. Throw dogs and cats into the equation and even fewer species survive the changes.

We're both grateful to have been involved in the Rainbow Region (north coast region of New South Wales) during the 1980s, before the big money arrived and changed the local culture irrevocably. Now, we perceive the area as more of a 'fishbowl' than a country lifestyle. Still, living there coloured our ideas about eco-management, alternative lifestyles, and housing options. But if we did this project in Byron Shire, we'd be just another 'green' hobby farm. Conversely, 'Euphoria' exists in a community that is made up of traditionally conservative, regional working class families, where the biggest events of the year are the annual rodeo and the local show. To espouse environmental values in such a community is still a radical act. The farmers out here are hurting because of market deregulation, and are traditionally suspicious of 'greenies' and fearful of tree-clearing legislation. Just putting a sign on our gate and (in Kim's case) sculpting local animals in local timbers and (in Liz's case) writing about the bush and its spiritual and aesthetic values are – we believe – acts that can break through people's fears and

prejudices where talking can't. We've become convinced that the best way to change people's thinking about how they treat the environment is by example. Here, this means treating habitat as the valuable resource it is, (instead of viewing it as useless if it can't be ploughed or used for cattle). Natural habitats wonderfully inspire art and are a joy to live in. We know some of our neighbours scratch their heads and wonder why we'd choose to live in a tiny house up amongst the trees, when they prefer to clear all the native bush and build large houses surrounded by lawn. We're glad they wonder, and hope one day they'll notice that *we* aren't spending *our* weekends sitting on the ride-on mower! And that 'Euphoria' is where the animals hang out! At last count, we've positively

The first of the steel posts arrive

identified 45 species of birds, 7 mammal species, 13 types of tree, 9 ground covers, 10 species of snakes, lizards and frogs, and dozens of insects. We expect these numbers to increase as we implement our nestbox programme to supplement the natural tree hollows.

September 9th, 2002. We have now been on the property for two years and three months. The house is at framing stage. As I write this, chainsaws growl from one of the properties adjacent to us and at least 8 large trees have been felled in the last few hours. We have spotted one koala on our block about a year ago and the number of observed bird species continues to climb. We have survived two bush fire seasons (without insurance because the house is still unfinished) and are entering our third. Last year some few thousand small bush fires were put out in a matter of weeks within 20 kilometres of us, many of them lit by schoolkids and fanned by the September winds. We understand the motivation to clear by those afraid of bush fires, but, for us, the risk is not sufficient to cause us to wipe out native habitat in order to lower the odds. Bush fires are a fact of life in Australia that has to be accepted and worked around.

The building process has been slower than expected but this is hardly a novel experience for most house builders. Life still has to go on while such projects progress. The roof is up and the verandah finished so at least we can enjoy a cup of tea at tree level and dream of plumbing and a bathroom. Despite the worst drought in 100 years we have managed to keep our fruit trees and garden alive by hand watering by bucket. Our young trees have survived two seasons of frosts while near neighbours have lost many trees. There are two reasons for this: the gentle slope of our block and the upper canopy of the surrounding forest, which prevents frost forming at ground level. With luck, we look forward to living many happy years out here observing the wildlife, enjoying fresh fruit, herbs, and vegetables and soaking up the healing ambience of the forest.

Stop press:
Various friends have helped enormously on the house building and it's slowly all coming together. Our creek ran for several days (VERY exciting), and we've had our first visit from a koala (EVEN MORE exciting)! Froglife is so loud lately it's like a symphony! Who needs cows when you can have koalas?

With a little help from our friends

Living underground
Alan Dearling

*"For those that understand the mystery,
no explanation is necessary;
for those who do not, none is possible."*
(*www.crosswinds.net/*)

Caves are fascinating natural dwelling places. Their very existence exudes a kind of magick.

It is estimated that some naturally formed caves were lived in by our distant ancestors half a million years ago in Europe and China. Myths and legends surround 'cave history', with Mithra and Zeus both being born in caves, depending upon which accounts you read. Caves also furnished the mythical entrance to the underworld, entered by Orpheus in search of Eurydice. Hitler and Himmler were inspired to new heights (or depths) of Aryan nationalist fervour by the pagan Externsteine limestone rocks near Detmold in West Saxony (see right). Although Christianised to some extent, the site is closely linked with a local hero, Arminius, who led a rout of Roman troops. Hence, the Aryan legend. Closer to my home, Alderley Edge in England's Cheshire has long been associated with the King Arthur legends: blowing the appropriate horn, it is said, will once again summon Arthur's slumbering Knights to do battle for the their king and Merlin, the wizard.

The French Cave complex at Lascaux, discovered relatively recently in 1940, led to a far greater understanding of the religious and cultural significance of caves, through the analysis of the 65 tableaux of rock paintings, dating from about 15,000 years BC. The Trois Frères cave at Arriege provided artistic links with the Native North American and Australian Aboriginal rock paintings. In each case the images show the ritual and sacred significance of cave dwellings to nature, man and animals. This is equally true of Uluru in the red centre of Australia or Altamira in Northern Spain. And today, across the globe people still tunnel out their own troglodyte dwellings for a variety of reasons, and in variety of styles. Most are dwellings constructed at least in part, through removal or extraction, as opposed to addition of materials.

Rock houses

For myself, when I was living afloat in a narrow boat, one of my favourite mooring places was the village of Kinver, Staffordshire in the English Midlands. A couple of miles inland from the canal lies Kinver Edge, a magical, mystical place which also

Exernsteine in West Saxony

happens to be the site of England's last inhabited cave homes. Dug out of the red sandstone of the 'Edge' (now a 200 acre National Trust park) the troglodyte homes were mentioned in the 1671 parish register, and probably have a much longer history. They enjoyed a particular boom-time in the mid 19th century when 12 labourer families moved into Kinver for work in the iron and steel industry and as beesom makers. The Holy Austin rock houses are now the most prominent and have been re-modelled as show houses by the National Trust. The last remaining permanent inhabitants were evicted from the caves in the 1950s.

A few so-called hippies used the caves on an ad hoc basis in the 1960s, and a café existed there until 1967, but officialdom had its way and the neat, tidy homes with their own wells were deemed a environmental health hazard. Sadly, their demise marked the end of an era in the UK, although there are a number of

Cave paintings at Lascaux

The Kinver Edge houses before they were closed up

modern caves and underground dwellings elsewhere around the world.

Earth buildings

Earth sheltered homes – those with earth roofs as well as sides – and earth bermed homes, which use conventional roofs, are becoming more and more popular around the world. Properly designed and constructed, these homes can supply plenty of natural light, fresh air and are exceptionally energy efficient, especially those with earth roofs. Whilst not exactly caves, they are certainly forms of underground shelter. 'Molecules' is the name given by Stuart Bexon to the underground prefabricated homes which he built in 1999 on the Roseland peninsula in Cornwall. He designed them as underground, earth covered replacements for static caravans after gaining support from environmentalists. The *Times* (24/4/1999) described them: *"After landscaping, they look like a gentle mound from*

the rear or sides," with only the front wall and windows visible. Environmentally they are warm in winter, cool in summer, have natural sound insulation, have no foundations and are, according to Stuart Bexon, virtually maintenance free. Also, compared to caravans they are expected to have a four to five times longer lifespan. Stuart was quoted in the same *Times* article saying: *"I have a dream that on my tombstone it will say 'the man who buried the holiday caravan' because they are the ugliest thing ever invented."*

In a quarry near Padstow in Cornwall, Simon Ormerod built himself an earth sheltered home, which has finally been given planning permission. Selena Merrett who is co-ordinator of the organisation *Dwell Well,* says of it:

> *"This type of building is very energy efficient, requiring little or no heating in Winter and maintaining an ambient temperature of around 21 degrees centigrade all year round. This is achieved by a passive solar conservatory area absorbing in the Sun's heat and a backing to the house of thick earth or rock, which holds the heat in the space."*

In some ways, along with the first UK earth-sheltered housing at Hockerton, near Nottingham in the UK (partly the dreamchild of the Brenda and Robert Vale, whose contribution to this book is the previous chapter, *Autonomous living*), these are Anglicised cousins of the earth covered, used-rubber-tyre constructions, know as the 'Earthships' of Taos in New Mexico. There, the Greater World Community has lived utilising solar power and 'off the grid' for thirty years. Many see it as the solar capital of the world, but it also reflects a link with the past, using the local indigenous adobe mud mix as the outer coating for the dwellings. In building and architectural terms, what makes these dwellings different from ordinary structures is that their construction

Simon Ormerod's earth sheltered home (Selena Merrett)

depends more on the removal of earth materials, rather than the addition of new ones. It's what Rodofsky in his classic *Architecture without architects* (1964) called, *"Architecture by subtraction."* At its most extreme, as in the Mesa Verde, Chaco Canyon and Pueblo Bonito in the southwest of the United States, the Pueblo people built, *"many multistorey pueblos of hundreds of rooms."* (Rapoport in Oliver, 1969)

Troglodyte dwellings

Amongst the many examples of man made caves around the world, the stone hewn caves of the Murgia of theTrulli in the 'heel' of southern Italy; the fairytale cones of Cappadocia in Turkey; the desert dwellings of Matmata in Tunisia and the opal miners' underground homes of Coober Pedy in Australia are amongst the most famous. The following provides a very brief overlook at these spectacular sets of cave homes

Cave dwelling near Fethiye

Massafra

This southern Italian village still has cave houses which are inhabited, unlike many of the abandoned underground tunnels of the surrounding area of the Murgia of the Trulli. Apparently over thirty thousand people at one time lived in these dwellings hewn from the stone known locally as Tufo. Residents are not being encouraged to remain and as Edward Allen says,

> *"Presently its inhabitants, many unwittingly, are being moved to new, faceless apartment buildings on the plain above, and their cave houses are blocked so they cannot go back."* (1969)

Massafra cave homes

Cappadocia

Turkey has many cave houses cut into the rockfaces of the mountains which encircle many towns and villages. I have been lucky enough to visit a number. The photograph on the left is of a house close by Fethiye on the Mediterranean coast and is typical of the modest entrances into quite substantial living areas.

However, it is Capaddocia which really captures the hearts and imaginations of visitors to the Anatolia region of central Turkey. The natural minarets of the area are made of a soft volcanic stone called Tufa rock, which is much more suited for hollowing out into cave-shelters, rather than being used as a building material. A local subsistence level economy existed in the region throughout the twentieth century, but this has been supplemented from tourist income as the visitors arrive in their coach-loads to wonder at the man made labyrinths of Nevsehir, Kayseri and Goreme. Sadly, as Paul Oliver noted in *Shelter,* the locals' modest, rational way of life *"may not gain much from the dubious benefits from an economy based on tourism."*

Capaddocia's fairy castles

Matmata

I first visited Matmata, a Berber mountain village to the southwest of Gabes in Tunisia towards the end of the 1970s. It wasn't a major tourist attraction back then, but I was in awe of the strange 'other-worldly' feeling of its desert dwellings carved from the inside of craters in the red sandstone of the desert. Sure enough, so were the creators of the *Star Wars* film who used the Matmata dwellings for some of the early scenes featuring Luke

My visit to Matmata

Skywalker. The bar and the dining room at the small Sidi Driss hotel are now a shrine to Matmata *as depicted in Star Wars!*

Nowadays, the one hundred 'typical' Matmata cave houses, which consist of a courtyard dug out vertically downwards, with small rooms tunnelled off, are mostly used for tourists in one way or another. The 5,000 or so residents nearly all live in more conventional houses in the surrounding area. Because of the softness of the sandstone, the majority of the troglodyte homes are not very old – they erode quickly – but new rooms can equally easily be tunnelled out to create new accommodation or storage areas.

Coober Pedy
Desolate, arid and searingly hot are three evocative ways of describing Coober Pedy. Its location is a post-apocalypse 500 miles north of Adelaide in Australia. Quite literally it is in the 'middle of no-where'. The name Coober Pedy is derived from the Aboriginal *'kupa piti',* which literally means 'white man's burrow'. It only exists because it is where 90 per cent of the world's opals are mined. In excavating for opals, the miners soon realised that the underground tunnels provided a cool respite from the scorching heat, and since the first discovery in 1915, many have constructed themselves underground homes. Some have even found more opals while digging out there own dwellings!

Even today, new homes are built by miners and others wanting to live in this extreme spot – not all are called Mad Max or Priscilla, Queen of the Desert! Like other sites with underground dwell-

ings, it has become a tourist Mecca. Tourists get a taste of underground living in hostels and backpackers' hostels such as Radeka's and Joe's. Then there are underground shops, a church and Crocodile Harry's dugout home – a decidedly leftfield tourist attraction. Harry's ideas of underground furnishings stretch to eight foot headless 'Sheilas', with melon-sized boobs, sculpted lovingly by Harry himself. Then there's his 'Virgin collection' – a collage of over 1,000 women's names. Harry recently told a local newspaper: *"They can be near virgins, I'm not that fussy."* Perhaps not your Ideal Eco-Home!

And...in China...
Less well known, but much more extensive, are the Yaodong cave dwellings in China, which are the focus for the next contribution from Liu Jiaping, David Wang and Yang Liu. With their natural

Inside a Coober Pedy home

insulation and use of readily available materials, these dwellings are famous in their own country but only now are becoming of interest to environmentalists and architects elsewhere.

References
Allen, E. (1969) *Stone Shelters.* MIT Press.

Rapoport, A, 'The pueblo and the hogan' in *Shelter and Society,* edited by Oliver, P. (1969) Frederick A. Praeger.

Rudofsky, B (1964) *Architecture without architects,* Doubleday.

Shelter (1973) Shelter Publications.

A New Generation of Sustainable *Yaodong* Cave Dwellings in China.

Liu Jiaping, PhD
Director, Green Architecture Research Center
Xi'an University of Architecture and Technology

David Wang, PhD
Washington State University

Yang Liu, doctoral student
Xi'an University of Architecture and Technology

The *yaodong* cave dwelling is one of the most important expressions of vernacular architecture in China (Figure 1). This is not only due to its sustained use in history (*yaodong* dates back to the Qin dynasty, c. 220 BC); it is important simply because of the number of people still living in them. In the vast rural landscapes of the Loess Plateau in north

Figure 1: Yaodong caves

central China, the *yaodong* population easily numbers in the millions. This article reports on an important attempt to continue this tradition by designing and building new *yaodong* units in accordance with the principles of 'green' design.

The term *yaodong* (pronounced yow-DOAN) literally means a tunnel dug into the side of a mountain, and this aptly summarizes the construction of these dwellings in history. The high silt-clay content of the Loess Plateau is structurally conducive for excavation into the land. The interior is thermally stable because the mass of the terrain acts as an ideal insulator against both winter cold and summer heat. The ease of construction coupled with the abundance of material – the land and terrain itself – makes the *yaodong* a decidedly vernacular phenomenon.

Figure 2: Yaodong farms

The future of this housing type is of particular interest now, at the turn of the twenty-first century, in light of China's nationwide push towards modernization. In matters of the built environment in China, modernization often translates into a fascination with Western technological prowess and size, perhaps without enough regard for the aesthetic and symbolic values that come out of China's own profound cultural traditions. For example, the Beijing of even as recently as the 1980s is not the Beijing of today. Ultra modern skyscrapers, at once impressive as well as anonymous, dot the city's skyline. With the recent announcement of Beijing as host city to the 2008 Olympics, the push for modernization will be even greater.

The *yaodong* reality in many ways swims against the tide of the trend to modernize. While modernization occurs largely in China's cities, the *yaodong* is exclusively a rural phenomenon. In Zao Yuan Village, where new sustainable *yaodong* prototypes are being constructed, 70 per cent of the 680 persons are farmers. Or again, while modernization is necessarily a 'professional' effort, *yaodong* construction even today is largely realized by local people. In Zao Yuan, the communal government decides when and where people can build new units; members of the community apply by drawing lots if there are more people than sites available at any one offering. Communal efforts then help keep construction costs down. Finally, while modernization tends to look to fossil fuels and non-replaceable energy sources, the *yaodong* typology offers possibilities for a sustainable approach to energy use and conservation.

Since 1996, the Green Architecture Research Center (GARC), based at the Xi'an University of Architecture and Technology, has been designing sustainable *yaodong* units in Zao Yuan Village, some 300 kilometres north of Xi'an, outside of the city of Yan'an. To date, some 100 such units have been built (Figure 2). The aim of the GARC is to improve life in the *yaodong* community by introducing current methods in architectural technology to the design and construction process. But it does this with the goal of not compromising the emphasis upon local cultural values. It makes for a provocative mix of 'professional' intervention tempered with a guiding respect for vernacular wishes. For instance, the GARC produces its designs by sending a team to live among the *yaodong* population for sustained periods of time. Meetings are held with the local people and leadership (Figure 3 above), surveys and questionnaires are filled out, and what is most impressive, the local population is given input into design proposals. A recent idea for a greenhouse front on a new unit was rejected precisely because the arched cave opening, so culturally meaningful to the locals, would not play a prominent visual role. This illustrates how a 'green' concept in the abstract (the greenhouse would have increased thermal performance in a sustainable manner) still did not pass muster because of human preference – and hence human behavioural – factors.

Figure 3

From its early beginnings, the *yaodong* typology has evolved through several generations: from the addition of masonry construction at the signature arched front, to *yaodongs* only partially engaged into the mountainside (this is the 'lean-to' yaodong, or *kao-shan yao*). Next to emerge are actually free standing 'caves' that

nevertheless retain the distinct arched front and connection to the land (Figure 4, right). These progressions illustrate formal change indexed to indigenous cultural factors. For instance, the use of masonry denotes increased financial standing. But because they are indigenous, the changes can be said to be 'true', and it is instructive how the formal changes do not compromise the essentially agrarian spirit of the cave typology.

The GARC designs continue this evolution by introducing a *second storey* in the new units. This move immediately accommodates modernity – for instance, upstairs bedrooms accommodate the

Figure 4: Kao Shan Yao

need for *privacy* – but not without violating the vernacular spirit. The form brings new possibilities for sustainable applications, such as increasing opportunities for cross ventilation, deeper penetration of natural lighting into the interiors, roof planting, and thermal mass (Figure 5). Historic lifestyle practices are retained in the newer units. For

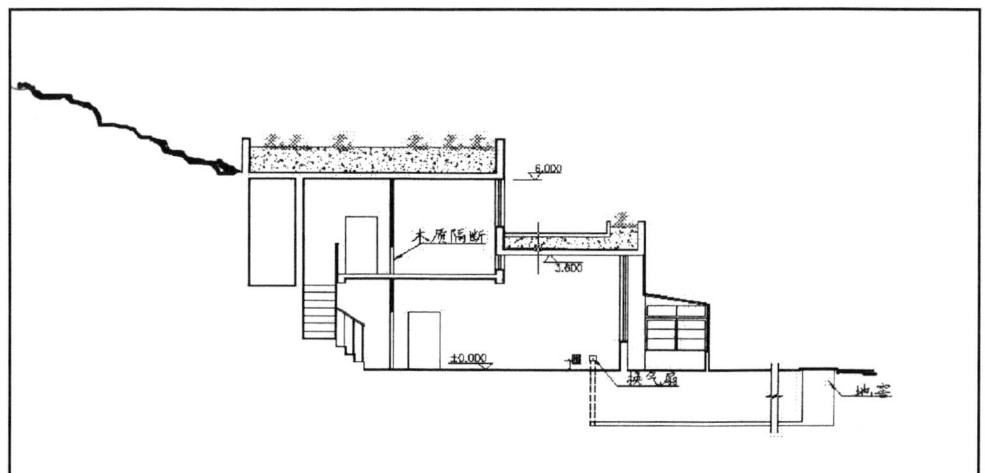

Figure 5

instance, the older yaodongs locate the cooking flue underneath the raised sleeping area to generate warmth (Figure 6, below). In retaining this practice, the new yaodong designs illustrate how a historic practice is continued for its cultural meaning as much as for its functional value.

This is perhaps the most important point the GARC approach contributes to the larger discourse on 'green design', to wit, that true sustainability involves not only the conservation of material resources, but also the continuation of cultural values as well.

As of this writing, the GARC's work has progressed enough for them to do some 'post-occupation evaluation' studies. While the cost for the new units is still prohibitive for a local family to take on, more and more units are indeed being built to the great satisfaction of the population. Perhaps the most encouraging indicator is what young people who have left the village to live in the city have to say. They report that the new units are more comfortable than traditional apartments in the city. This, coupled with the mayor of Zao Yuan's explicit appeal to them to come back and *"return to nature",* may result in even more demand for sustainable yaodong units in the years ahead.

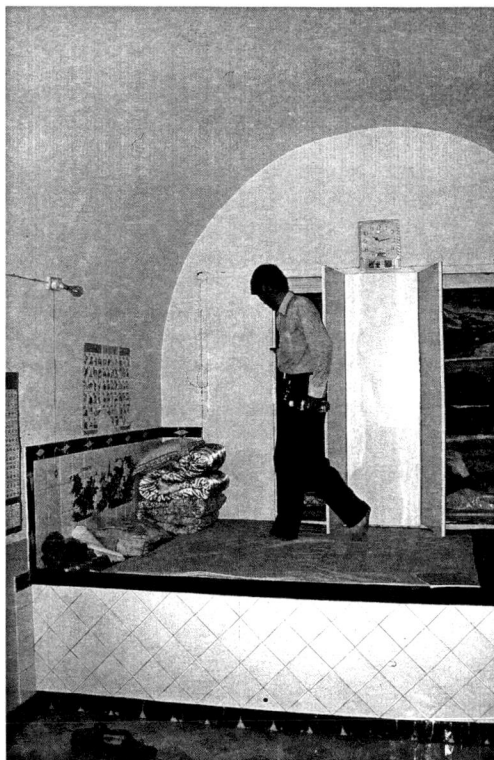

Figure 6

Willowater – Roger Dean's Home for Life project
Alan Dearling

The Sunday Times described Roger Dean's designs for future eco-homes as *"disturbingly like a Teletubby hideaway"*, but in fact they are practical, elegant and capture the imagination of adults and children alike. Anyway, at a time when Tolkien-mania is alive and well, these homes are possibly more akin to futuristic Hobbit-homes.

Bishop's Wood prototype

Roger Dean is well known around the globe for his fantastical designs for album covers, especially those for the band, Yes. However, he has recently been using his eye for detail and imagination to design an entire eco-village, called Willowater. Co-ordinator of the project, John Talbot, is currently using the prototype at Bishop's Wood educational centre, near Stourport in Worcestershire as his temporary office.

John explained to me that he hopes that *"Roger's*

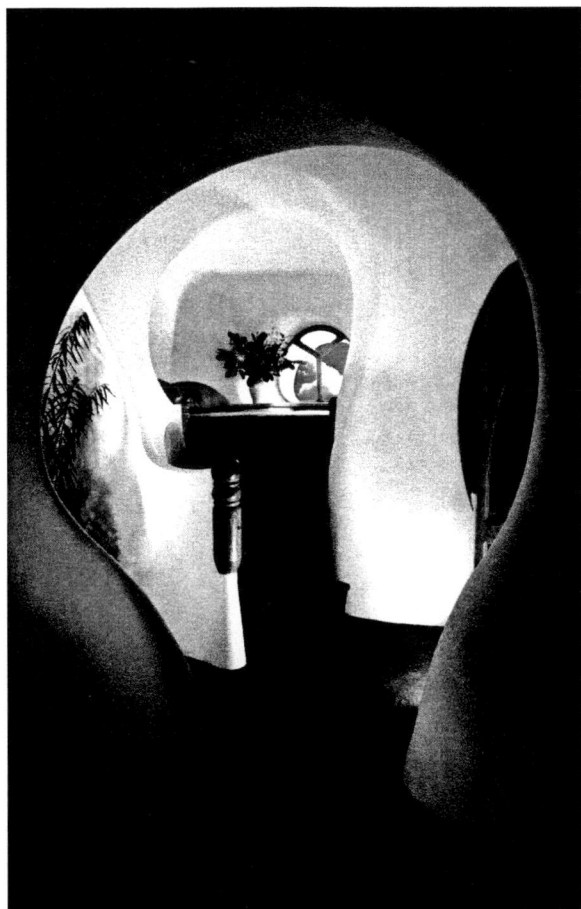

Home for Life hallway

architecture gets taken seriously". The prototype, like the eventual village is built from modules. These start life as curved mouldings, and each 'Home for Life' as they are called, can be tailored to meet individual needs, from a one bedroom unit up to a planned 150 room hotel and huge bio-dome housing indoor food crops and a swimming pool. John reckons that the homes would typically cost 30-40 per cent less to build and the process would take weeks rather than months, because once the foundations and services are constructed, the shells for living units are shipped to the site, assembled and then sprayed with insulation and gunnite concrete. The aim is for affordable, but unique dwellings. Internally, fittings have to be individually built to fit with the curvature of the rooms and passageways.

Roger Dean describes his concept and vision for Willowater:

"The village style community we propose to create will be a highly inspirational neighbourhood, a role model for community building. It will effectively address many of the critical issues sometimes overlooked; issues such as security, communications, the environment, sustainability, practicality, children and the less able, spiritual amenities and materials.

'Home for Life' is a concept that embodies the results of many years of research into the way people respond emotionally to interior spaces – the sort of spaces that produce a sense of security and well being as well as being practical, spaces that are peaceful and tranquil, such as bedrooms and home offices and kitchens that inspire and energise."

Both John and Roger have been particularly struck by the positive reaction of visitors to the prototype and the touring exhibition that visited the International Ideal Homes Show, Tomorrow's World Live and the Royal Show. Typically, visitors say: *"I want to buy one"* and *"I really feel at home"*. The plans for Willowater also include a village school. Roger has, for a long time, been involved with young people and in designing the £600,000 Natural Learning Centre for Worcestershire Council at Bishop's Wood, he has listened to their frank and uninhibited views. Trees and the natural environment are intertwined holistically into the design for the school. The same will be true at Willowater, which will be an example of earth-sheltered architecture.

determined ideals. We expect Willowater to be a learning process and we are sure to fall short of perfection. We also expect to build something incredible, using all the best practices and knowledge that the project team has acquired. Something amazing that will be a huge step forward in our understanding of what a community can be. A real achievement and a real inspiration to both the people who live there and to others who will dare to develop new communities in the future."

With more than a touch of humour, John Talbot says, *"I love working on projects that I really love…what the hell, I enjoy my life…if Willowater happens, it will take care of my retirement years!"* I really hope so for both of them and for the potential future residents of Willowater.

To find out more about the project, see:

www.rogerdean.com and www.homeforlife.co.uk

or write to:
The Willowater Project
Astley House
Dunhampton
Stourport-on-Severn
Worcestershire
UK DY13 9SW

A Home for Life bathroom

External photos of the prototype Home for Life by John Talbot, and internal photos by Martyn Dean, Roger's brother.

John explained to me that there are already *"a hundred or so folk who really want to live in a Dean home and are suggesting the formation of some form of co-operative."* To turn the dream into a reality is the next stage. John and Roger are actively talking to local authorities and planners to find an appropriate site for the full Willowater community project. Roger says: *"Providing we get the right site, I think we would have the local authority support and I think we would get financial help."*

He added,
"Utopian dreams are seductive and invariably fall short of pre-

Another view of Bishop's Wood

Putting heart back into our homes
© *Tom Bender*

The places we make are some of our most visible actions – ones that speak clearly to the rest of Creation what is in our hearts and the sources of our love and joy. When I graduated from architecture school, I looked at what I could design, and felt emptiness and sadness in my heart. My designs were lifeless and barren, somehow, and felt very wrong. I didn't like what I'd been taught. As I looked further, it wasn't just me, it was our culture. It didn't know how to touch the heart of things, and therefore couldn't teach it, and the work of my classmates and practicing architects alike suffered equally. As a result, I've spent most of my career trying to learn anew how to put heart back into our homes and into our lives.

In retrospect, it's amazing that it took me, and all of us, so long. It seems so obvious. But it isn't, when you're a product of your culture and its oddness has a seamless internal logic. It wasn't architecture that needed to change, it was everything, and we had to feel our way out of the box piece by piece, transforming the whole web. So my life has been a curious dance, going as way opens – between the magic and the mundane; theory and practice; economics and technology and art; words and hammers and nails.

One of the things I remember that brought my path into focus happened while teaching architecture in Minnesota in the early '70s. Change was in the air, the Whole Earth Catalog, Domebook, Radical Software, and other publications networking a heady brew of new visions and action. I would look at the seductively beautiful transparent geodesic domes that people were building in California, and say to myself, *"Gee, I wish I could do that here, but it's too cold, and too…and too…"*

One day, a new issue of one of the magazines arrived. In it was an article on the building of a dome, and the wonderful things learned in the process about heat flow in domes and their special value in cold climates. This dome wasn't in California. It was in northern Minnesota, an even more rugged climate than where I lived – minus 40^0 centigrade temperatures, mosquito-filled summers – you name it. So I could have done something where I was, and hadn't even tried. I played back to myself what I had been saying… *"I can't…I can't…I can't…"* "O.K.," I said, *"that word isn't getting us anywhere. Time to throw it our of our vocabulary."*

I asked myself then what the most important thing was that our world needed that I might possibly be able to help achieve. Then I learned not to look at what we are lacking to change the world, but to look at what we *do* have, then figure out how we could use what we have to help accomplish what was needed. The third thing, I learned from Bucky Fuller – to look for *big* changes, not small ones, and that it usually takes twenty-five years for a real change to become part of a culture. The fourth was that we learn by *doing*, and that learning spreads when people can see and touch and feel that something *does* work, *does* feel right, *does* touch them in their heart.

I was teaching architecture. Many of the students and a few of the faculty felt it was important to change 'education'. What did I have? Classes to teach. Money? Grants? Curriculum? No, but I could give academic credit! In one class, I 'paid' advanced students with academic credits to help teach things that weren't in the curriculum. In another, I was assigned to teach a history course in 'Renaissance Architecture'. I had said when I was hired that I didn't like Renaissance architecture and didn't want to teach it. A creative reading of the course description revealed that it didn't mention anything about having to stick to European Renaissance Architecture. And of course the school taught virtually nothing about the architectural history of other cultures. So the first day of that class, I announced that we would be looking at the exciting renaissance of architecture that had occurred in Japan, Persia, China, and India at the same time as in Europe!

All this may seem a long way from designing and building homes, but it explains in part what designing and/or building a home is to me. If building my own home is what is on my plate, then my question to myself is, *"OK, what can be achieved through this? What resources, what opportunities do I have, and what might I be able to achieve with them?"* When our house burned down the day we finished building it, then that was what was on my plate, and my question to myself was, *"OK, what can be achieved through this? What resources, what opportunities do I have, and what might I be able to achieve with them?"*

By the time I did get to building a house, it was part of many strands of a new web that was building in and through my life. Using what resources I had (students, academic credits) we had built one of the first regionally self-reliant demonstration houses – the Ouroboros Project in Minnesota. Using some university land that was somehow exempt from building codes, utilizing student labor and skills, recycled and begged materials, we built a pioneering house that demonstrated the viability of renewable energy and energy efficiency. At the same time it *also* demonstrated a new ecological economics that showed that 1+1=3. The right things put together achieve more than they can individually.

Reducing our energy use by an order of magnitude was one of the things I felt we needed to do to achieve sustainability. What could I do? Show it was possible on paper. What resources did I have? An old typewriter. Out of it came *'Living Lightly: Energy Conservation in Housing'*, a path-breaking monograph which showed that we could reverse accepted trends and achieve order of magnitude improvements in how we do things. *Ouroboros* showed that the theory worked. This seed, a couple of decades later, became today's new *'Factor-10 Economics'* which is applying the process developed in Living Lightly to transform all sectors of our economy.

Ouroboros: Earth-sheltered construction, super-insulation, efficient windows, night insulating shutters on the windows, sod roof, and building geometry reduced the energy needs of the Ouroboros house enough that a combination of active and passive solar heating (with snow reflectance), a solar greenhouse, and wind-generated electricity was able to heat it even in Minnesota's harsh climate.

This was followed by articles – self-published, then reprinted in *New Age, Utne Reader, East-West Journal* and other publications – that introduced first my students and then our culture to the chi energy based Chinese practice of *feng shui* and its geophysical basis, and to the concepts later termed *sustainability*. Another door opened and I was suddenly doing energy research and writing energy policy in Governor Tom McCall's office in

Oregon. Nobody else, it seemed, had figured out both that we could reduce our energy use greatly, and that life might be better, not worse, in the process!

After that, some friends were doing an environmental education newsletter, called *RAIN*. Its grant was running out, and the university center it was in was closing. What could we do with this resource? Outside of academia, it became a resource networking publication spearheading the development of more appropriate technologies, resource efficiency, recycling, organic agriculture, and community economics.

It was time again to put words into action, and our feet where our mouths were. So we built a house. Today, thank goodness, many aspects of its design have become common practice and no longer seem innovative. But for the mid-seventies, it did okay. One of its goals was to make ourselves self-reliant for our housing needs, avoiding mortgage costs through sweat-equity, so we could live simply and free our time to do interesting things. The things that I was interested in were, of course, unfundable because nobody understood them yet. Wasting time searching for funding didn't seem worthwhile. People rarely fund the early stages of new developments. This part of the house isn't really visible in its design. Another goal was to demonstrate and experience simpler living patterns – no-commuting, working at home; compact, innovative use of space; simpler and more earth-friendly technologies; more direct ties with the rest of nature. A third goal was learning construction skills. A fourth, applying in our own lives, testing, and developing resource efficient ways of building.

It hardly seems radical now, but local people had never seen 2x6 advanced framing wood construction. They refused to put insulation into walls underneath windows, because those areas seemed prone to rot in our very wet climate (from condensation on the glass of single-glazed windows, it turned out). Our house must have seemed odd to some – more than twice the insulation normally used; wood heat from one of the first air-tight Defiant woodstoves (made from recycled automobile engine blocks); an owner-built squat compost toilet and graywater system (built as part of a state testing program which legalized their use); a solar hot water system made with recycled printing plates; an outside-vented 'cool box' instead of a refrigerator; insulating shutters for the windows; passive solar heating; water- and energy-conserving foot-pedal faucets; recycled wood walls, window glass, plumbing fixtures, stove, etc.; whole walls of the house sliding away to open to the outside; floor sitting on carpets, futons, and cushions; earth cement entry floor; high-efficiency lighting, native plant landscaping. Spacious room for a family of four, plus two offices, in under 1200 square feet.

This house, and those that followed, were learning laboratories for what focused attention can do in the process of design and building as well as in other work. Attention is a Zen practice of not letting our minds wander from what we're trying to do, keeping our intention clear, and listening to what comes out in the process of work that suggests one thing or another is right, or wrong, or inessential. I wasn't a Zennie, but was trying hard to learn what touched

Bender kitchen: Eliminating the mechanical noises of furnaces, toilets flushing, refrigerators, TV, and dishwashers made possible a silent and peaceful house, which showed that living simply didn't mean living primitively.

my heart or didn't – and why. I've written a lot about what I've learned – in *The Heart of Place; Silence, Song & Shadows; Building with the Breath of Life* and elsewhere. Before building this house, I'd wondered how to know whether a particular design detail or idea was right or not. I learned the obvious, of course. Build it, and it will tell you. The results will bother you, and you rip out what you've done; you love it, and your heart skips a beat every time you come into the room; or you forget about it and learn that it didn't matter! The learning with all three options goes beyond just doing it.

[I knew I was going as deep as I could to find soul when I built this house. In the process, of course, I learned that we can't go deeper than *we* are. I would keep trying to add some richness to a design, then it wouldn't feel right and I'd remove it. I couldn't do it right until I was right. Eventually, as I did deepen, so did my work. Each job was a teacher, with both expected and unexpected lessons, both of which opened new doors and deepened the harmony].

I did achieve something in this house that I wasn't consciously trying to do. It was probably the most important thing accomplished in the project, though I wouldn't learn it for almost twenty years. It had nothing to do with the techie-toys, though they were probably necessary elements. It had little to do directly with any of my conscious goals. Intuitively, I had somehow managed to actively work on an energetic level as well as the material one, and to create a place filled with healing and sacred energy; a place filled with the peace and wholeness that I had been seeking.

Wilson garden path: I wanted to show that houses can nurture people, surround them with love, other life, and the joy of connection with nature, beauty, and the skilled product of human work – even in a without a 'view' property.

It was probably a dozen years later before I was able to achieve the same thing consistently in projects for other people, using other builders, and dealing with other people's dreams. What was happening to me on the conscious level at the same time was that I was discovering that the vehicle for all the things I was trying to achieve was chi or life-force energy. It was the basis of the Chinese feng shui I had incorporated in my work years ago. Walking around in circles, I'd tripped over something for the second time – but this time finally understood its value!

One of the most powerful tools for working with chi energy is *intention.* And it was the clarity and strength of my intention in how I designed and built which gave power to the place. By this point, I didn't have to do any conscious energy work on the site or the building. I didn't even have to see or visit the site, or do anything special in the design. The design itself was empowered in some way to bring focus and power to the energy that emerged in the process of the building becoming material-ized during construction. Amazing…and more

Bender living room: Even in a region with 160 kph winter winds and almost three metres of rain a year, we showed it was possible to live more connected with the outside world.

Guest loft: We could happily live far more simply than this, but we wanted to show that luxury and fullness in our lives does not demand great financial and resource costs.

amazing the more I learned about life-force energy, how other cultures worked with it in their building, and how it affects our lives and health. It's reacknowledgement in our culture today is trigger-ing what is probably the most powerful positive transformation our culture has ever known. (See *Building with the Breath of Life* for details.)

I kept my mouth shut about this new development, and listened to people's reactions to the places I helped bring into being. People started to say, *"Wow, the energy is incredible in this house."* I'd respond, *"Yes, it has a wonderful view; it's a lovely spot…"* *"No,"* they'd reply, *"I mean the energy of the house is wonderful!"* At a local workshop I was teaching on feng shui, I started to say something about the energy of our own house. At that point, a woman put up her hand and said, *"I'd like to say something about the energy of Tom's house."* Okay. *"Well,"* she said, *"the first time I went into his house I almost threw up."* *"Oh, great!"* I replied, *"Can I use that as a jacket blurb on my next book?"*

A marvellous and sensitive yoga teacher, she had just moved to our area. In the process, she had put up protective barriers around her energy to buffer the disruption of moving. When she walked into our house, the barriers tumbled away because the house felt so safe, and it was that which had disoriented her.

Over the years, I have found many things that help put the soul back in our surroundings. Once un-derstood, almost all of them turn out to be con-nected with life-force energy. It is the telephone line through which we communicate with all of the rest of nature and become a connected part of its community. It is what breathes life into what we make, surrounding us with places filled with love and joy, rather than the deadness out of which I was taught to design buildings. It is what connects us with the spirit world; what energizes the things that manifest into the material world; and what nurtures and heals our lives and our communities. And learning its theory after how to do it was important. By the time I understood it, I had already forged new ways for our own culture to successfully apply it in our conditions rather than copying something without understanding from another culture.

So, building a home for me now is an opportunity for each of us to help heal our culture, our communities, ourselves, and our relationships with other life. It is an opportunity to affirm wholeness, the sacred, the wonderful cosmic dance of which we are again part.

It was an odd search, not knowing what we were looking for. And we couldn't know, because we were lacking it so totally. The only way possible to

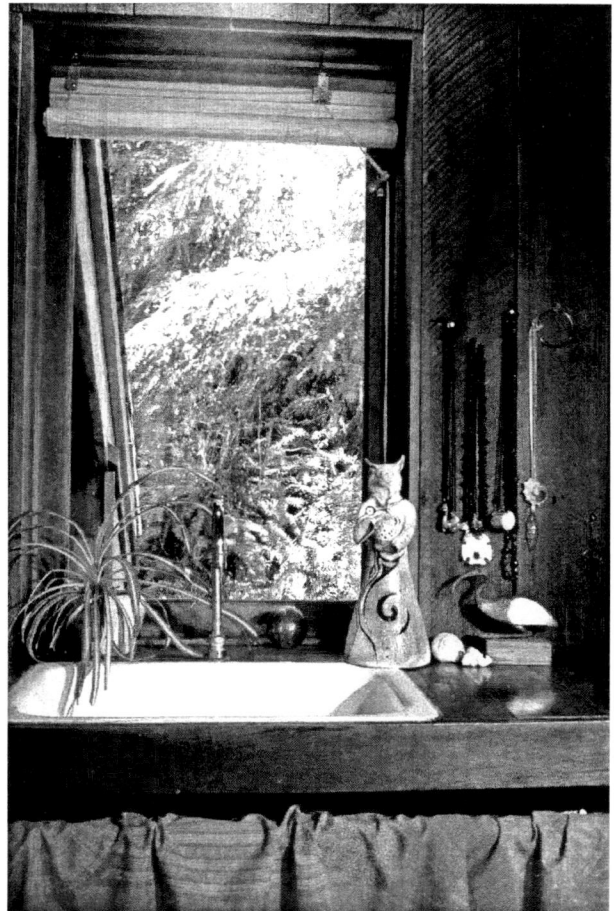

Bender bath: Replacing bathroom mirrors with a window changes the energy with which we start a day, and eliminates our 'morning-hang-over' negative self-images.

find it was to discard what we knew wasn't it, and hold on to each little piece that seemed like it might be a piece of what we were lacking. Like a jigsaw puzzle, the answer came together piece by piece, until suddenly we saw the connections that gave us wholeness again.

More information on Tom Bender's work with chi energy and building can be found in his books – *Silence, Song & Shadows, Building with the Breath of Life, The Heart of Place,* and his earlier *Environmental Design Primer* – as well as articles on his web site, www.tombender.org. He can be reached at tom@tombender.org. His current book-in-progress is *Learning to Count What Really Counts: The Economics of Wholeness.*

MacNaughton Porch: It happened suddenly, in one house, where the plumbers, painters, and other contractors working on the unfinished house would come up to me and say, *"Wow, there is something incredible in this house. When I come in the door, something in me relaxes and starts to sing, and I feel a wonderful peacefulness."*

73

Life in the Bat House
Alan Dearling

"The volume scale shudders on my personal, mental amplifier. It is hitting around 8 or 9, with 10 being maximum. I'd been warned that I might get cut off at the Australian Tropical Rainforest Research Centre, but it feels as though it is now really happening. I'm lying here in my bunk bed at just past midnight. Thunder is providing the punctuation in between the harsh swathes of sheet lightning. A pretty impressive natural light show! The rain on the corrugated roof sounds every bit like a tidal wave. The gods are having fun with us tonight and it is easy to understand why this area is sometimes referred to as one of the most hostile environments in Australia."

(from Alan Dearling's personal diary, 21-1-01, Daintree Rainforest, Cape Tribulation.)

Dr Hugh Spencer and one of his bat colony

A bit of history about the Cape Tribulation Research Station

After visiting the Australian Tropical Research Foundation's website (www.austrop.org.au) I had an informative and amusing dialogue with the Foundation's co-founder and director, Dr Hugh Spencer about this book on eco-dwellings. Hugh said: "Well we certainly are the right place for your book – environmental sustainability is our big interest – and we have a range of buildings from utilitarian to just plain funky!"

How could I resist going to visit them?

To discover Cape Tribulation for yourself involves a process of personal discovery which turns it into your very own 'special' place. Located like a gemstone in heart of the Daintree lowland tropical rainforests, it is now a World Heritage site encompassing some of the most complex and diverse plants and trees in the world. Even so, as a result of a sell-off of 1,200 plots of land (about 7,800 acres in all) along the coastal belt by the 1980 Queensland government of Joh Bjelke Petersen, the spectre of increased settlement, possible connection of mains electric power and increased tourism all loom large over this area.

The Cape Tribulation Tropical Research Station was founded in 1988 amidst the furore and political debate surrounding the development of the area and the future of the rainforest. It was, and is, the dream and reality of some highly committed individuals. Hugh Spencer had been a scientist and staff member at Woolongong University, and he and his then partner, Brigitta Flick, bought the 25 acres of regeneration and primary rainforest land on Mason's Creek, Cape Tribulation. Their purpose was to create a base for scientific investigation, study and education for researchers, students, the local community and visitors to the area. Together

The main social and eating space at the station

with its umbrella organisation, the Australian Tropical Rainforest Research Foundation, incorporated in 1993, it is also actively involved in the conservation, regeneration and protection of these tropical eco-systems. As Hugh Spencer puts it, "It is always work in progress."

The research station

When you see the pictures of the research station buildings, they appear to be lushly remote. In some ways they are. The station lies an hour north of the Daintree River, which requires crossing on a ferry, and that is another hour north of Mossman, the nearest medium size township. But, the station's buildings actually start at the roadside with the passive solar Bat House – the interpretative visitor centre – which offers a friendly

Inside Hugh's personal space

and inquisitive flying fox (old world fruit bat) along with displays of information concerning the rainforest and eco-systems and the bio-diversity of the whole Cape Tribulation rainforest and reef area. And the Bat House itself is next to a small hamburger shop cum café, and opposite the 'full-on' party atmosphere of the rainforest backpackers' village called PK's. It is only when you take the walk a few hundred metres down the forest track that you exit from relative civilisation and enter into the real world of the Cape Tribulation Station.

Altogether, the station has planning permission for nine self-contained buildings as well as the labs etc. At present there are a number of separate buildings on the site, none of which could be considered self-contained! Hugh Spencer is an inveterate 'scrounger' of materials. As he says, "I have to be to operate and build a research station on the equivalent of a lecturer's salary!" Many of the buildings have been constructed from

reclaimed clapboard and wood from a variety of building sites, including an old film set. They include:

- the living zone, which incorporates a raised wooden floored breezeway and seating area for up to 20 people (for all meals and some work purposes), which has a roof above it suspended between two ageing 'dongas' (40 year old ex-Mains Road Department portacabins) which in turn house the kitchen, Hugh's office and the small station library.

- the 'Dunny in the sky' (pictured below) – a Dowmus-style accumulator system composting toilet under which is laundry with a the washing and gas/electric drying machine. Kitchen grey water is processed through an aerated digester system of station design. There is a solar heated shower and all water comes from a natural spring;

- three sets of living quarters including the guest building where I stayed, which is affectionately known as the Hilton! All were assembled by volunteers from designs made by Hugh (see picture on left). They feature sloping vented rooves, and are quite airy and fairly comfortable in a rustic sort of way. Because of the extreme 80-100 per cent humidity, high rainfall (on my one night there, described in the diary extract, we had 137 mms in five hours), and high temperatures, problems of mildew, condensation and fungal spores are extreme. Therefore, it

The dunny in the sky

is essential that all the buildings are kept well insulated and aired. The rooves are lined with a simple 'sisalation' (a sandwich of aluminium foil with a bituminous paper filling) and there are no glass windows, just simple mozzie mesh, which together with roof vents and one metre overhanging eaves, ensures free airflow, maintaining the essential low thermal mass;

The big solar tracker

- the Bat cages, which are home to up to 30 flying fox bats who have been orphaned in domestic circumstances or are damaged in some way and cannot be returned to the wild;

- the station has a Renewable Energy Remote Area Power Supply (RAPS – top right)) with two solar trackers with 22 panels to provide the nine kilowatt hours of energy required by the station, with back-up coming from a small diesel generator. Power is stored in a 24 volt bank of batteries and converted to 240 volts AC through an inverter. The refrigerator and the station laboratory are the biggest sole users of energy;

filtered, dehumidified and slightly air conditioned. Overall, it is designed to use less power than a conventional fridge. It allows the station, in Hugh's words, *"to use decent science methods, processes and equipment…for microscopy, biochemistry and electronics."* It is equipped with up to date specialist equipment for a whole range of applications. Because of energy constraints, the station only uses lap top computers, which have proved to be the only kind to work successfully in an environment that causes rapid deterioration and destruction of all electrical and optical systems. Living on a very restricted power budget makes the

Johan, one of the station researchers, in the laboratory

- what Hugh calls the 'pièce de résistance' is the station's novel dry laboratory and machine workshop (middle of page) – the only building that is primarily constructed of new materials (except for the foundations and roof). This is built along the lines of a large walk-in cooler, with a three inch polystyrene foam-'Colourbond' sheet sandwich, incorporating a water-to-air heat exchange to dehumidify the air. It offers an environment that is sealed, air-

station very conscious of what Hugh refers to as, *"demand side management – turn it off if you ain't using it!"*

- the Bat House is the station's interface with tourists and visitors and helps to both maintain an external public profile for the station and generates essential income through donations. Partly because it is physically separated from the research buildings, it has its own solar

76

The Bat House visitor centre

energy system. Pictured above, the Bat House offers a range of displays and exhibits which help to generate an interest in the fragile local eco-system.

Life and work at the station

The station is financially sustainable and has developed through the dogged determination and perseverance of its founders and directors over 13 years. Its development has been, and remains, very dependent upon the many (averaging 50 per year) researchers, students, interns and volunteers who have stayed for varying lengths of time at the station. None have been paid, and Hugh has never received any salary. In fact, all make a financial contribution to the running of the station, which requires about AUS $80,000 in any one year. About a quarter of this comes from donations made at the Bat House and other amounts are received as capital and research grants and donations from agencies such as the Goldman Environmental Foundation and the Wet Tropics Management Authority (WTMA). Running costs include food for humans and bats, operating vehicles (very second-hand) and capital expenditure includes computer and scientific equipment and one-off schemes such as the extension to the Bat House, the establishment of the laboratory and the planned new storage area to protect station property from excessive decay.

From my stay there, it was quickly apparent that Hugh is very much the dominant person in all ways at the forest station. As he says, "I have to be!" This impacts on life inside the station and on its relations with the outside community. Hugh said, *"Cape Tribulation is mostly a blue collar community, very anti-intellectual, full of small-minded business people."* According to Hugh, even those locals who are environmentalists and living and working in the area have, *"isolationist mind sets".* Hugh added, *"This place (the Daintree) also plays absolute hell with relationships. It eats marriages."* For some period of time this seems to have left the station without any strong community base for its work, but this has partially changed since the station has run courses on renewable alternative energy for the community. These were established following a station research survey, conducted by Jonathon Cowie, on the views of 129 residents in the Daintree area on renewable power systems.

Living at the station isn't easy. Hugh says: *"The people who come here range from the sublime to the ridiculous. There's the full gamut – girls escaping love and angry young men, as well as wonderful people who make a major seminal*

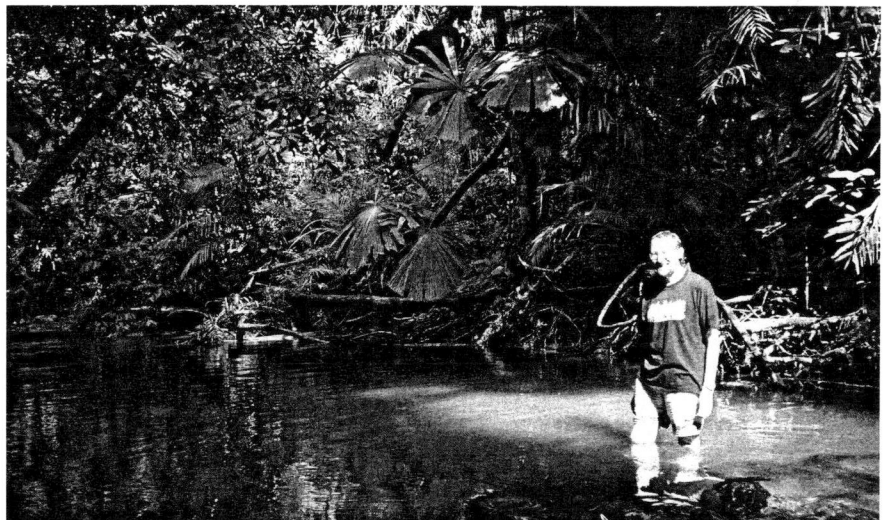
After the tropical rainstorm, this is Alan getting his feet clean!

impact on the station – mostly the latter."

In the local community and for the mostly young staff members, Hugh can sometimes seem intimidating. Johan Siverklev, who is one of the

77

station researchers, said, *"My impression is that local people tend to feel patronised or run-over by Hugh's way of discussing, and his sometimes overbearing manner of arguing can easily intimidate people – as I was intimidated in the beginning. It took me seven weeks living with Hugh to understand these things, and stand up to him in a serious discussion…I've realised that this is simply his way of trying to provoke a discussion…I can be pissed off at times, but I respect Hugh enormously for the knowledge and the dedication he has."*

Dr Hugh Spencer in an expansive mood

The station is its own form of intentional community, albeit a rather fluid one. Hugh is its anchor, what he calls, *"the ultimate backup for everything."* One of the biggest problems in its community can occur when volunteers arrive expecting it to be a kind of 'backpackers' hostel'. The Daintree area is also what Hugh describes as, *"a very complex place"*, and understanding precisely where the station, its occupants, and its work sit in the politics of the area is very difficult, and beyond the scope of this piece!

Other research projects
The range of research projects which can be tackled by the research station is very diverse, but much is focused on conservation biology. The flying fox bat colony has provided the basis for at least two projects. Project Gondwana from 1995 to 1996 was an extensive bat faunal survey for the WTMA. At the time of my visit, Hugh and Johan, the Swedish intern, were working on an energy conserving air exchanger project. The station has also produced significant research on fig biology, bat biology and is working on topics such as the effect of wild gingers in the forest eco-system, a radar based bat deterrent designed to emit flash charges to dissuade bats from entering fruit orchards, and other research topics which depend on the interest of visiting researchers and students.

Hopes for the future
Before I left Cape Tribulation I asked Hugh to 'dream a future'. His reply related both to the Daintree forest and the station. He told me, *"I'd like to see as much land bought back as possible – have it put into a public trust – a community land trust, rather than National Parks. There's an* amazing amount of local support for this idea."* Then, on the future of the station, he added, *"I'm hoping that some of the energy-related research that we are currently working on is able to be exploited, to produce a significant and stable cash flow for the Foundation – then the station can actually purchase the property it occupies (which will permit tapping into other Government funding), and even fund students. It has the potential to be a show case of appropriate technology and biological research in Australia."*

Finally, just before I bade my leave, Hugh said, *"I'm going to stay here and die here. It's my life."*

Lanzarote: the home of César Manrique
Alan Dearling

"Man was not created for this artificiality. There is an imperative need to go back to the soil. Feel it, smell it. That's what I feel."

César Manrique in 1964 visiting Andy Warhol and others in New York, and being nostalgic for his homeland of Lanzarote.

A very personal discovery

It was at the beginning of the 1990s that I spent a holiday on the Canarian island of Lanzarote with my partner, Christine. Frankly, I wasn't looking forward to it much, anticipating a package holiday destination with more than its fair share of lager louts and half-built multi storey hotel complexes. Staying in the old town area of Puerto del Carmen close to the harbour, and travelling from there to the 'tourist' spots, I quickly revised my opinion. Sure, there were plenty of tourist bars and shops along the long seafront which snakes around the bay northwards towards Arrecife airport, but there were no high rise monstrosities and the majority of the houses were a charming traditional array of whites, blues and greens. Hardly 'touristy' at all.

And as we visited the spectacular island viewpoints such Mirador del Rio, Del Diablo restaurant and viewpoint in the volcanic Timanfaya national park, and the acutely sensitive adaptation of the lava flows in the underground grottos of Los Jameos del Agua, we began to comprehend the all-embracing influence on Lanzarote that one man, artist, César Manrique, has had. In the architecture section of his official web site (www.cesarmanrique.com) it accurately, if boldly states that:

...even Puerto del Carmen is low-rise by comparison

Manrique in the desert landscape near his home

"Lanzarote is César Marique's most important work of art. His work and his influence have marked the external aspect of the island. The natives say he has 'made' Lanzarote."

Manrique's one-man environmental crusade

Each of Manrique's large scale environ-mental projects has effectively preserved a major part of Lanzarote's natural landscape. Each venture has provided the island with an environmental heritage site and their scope is breathtaking. They range from the founding of the massive Timanfaya national park through to the establishment of El Almacén, the Museum of International Contemporary art, which includes works by Picasso and Miro, and his last completed project, another personal passion, the Jardin de Cactus,

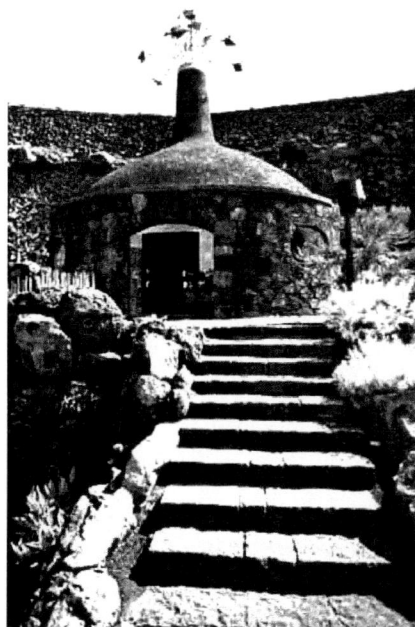
Jardin de Cactus

79

opened in 1990, two years before his untimely death, aged 73, in an automobile accident. With over 9,000 cacti and succulents growing in black volcanic sand known as lapilli, the gardens encompass 1,400 different species and celebrate what in the past was Lanzarote's main agricultural crop, cochineal, the red dye extracted from the beetle which lives on the prickly pear (tunera) cactus.

We also managed a visit to the house Manrique built in 'typical' Lanzarote style on his return from the USA. It's called, Casa del Campesino. In a similar fashion, his own house is situated within the striking volcanic inland area of Taro de Tahiche. In its simple lines, white exterior, its artworks and installations, there is a seamless blending which is totally in keeping with its natural location. The house for me represents César Manrique's intentions at their clearest. He said in his 1982 book, simply entitled: Lanzarote, that,

"Nature was generous to me. I can recognize many things others neither see nor understand...At last my stay on this mineral-rich island of frozen lava is nearing its completion, the contemplation of this volcanic baroque, with its deep crevices filled with cacti, with its living beings and plants – the emerald lizard in the sun and mossy lichen – all this brought me to the realization that the living beings on the earth have been created and endowed with an incredible sense of order by an unknown energy called 'life'."

Manrique's Tahiche house is a highly personalised lifestyle statement. It is an eco-dwelling built well before the term had acquired

Mirador del Rio: a spectacular outlook point

any meaning. This house is now home to the Fundacion César Manrique. It is also one of Manrique's clearest statements of intentionality. He wrote in 1982:

"Lanzarote was born some 15 years ago when it stepped out of its previous anonymity. Before this, life on the island was tough, even wretched...My battle to save the environment and the originality of the island has been violent...we contemporary artists – and those who perceive that harmony and beauty is at the highest level of our natural culture – have the moral and ethical duty to save our environment by all means at our disposal...I want to show my way of life and the way I feel quite openly, since I believe it will help all those possessing a constructive, free and healthy conception of life to defend this fascinating planet on which we live, no matter what the cost."

Among the aspects of the Fundacion house which left the deepest impressions with me were its snaking, circular subterranean tunnels. These interlink the rooms together, some of which are dome shaped. Everything inside and outside of the low sprawling dwelling is painted white, but the rooms and passageways are punctuated with completely natural rock formations, running waterfalls and all pervading cacti and succulents. Then there are the vast windows – a characteristic César Manrique signature – providing panoramic outlooks across the natural volcanic vista.

Now, that landscape which was so dear to Manrique, provides something of a national shrine to his memory, visited by over

The built environment and the natural world blend seamlessly at Casa del Campesino

300,000 visitors per year, as well as being the base for César Manrique Foundation, founded in 1992.

The surreal volcanic vista from within the Tahiche Fundacion César Manrique

Jameos del Agua

The lasting legacy of Manrique
The Foundation continues Manrique's life's work and concentrates on projects which:
- help to conserve nature and introduce people to the work of César Manrique;
- promote artistic activity and cultural reflection; and
- aid the development of activities that respect the natural environment and the order of the landscape.

It also offers annual awards to environmental projects in the Canarian islands which celebrate and enhance the natural heritage of the islands.

(My thanks To Daniel Poch and the Fundacion César Manrique for permission to use their photos along with some of my own)

The mural at the Fundacion

81

The seeds of eco-tourism
Alan Dearling

It is a brave and not always responsible band of entrepreneurs, who tread the delicate balance between opening people's eyes to the beauties and intricacies of nature, and despoiling the natural environment. The latter half of the twentieth century witnessed the rapid expansion of world tourism. The new century and millennium shows no let up, especially since so many countries' economies now rely heavily on tourist income. One developing component of this worldwide industry is the anachronistic, 'eco-tourism'. And as the fastest growing sector of the tourist industry, the United Nations actually declared 2002 as the International Year of Eco-tourism.

A matter of scale and motivation
The trouble with 'eco-tourism' as a concept, as well as the practices it encompasses, is that its meaning is not clear or universally 'shared'. The biggest problem is that unscrupulous large-scale tourist operators have frequently pirated the term eco-tourism to describe projects and holidays aimed at the richest of world tourists. Usually these are detrimental to local communities, indigenous populations and natural environment and bio-diversity. The World Tourism Organisation estimates that 'nature tourism' accounted for 20 per cent of all tourism in Asia-Pacific and South Africa by the end of the 1990s.

A 2002 study by the International Hotels Environmental Initiative found that 80 per cent of Britons say that they are prepared to pay more – between £30 and £70 per fortnight – to book into a hotel with a responsible environmental attitude. These practices could include using the heat from shower run-offs to heat other water tanks and more use of 'grey' water for irrigation and recycling through reed-bed type schemes.

Most of the worst examples of schemes under the banner of eco-tourism are large-scale and are blatantly exploitational. In the Mekong Sub-region of Burma, through Cambodia, Laos, Thailand, Vietnam through to China, the development of eco-tourism is based on the construction of major new highways – development corridors – and the relocation of 60 million highlanders from their homeland. The Asian Development Bank has suggested that they can be compensated with jobs in eco-tourism, while a coalition of non-governmental organisations (NGOs), the Tourism Monitoring Team (TIM), has described the development as creating 'human zoos'.

In Botswana, the indigenous bushmen are being moved out of their wilderness home to make way for more tented safaris in the Central Kalahari Game Reserve. Stephen Corry, director of 'Survival International' described the move as *"...the Botswana government exploiting land for private gain."*

Closer to my home, the 2002/1 issue of the *Friends, Families & Travellers' Newsletter* reported that Swindon Council in Wiltshire are proposing to redevelop the splendid double ramparts of Barbury Hill Fort, perched at 900 feet on the Ridgeway, as a theme park.

Treehouse holidays
I've been an enthusiastic visitor to Turkey for more than a decade. I find the people, the scenery and the environment all to my liking. However, even in the most celebrated of natural resorts like Patara on the Mediterranean coast (home of St Nicholas – our Father Christmas) there has been a tendency towards building monstrous hotels like the Beyhan, which

Some of Kadir's famous tree houses in Turkey

serve to destroy the natural beauty of the landscape and swallow up the limited water supplies needed for local agriculture.

Further west, in the shadow of one of the twelve Mount Olympos's in the world, at Çavusköy, is a very different type of low-cost accommodation set amidst sweet smelling pine trees and plants. There are 200 beds available in the treehouses and all are individual, unique constructions. Built by Kadir

Kaya in the late 1980s, locals thought that Kadir was mad to move away from the usual formula of hotels and guest houses. Yet he's been proved right many times over, remaining busy throughout the recent recession in Turkish tourism. His tree-homes appeal to the more adventurous travellers who fancy experiencing nature at close quarters and doing so in an ancient landscape of a Byzantine city's ruins and a Genoese fort – all of which is only about 2 km from the beaches. In 2002 the most expensive accommodation in a tree house is still under $10 US, and that includes both breakfast and dinner (with an emphasis on vegetarian food)! E-mail: enquiries@olympostreehouses.com

Part of the sustainable futures demonstration at the UK's Big Green Gathering

Respect and appreciation of the environment

The spectrum encompassed by 'eco-tourism' is incredibly broad. Included are an increasing number of people who want to share their environmentally-oriented lifestyles and homes with other people. Theirs is a much fluffier, acceptable and proactive form of eco-tourism. Most are aimed at practically demonstrating that we can and must respect nature in all its diversity and learn about how we can live more simply and sustainably. Arguably, without such schemes such as WWOOFers (Willing Workers on organic farms: www.phdcc.com/wwoof), festivals such as the Big Green (www.big-green-gathering.com) and Northern Green Gathering (www.ngg.org.uk) in the UK, and the ConFests and Woodford Forum (qff@woodfordfolkfestival.com) in Australia, many fewer people would learn about sustainable lifestyles and meet the people who are trying to bring about changes in attitudes.

During the compilation of Another Kind of Space, I met and heard about many people whose dwellings are a statement about the way they want to live. Many feel passionately about sharing these 'lessons being learned' with others.

The pros and cons of this industry cannot be simply stated. One view is that a few people visiting an area, whether it is in the mountains, the forests or the seaside, constitute a benefit to both the indigenous population (through income generation and funds to conserve their area), and to the visitors who learn about different environments, appropriate dwellings, lifestyles and cultures. The trouble is that it is mightily difficult to regulate – to set a limit to growth. When it is developed sensitively,

"Eco-tourism focuses on local cultures, wilderness adventures, volunteering, personal growth and learning new ways to live on our vulnerable planet. It is typically defined as travel to destinations where the flora, fauna, and cultural heritage are the primary attractions. Responsible eco-tourism includes programs that minimize the adverse effects of traditional tourism on the natural environment, and enhance the cultural integrity of local people.

Therefore, in addition to evaluating environmental and cultural factors, initiatives by hospitality providers to promote recycling, energy efficiency, water re-use, and the creation of economic opportunities for local communities are an integral part of eco-tourism." (GDRC, 2000)

I originally wrote this next piece in the gateway to Australia's eco-tourism – Cairns. With nearly a million tourists visiting this city annually, tourism is by far the biggest local money spinner and every conceivable tourist trip, service and facility is on offer, ranging from the predictable trips to the Great Barrier Reef and the rainforests in Mossman and Daintree, through to 4 wheel-drive 'adventures' taking the backpacker 'ultimate party' crew out on a collision course with the natural world. While in Europe or North America probably no-one would think of describing a five day bus tour as 'eco-tourism'. However, such trips are frequently 'sold' in exactly this way in Australia or Africa, where many tour operators thrive on taking groups out 'bush' in a gas-guzzling Mercedes truck or Land Rover.

In this next section, we meet Steve Caught, who is trying to breathe life back into a small eco-tourist rainforest resort in the Barron Falls/Kuranda area, 35 kilometres inland towards the Atherton Tablelands. Such ventures are becoming more common globally. The motivations of their owners varies considerably. Some are environmental conservationists who want to spread the word by giving more people the personal experience of getting close to nature, even for one night. Others have seen it as an obvious marketing opportunity, 'selling' the forest experience, or whatever environment it is, on a purely monetary basis. Usually the 'truth' is somewhere in between.

So, now you own a rainforest?
Alan Dearling

From yuppy tourism to...

"Looking for something unique? Experience the magic of Kuranda's World Heritage Rainforest first hand by staying in an innovatively furnished, fully screened cabin style tent, deep in the rainforest. Sit back, relax, take in the wonderful sights and sounds of the forest."

Kuranda Rainforest Eco Retreat advert, 2001

This is the bit of rainforest paradise that Steve Caught now owns. He bought it following a re-possession which ended the five year existence of 'TENTative NESTS' lovingly built and developed

The train heading towards Barron Falls and Kuranda

from 1995 to 2000 by Joell Bacon and Tina Kennedy. No-one wants to go bankrupt, and for Steve it a sad way to inherit a property, let alone a potential business. He's also purchased it without ever even meeting the people who dreamed the place into existence.

Now, to put not too fine a point on it, Steve knows what he doesn't want to do both in his own life and with the property. He told me,
"I don't want a place full of yuppies, I'll bring the price down and try and make it affordable for anyone who wants to have the experience of staying in the rainforest...I'm not going to put up with people who expect to be waited on. It's not going to be that sort of place. If they don't like staying in a tent and having simple facilities they shouldn't be here."

Rainforest Retreat barely visible through the lush Kuranda rainforest

It may seem a bit odd to start by describing the 'problems' facing Steve before exploring the property and its dwellings. However, it will make sense, trust me!

The advert for the re-named Rainforest Eco Retreat was placed in the Kuranda guide booklet back in 2000 when Steve thought it would be a quick and straightforward job to get the place up and running. He expected that it would be nothing more than a general clean up and some renovation and replacement work. The trouble was that Steve had (and has) a relatively well paid job at the opulent end of the casino/hotel/islands tourist industry. He fervently wanted to escape from that world

84

The badly damaged bridge

and involve himself in something of his own that he believed in. The plan had been for him to sell his Cairns' apartment to finance the necessary work on the Kuranda property, and allow him the capital to make the move over into his new existence as an eco-tourist host. But the Cairns' property market is in a temporary or permanent slump. So, this means that Steve can't realise his capital and is left with two mortgages and a six days a week, full-time job, half an hours drive away from Kuranda back in Cairns.

The next problem lies in the property itself, where a cyclone and river flood has relocated the bridge, and effectively split the seven acre property in two. This has denied access for visitors to the area where the sleeping platforms and tents would normally be – and being rainforest, the paths, and indeed the whole property, has become engulfed in lush new tropical growth. Paths, platforms and whole buildings are virtually lost in the jungle.

Finding out about the past
Walking around the buildings and the rainforest site with Steve was a fascinating experience. *"I'm really envious of what you've got here",* I blurted out at one point on the tour as we moved once more from a building into the verdant richness of the forest. Steve replied, *"…but no-one I work with is interested in what I'm doing here."* And that sense of personal isolation is intensified by the fact that Steve doesn't yet have roots into the local Kuranda/Barron Falls

The leaf-strewn entrance into the main guest building

community. In fact, local Aborigines living across the road from the property have continued to use the area as 'their own' during the time of the TENTative NESTS, through into Steve's occupancy. Small scale vandalism and petty theft from the site have occurred sporadically in the past year, partly no doubt, as a result of Steve's infrequent habitation. There has also been a squatter living on the property who has taken it upon himself to cut down some trees to ensure an unrestricted view of a particularly striking dead tree. Finally, Steve is only gradually building up a picture regarding how the place was organised in the past, both in terms of practical land management things like how the Rota Loo composting toilets and the irrigation system work, through to how daily life used to run during the TENTative NESTS regime.

Some of this knowledge can be rebuilt from material that has been available on the Internet. Visitors had been encouraged to make comments on their stay in the 'nests' and from these we can glimpse the positive side of effective eco-tourism:

"We saw platypus and other species and it really is too much for words."
Bill and Babs Joseph, New York, USA.

"We never imagined rainforest so beautiful. We recommend it to all our friends." Brandt and family, Germany.

There are three main buildings on the site:
• The reception building in which Steve is currently living, having made it more secure, if less airy, with the installation of windows and glass patio doors.
• The main guest building which was described in the pre-Steve days as: *"Upstairs there is a lounge, adorned with interesting artefacts and a library. Downstairs is a clothes washing area, hot showers and composting toilets."* It also appears to be a natural communal cooking area. As you can see from the photo, the forest is gradually claiming its own!
• Across the creek where the bridge used to be, lies the main (presently difficult to access)

85

section of the property. Within it is a large canopied dining and social area. Water and electricity are laid on to this section of the site. It includes various walking paths, originally used for night walks, a small 'back to nature' campsite, and the eight sleeping platforms, built (to quote TENTative NESTS):

"One or two metres above the ground depending on their location. They are large enough to include an enclosed veranda and contain floor-level mattress beds. The nests are covered with a high quality canvas with a vinyl protective layer to give it extra protection from the frequent rain…Treated plantation pine was used to construct the tent platforms. All other structures are made of timber salvaged from old railway buildings and sleepers and concrete and corrugated iron from local suppliers…Some bush tucker species such as quandong, Burdekin plum, chocolate peanut and lemon myrtle were also planted as an educational feature."

Steve hasn't inherited the tents or beds – indeed it is nigh on impossible even to locate the tracks and platforms. Getting the bridge rebuilt, is, therefore, one of the priorities, but not easy to accomplish in a part of the forest which is so hard to access.

Looking to the future
Amongst the questions, decisions and options facing Steve Caught as he looks to the future of his rainforest dream are:
• How can he raise the finance to enable him to stop working and to start living his life full-time at his Eco Retreat?
Options include obtaining capital finance from a new partner or partners; renting one of the buildings at the Eco Retreat on a semi-temporary basis; inviting 'volunteers', possibly through the WWOOFers (Willing workers on organic farms) scheme to come and help with the renovation of the property and forest. Volunteer workers might

even be prepared to pay something for the experience, as do the visitors to the Daintree Rainforest Research Station.
• What sort of visitor/visitor experience should be the focus for the facility?
Options include re-focusing on backpackers; building links with local Cairns tour operators; offering 'package' deals including activities like guided walks, night experiences and vegetarian food. Previously the TENTative NESTS and the grounds were marketed as being alcohol and smoke free – Steve will possibly have other views.
• What sort of structures to put onto the platforms?
Options include up- or downgrading the original mix of tents and beds, especially with a view to combating the high humidity and mildew/fungal spoor problems associated with rainforest.
• What sort of lifestyle and community does he want to be a part of at his Eco Retreat?
Options include viewing the property as something special that is held in trust for the future; expansion of the number of properties on the site; sharing the dream with other partners/participants as the eco-tourist resort is rebuilt and restructured.

There are no easy or soft options for Steve, but then, owning a rainforest brings with it a challenging array of both rights and responsibilities.

References
Global Development Research Center (GDRC) (2000) *Defining Eco-Tourism* at *http://www.gdrc.org/uem/eco-tour/etour-define.html*
WWOOFers info for hosts and volunteers at www.wwoof.org

Steve Caught in the guest building

Part Two:
Free spirits: Gypsies, Travellers and Nomads

Back to the Road
Jake Bowers-Burbridge

"I'm a Romany Rye
I'm a true didikai
I build all my castles beneath the blue sky
I don't pay no rent cause I live in a tent
And that's why they call me the Romany Rye"

My granny sung this verse to me one of the last times I saw her. I was sitting in her caravan at the council run Gypsy site that she had lived at for the last years of her life. The site was called 'The Hatchin Tan', which means the stopping place in Romany. The site, of which she was the warden, proved to be her last stopping place. She had lived there with my granddad, the man she had eloped with when she was sixteen, but he had died 6 months earlier of a heart attack. Her last hatchin tan was similar to many other Gypsy sites in England – a concrete plot surrounded by barbed wire, a cultural Auschwitz where the last of my people live together to enjoy some sense of community with their culture under threat and way of life outlawed. With her died knowledge that I will never know and a story that I had just begun to listen to. When we lowered her coffin into the ground I realised that the thousand year trek of the Romany people will come to an end if we – her grand children – do nothing to ensure the survival of our people.

My grandmother, Julie 'Billy' Bowers (third from left) in the hop fields of Hampshire

It's difficult to know where to begin this story. Perhaps I should begin with myself. I am a didikai. Half Romany and half Gorjia (non-Gypsy) by blood – a real half breed. I spent little of my childhood living a Gypsy life. Although from the age of 13, when my Romany father introduced me to many of my 17 half brothers and sisters I began to have a lot more contact with Traveller culture and people.

In August 1997, I decided to honour the memory of my grandparents by living the way they had as young people. I came to England with some money I had saved in Sweden and began the process of finding a horse and a traditional bow-top wagon. I knew nothing about horses and even less about living in a traditional way on the road. Six weeks later I had spent £3,000 on a kushti grai (good horse) and a kushti vardo (good living wagon) and embarked upon a project that has transformed my life.

The horse was bought from Alf Selby, a horse dealer and breaker in Kent and the wagon from Eli Frankham, a Romany poet, activist and distant relation. The horse I bought was called Sally – a black cob mare measuring 14,3 hh (150 cm) at the withers. She is 3/4 cob and 1/4 shire and has everything I was told to look for. I needed a horse with a 'bomb-proof' temperament, a 'foot in each corner' and 'four big hairy feet'. I found Sally working for Alf where she and Alf taught people to drive. Sally had the patience of a saint and the strength of a tractor. She was exactly what a novice on a very steep learning curve required. As a cob she was also a traditional horse doing a traditional job.

My horse Sally – still going strong!

The wagon was built in Sussex in 1926 and had travelled many miles through English lanes in the service of many Romany families. Eli had recently re-painted the caravan and replaced its canvas. I spent a couple of days with Eli and his wife Gert in Norfolk. I listened to his stories and poetry and heard him play the harmonica. A week later I fetched the wagon and was wished *"Kushti bok"* (good luck) by Eli. It meant a lot to me that I had bought my wagon from a distant relation and a Traveller, who is very well known and respected within the Romany community.

I had a fair deal of 'kushti bok' that summer but never really made it out on the road. This was largely because I had decided to start travelling from a village called Three Oaks, which lies in a very hilly area in southern England. The horse was totally unused to pulling a one-ton wagon through hilly terrain and the harness we had bought just wasn't up to the job. Autumn was coming and by the time November came, we decided to take the caravan and live the sedentary Romany life in a horse paddock outside Three Oaks. We did all the things my ancestors had done for hundreds of years, like gathering wood and eating wild food.

The autumn was dark and cold, but living next to a railway embankment provided an almost limitless amount of well seasoned, ready chopped logs to burn.

That autumn I felt like a failure. I had invested thousands of pounds and three months of my life in a project that had covered a grand total of one mile. I was parked outside Three Oaks in a horse paddock. It was cold, damp, no one came to see me, and I had nearly run out of money. Even the horse looked miserable as she stood alone staring into the flames of the campfire. In hindsight, I'm glad that I was forced to perfect the skills that I learnt during that period, from handling and driving the horse to making a fire after a week of torrential English rain. It was anything but romantic but it was nothing compared to what my grandparents had experienced. It is nothing compared to what Gypsies face everyday from Wokingham to Wallachia. The police left me alone, the locals weren't hostile and I was never short of money or food. I was never forced to go out and knock on doors, never forced to beg or defend myself from physical attack. I had no children or elderly people to care for. There were no neo-nazis trying to kill me or Gestapo trying to root me out. Life could have been better but also so much worse.

After Christmas, I decided to take the horse and caravan to Sweden. This was my long-term intention because I knew that travelling in the UK was hard. The Criminal Justice Act of 1994 basically criminalises a traditional nomadic lifestyle. Three months prison for 'criminal trespass' and other executive powers have given local authorities the power to culturally 'cleanse' the English countryside of Travellers. I am full of admiration for those Travellers who still travel in Britain today and maintain their right to do so. Their daily defiance is mind blowing and great proof that we are the most ungovernable people on earth.

Sweden – a promised land for Travellers ?
In January 1998, I loaded Sally onto a horse lorry bound for Sweden. Behind the lorry, on a trailer generally used for transporting cars, sat my vardo, my home and container of all my worldly goods. I travelled with them and John Ryan - an Irish horse dealer who exports piebald and skewbald Irish cobs to Sweden. I have lived and travelled in Sweden for two years. First with an ex-girlfriend Anna Pulvirenti in 1998 and then with my wife Claire in 1999.

Winter has always been a tough time for Travellers in northern Europe. Harsh weather drives the hardiest of people indoors, many animals choose hibernation or fly south for the winter. Such luxuries were not available for Romany people traditionally and they would establish winter camps where they would wait for the dark cold months to pass. The coming of spring would mean freedom to move on because it brought the beginning of the agricultural year and fresh grazing for the horses. Finnish Gypsies are known to have continued travelling through the winter in open horse-drawn sledges obtaining hay for the horses where they could. Swedish winters are every bit as severe as Finnish ones and the thought of travelling with a horse and wagon in temperatures that often drop to minus 20 centigrade was not one I relished.

Because of its high latitude, spring does not come to southern Sweden until April and good grass growth cannot be guaranteed until May. So in May 1998, I set out on the road with Sally. It felt really good to finally be able to see all my plans about to come to fruition. After transporting the caravan 15 km to a farm where I could stay as long as I liked, I set about getting Sally, the caravan and myself ready for a summer of travelling. This included getting Sally used to pulling heavy loads, painting and cleaning the caravan and making myself fit. I knew that I would spend a lot of time walking beside the caravan and I intended to travel at least 300 km.

You might wonder why I decided to buy a vardo when I went back to the road. Why not buy a pick-up and trailer like some of my siblings and cousins have? The answer is simple. After 5 years experience fighting road-building schemes across Britain, I didn't want to contribute anything to the petrol economy. The internal combustion engine is wreaking havoc throughout the planet, from road-building to oil exploration and global warming. That said, if anybody has the right to use cars, mobile phones and even disposable nappies, Travellers do. I fully understand why the vast majority have embraced modern convenience.

Horses are effectively solar powered (they eat plants) bio-engines. They are also great company and the emissions they leave are good for the earth rather than harmful to it. Then of course there is the added bonus of being a 3 mile an hour road block which slows down the rest of the trafffic. On a practical note, horse-drawn living is also cheaper (no tax, fuel, insurance or licence). It's also less offensive to the settled population you are dependent upon.

Vardo living means a lot of walking without having to carry your things on your back. You can walk hundreds of miles and the horse takes the strain of

Tidaholm. I had been accepted at an art school there to study silversmithing. I needed a skill that could easily produce crafts that could be transported and sold from the wagon and silversmithing seemed to fit the bill. Right from the time the Romany people left India they are

Claire with Jake on the roads of Sweden

your belongings. What you take with you is essentially a bedroom on wheels. You sleep in your wagon, but spend the majority of your time under the sky. It's a physically demanding life, especially in the colder months, but highly ecologically friendly. The consumption of resources is minimised. I had a solar panel on the top of my vardo, which powered a radio and lights. Your fuel is scraps of wood that nobody else would bother with and the even the water you consume is cut right down when you have to go and fetch it yourself. Horse-drawn travellers are essentially modern hunter-gatherers taking only their basic needs from their environment. They must have one of the smallest 'ecological footprints' of any citizen. You can't have too many possessions because that would be unfair on your horse.

My goal was a little town in western Sweden called

reported to have worked as smiths. Indeed a very common name amongst British Gypsies is Smith and one of the largest Romany groupings in Sweden and across much of the world are the Kalderasha, which means Coppersmith in Romany.

One of the biggest reasons for the decline in traditional Romany culture, aside from forced assimilation and genocide, is the fact that much of Europe no longer has an agricultural economy.

Traditional Gypsy skills, such as herbalism, horsemanship, entertaining and craftsmanship have become redundant in an industrial age. In many countries, Romany people are becoming assimilated into society as unskilled labour where they, having lost their unique culture, lifestyle and language, face a future of being nothing more than industrial cannon fodder. Our survival therefore depends as it always has on finding an economic niche for ourselves so that we can maintain our economic and cultural independence from mainstream Gorjia society. For me, silversmithing is one way of doing this because it is both traditional and modern. Jewellery will be wanted as long as human vanity exists, and that shows no signs of disappearing!

Silversmithing, however is unlikely to make you rich and in 1998 I was not a skilled enough craftsman to support myself with it. I therefore earned my living throughout the summer by editing and translating documents for the Swedish telecommunications company Ericsson. It was great to 'tele-commute' from a bow-top wagon whilst on the road. I worked in fields and laybys whilst the people I was working with sat in factories and office blocks. Perhaps information technology is a possible economic niche in the modern world for Gypsies that wish to remain nomadic. Unlike many of my brothers and sisters I was fortunate enough to have received a school education that allows me to take advantage of such opportunities.

I travelled over 450 kilometres during the first summer. I made it to Tidaholm much earlier than expected. In fact I experienced no major problems at all. The horse managed every challenge we gave her, no hill was too steep, no raging juggernaut too scary. She only ever lost one horseshoe and despite having no spare tyre we never had a puncture. In fact things went so smoothly that it seemed as if our path was blessed. I like to think that my granny and indeed all my ancestors might have appreciated what we were trying to do and smoothed our paths for us. All in all we had a very 'Latcho drom' (the Romany equivalent of 'have a nice trip' meaning literally 'good road') and a whole load of 'kushti bok'.

My trip from eastern to western Sweden attracted a huge amount of attention. Every local newspaper whose area we passed through wrote about the journey. Sally and I were photographed and video filmed every step of the way and we were always well treated by farmers who I asked to camp with for the night. In fact I only met one truly unpleasant landowner the whole summer.

I know of no Travellers in Sweden living a nomadic or traditional horse based lifestyle. The Swedish welfare state has given everybody the opportunity to move into houses in its desire to create the 'Svenska Folkhemmet' (Swedish People's Home) which, depending on your politics and perspective,

can either be seen as an attempt to create a socialist utopia or an Orwellian nightmare. Swedish Gypsies themselves, led by the Romany author Katarina Taikon campaigned very effectively in the 1960s for access to housing and education. I have been lucky enough to meet her uncle Aljosha Taikon. He lives in a flat in an immigrant suburb of Stockholm. He was born in a tent and lived as a traditional Kalderasha until the second world war.

In the two years I spent travelling in Sweden, I met many people that belonged to Sweden's diverse Romany community. I've met Finnish Kale Roma, Swedish Kalderasha Roma, recent Roma immigrants to Sweden and many Swedish Tattare (similar to Irish Travellers in ethnicity but with a language and culture that is very similar to Romany) but all lived sedentary lives. Gypsy communities in Sweden are to be found in larger towns living alongside immigrant communities. It seems as if official policy has been to assimilate Travellers through generosity, yet past policy has often been brutal; up until the 1960s Travellers were sterilised in Sweden.

The effect of this assimilation has been to remove Travellers from the Swedish rural landscape. Indeed the only person to recognise my wagon as a Gypsy wagon turned out to be an Englishman! Curious people were very happy to see the 'circus wagon' and many were surprised to hear that the wagon and its owner had Gypsy origins. "You're surely not a Gypsy!" many people would say after seeing my blonde hair and blue eyes. Gypsies, for most Swedes, are dark suspicious urban thieves, not blue-eyed, horse-drawn Englishmen encountered on dusty forest roads. This ignorance shows just how far assimilation has gone in Sweden and although sad, when you consider the thousands of Romany people that built up and maintained the Swedish rural economy, it is a situation that can be taken advantage of. The Swedish rural landscape is not only devoid of Travellers, it is devoid of suspicion of Travellers.

The fact that the inhabitants of the Swedish countryside are neutral towards Travellers makes it a great place to travel, particularly if you are interested in living a traditional horse-drawn lifestyle. But there are also many other reasons to live and travel there. Sweden is a large country with a sparse population with enough living space for thousands of Travellers. The roads are empty of traffic. Its law of 'allemänsrätt' (all man's rights) is a model law protecting the 'right to roam'. Everybody has the right to camp, gather firewood and walk in the fields and forests – provided they do not destroy any property or harm the environment. Everybody has the right to bathe in any of Sweden's many thousands of lakes and gather berries, herbs and mushrooms from the countryside. Although this law does not give the right to graze animals and park caravans, the spirit of it generally means that doing so is accepted, as long as the landowner's permission is sought.

In short, Sweden is a land where everybody has land rights. It is very far removed from Britain with its endless fences, Criminal Justice Act and feudal mentality towards land and class.

New challenges and lands

If Sweden can be criticized for anything, it is that life is perhaps too easy. This may seem like a strange concept, especially for those that have known nothing but struggle, but it is definitely the case in Sweden. Of course, Sweden does have its own problems, such as the spread of neo-nazi violence. But my experience is that travelling in Sweden with a horse can give you the annoying status of semi-celebrity. I have been photographed peeing at 7 o'clock in the morning by German tourists and treated as a member of a travelling freak-show. Swedes are by nature very kind and great defenders of human rights and justice. But on an individual level they can often be very conservative, boring and conformist, hence their great fascination for anyone that breaks the mould and lives in a horse-drawn wagon. The level of material comfort is so high that many Swedes cannot comprehend how anybody would willingly choose to live a materially basic nomadic life. The result can be that they are intrusive and do not respect that a caravan is actually your home. One day, whilst fetching some water for the horse, I saw, from a distance, a woman walk straight into my home as if it was a tourist attraction.

Gypsies, however, have always been masters of exploiting people's fascination for the exotic. We have always consciously weaved a web of wonder around ourselves. Partly as self-defence, but also as a business opportunity. You might say that we are some of the world's first PR experts and spin-doctors. Deliberately making ourselves more exotic, mysterious and romantic, makes our curses more potent and our fortune-telling more profitable. Gypsies invented modern marketing, it's not the product that's important it's the image and packaging that surrounds it.

Travelling in Sweden, I decided, could not only be fun but profitable. So at the end of 1998, after 4 months studying silversmithing and making

jewellery I travelled with Claire, my wife to be, to Bali in Indonesia. We bought lots of silver jewellery to complement what I had made at art school in Tidaholm in order to finance a trip back across Europe with the horse and wagon. As much as I love Sweden, there is an eeriness it. The woods are suspiciously silent and empty. The greatest thing that made us want to come back to England was the total absence of Travellers in the Swedish rural landscape.

So, in May 1999, when the grass started growing again. We set off across Europe. Our goal was to be St.Marie de la Mer in southern France but we never made it. We spent too much time making money and enjoying the sunshine of Sweden's west coast. When September and autumn came we had only travelled 500 km to the southern Swedish county of Skåne. I contacted John Ryan, the man who originally took me to Sweden, and brought everything back to England. We abandoned our original plan of going to France after meeting Stefan Kwiek, a Polish Kalderasha Roma, whose family are still metalworkers and live everywhere from Paris to Mexico. He told us that Travellers in France need internal passports and must report themselves to the authorities every 24 hours. We reasoned that if we were to be harassed it might as well be in a language we understood.

Back to Olde England

England is an old grey country. Everything about it is old. Its lanes, its houses, its politics. Like an old person, it is always far more inclined to look back into the past than forward into the future. It's a hostage to its past and England's past is not a pleasant one. It built the slave trade, it subjected half the world to its military might, its aristocracy and class system remains intact and it is the birthplace of industry - the economic system that destroys all forms of diversity, be it biological, or cultural.

In the time of Henry the 8th, England was a country that used to have the death penalty for simply being a Gypsy. Those Gypsy families that weren't expelled, transported to Australia or hung have survived by their wits. They have survived in an environment that is hostile to their needs not just because of legislation and racism, but because of its physical make-up. England is one of the most densely populated countries on earth with land-ownership as concentrated as that of any corrupt third-world country. Bad news, if you're a nomad that needs constant new grazing for your horses and free access to land for fuel and food.

You may ask why we returned to such an environment. We have also wondered this many times since returning. Maybe we felt like a challenge after comfortable Sweden, maybe we are gluttons for punishment or maybe it's just that you can run but you can't hide from injustice.

The things that make you a celebrity in Sweden define you as a pariah in England. When the English Home Secretary Jack Straw recently remarked on radio that all Gypsies, *"defecate on doorsteps"*, he was echoing the feeling of many a Briton. Travelling in Britain has proved to be a rude awakening for me. I always knew it was bad from my family but had never directly experienced it myself. Just 500 miles separates England from Sweden, but if you're a Traveller the gulf in attitudes is colossal. The laws that cover all aspects of a Traveller's life are dramatically different:

- ■ Camping on private land is a right in Sweden, it is an imprisonable offence in England.
- ■ Free street trading is acceptable in Sweden, in England street trading is only permitted within designated areas.
- ■ Swedish Gypsy children have the legal right to be taught in their own language, English Gypsy children do not.
- ■ Swedish Romanies and Travellers are recognised as distinct ethnic minorities by the government, British Romanies and Travellers are not even mentioned in the British Census.

Britain is without a written constitution and sometimes it seems as if the only rights Britain's citizens have are by default. Such as when a legal challenge to a law that forbids something is successful or when we gain rights on a European level. Even then, we seem to have no inalienable rights that can't be taken away by government policy or legislation. Such as the 'right to remain silent' which was abolished by the Criminal Justice Act in 1994.

The right to travel is not disputed in England. Anybody can use the roads if they have the documentation and vehicle required. It's the right to stop that is the problem. Most of the old hatchin tans are gone. Those that haven't had a ditch put through them by local councils, have been grabbed by farmers extending their fences or disappeared under the developers' relentless tide of concrete. A lot of the drove roads and by-ways,

which were perfect for moving horses and wagons, are now ripped up by 4 wheel drive vehicles or illegally blocked by landowners. The commons we used to use are being turned into golf-courses and plantations. The verges are forever made smaller by the widening of ever more congested roads. Travelling in Britain is only possible nowadays with an extremely intimate knowledge of the countryside and a willingness to trespass in defence of the right to live as our ancestors did.

Now that the places we had the right to stop by customary use have been taken away from us, we face a stark choice: settle, or engage in daily law-breaking in defence of our way of life. This ongoing struggle has got to be one of the longest running campaigns of civil disobedience this country has ever known. Trespass is a daily fact of life for any Traveller. The Criminal Justice Act however, not only made trespass a criminal offence, it also removed the duty of local councils to provide sites for Travellers. The result has been that Travellers' sites across the country have been privatised and closed. Even the few legal stopping places are decreasing in number and those Travellers that buy their own land in order to find some security find that they cannot do that either. The Town and Country Planning Act 1947, which was destined to stop the very developers that have stolen our traditional stopping places, also stops us from living in a caravan in a field. In short, the whole system has made our lifestyle impossible.

With such insecurity and living under the constant threat of eviction, the quality of Travellers lives is greatly affected, especially Traveller children. Very few Travellers are registered to vote, many do not receive education or access to health care. We are not even recognised as an ethnic minority in the British Census.

On our trip through England we experienced at first hand all the problems I've mentioned above. We hot-footed it through England to Dorset and then Kent, where we now live. Not only were we unable to stop but we were unable to trade. Everywhere we asked to stop on farmers land we were denied, everywhere we tried to sell our silver we were moved on because we didn't have a 'Street Trading Consent' issued by the appropriate authority. We felt hounded from town to town, an authentic Romany experience if ever there was one. Like a scene from black comedy, we were welcomed into the county of Wiltshire by a police car. The officer inside accused us of mistreating our horse and needing to know our names and final destination. We met other horse-drawn Travellers who had told us about being physically beaten by landowners and refused water by local villagers. In such a hostile climate, your semi-celebrity status is soon replaced by that of a pariah or social outcast. The red carpet treatment of Sweden had definitely run out. By January 2001, we had sold our trusty horse, Sally, and our wagon, but I hope to buy some new 'wheels' again soon. At about the same time (December 2000), Eli Frankham died, and I found myself writing his obituary for the 'Guardian' newspaper. There I wrote of him:

"Eli helped hundreds of Romani families fight the local planning regulations that stopped them from settling in caravans on their own land. Eli was both modern and traditional. He believed that education was crucial to Romani emancipation, but he also valued Romani tradition. He both kept and traded horses all his life, recorded old Romani stories and songs, and would not be seen in public without a diklo, or Romani scarf, around his neck. He was a powerful public speaker and singer, who never failed to entertain his many family and friends.

Many travellers referred to him as Uncle Eli; some of his younger relatives called him 'Uncle Badger'. I recently overheard a journalist asking another Romani activist if he had email. 'No', he replied, 'but I've got E-li'."

My journey of course has not come to an end. It's only just begun. I once dreamed of living in a horse-drawn community that would practise all our traditional trades and show the world and ourselves that we have a beautiful culture of which to be proud. That dream may yet be realised. I've lived the life of my grandparents, enjoyed its freedom thanks to Sweden, suffered its burdens in

Eli Frankham in a photo taken for a TV documentary

England. But, I've realised one thing. The Romany Trek is not coming to an end because my generation is failing to live the old-life. It is because we are unable to.

Every nation without a homeland has its promised land. For the Kurds it is Kurdistan, for us, it is Romanestan. But Romanestan is just an ideal, a utopia in time, if not in place. We may originally have come from India but I doubt that many of the world's eight million Romanies would choose to go back there.

If our culture is to survive it must be made possible through political action. By going to Sweden I've seen glimpses of Romanestan in the forests now empty of Travellers. By coming home I hope I can bring a little bit of it back with me to a country so in need of its promise. My granny used to chase away policemen that had come to evict her with a burning log and I don't doubt that she would have loved the freedom of Sweden.

What would have meant more to her however, would be to have this freedom brought home. The Swedish 'allemänsrätt' is the political equivalent of my granny's burning log. Now that I'm back in Britain, I intend to chase our imprisoners with it, and I'll be thinking of her as I continue that pursuit!

If you share any of the sentiments in this article, or would like to get in touch with me, please email: jake.burbridge@ic24.net

Ger a life!
David Renwick Grant

*In the autumn of 1990, the Grant family –
Kate and David, along with Torcuil, Eilidh and
Fionn, then 10, 8 and 6 respectively, left their
home in Orkney to begin a journey that was to
take them around the world, through fifteen
countries and across three continents by
horse-drawn caravan. They experienced war
in Yugoslavia, school in Slovenia, a court case
in Mongolia and expulsion from China. They
also experienced a great warmth and hospitality along the way earning them a place in the
Guinness Book of Records. Altogether they
travelled 12,360 miles in 2,570 days, from Scotland to Kazakhstan, China, Japan, the USA and
Canada. David kept a diary of those adventures
which has been published as 'The Seven Year
Hitch' (1999, Simon and Schuster). Here is his
account of the lifestyle and homes of the people of
Mongolia.*

You probably know them as yurts. I mean those
round felt tents, the kind that you associate with
Genghis Khan and that featured in blurry black
and white photographs in my school geography
book. The kind that, basically unchanged, are still
in use today all over Mongolia and beyond.

Ger is simply the Mongol word for 'home', but it is
also used by Mongolians as the particular name
for this type of tent. Any form of dwelling that can
last, in essentially the same form, for a period of
two and a half thousand years, has to be remark-

Erecting a ger

to more than three-quarters of the population of
Mongolia. Still more confusingly, though, Kazakhs
call them *yurta*!

During the course of circumnavigating the world by
horse-drawn caravan, my family and I saw our first
'live' ger in Kazakhstan. There, they are used as
temporary accommodation for shepherds and their
families while tending sheep on summer pastures.
We were fortunate enough to see one being
erected, which gave us a step-by-step view of how
they are constructed. The Kazakh model is rather
less sophisticated than the Mongolian, being

Inside a Mongolian ger

lighter and less ornate, but the basics are the
same: the *khana* – lattice walls made of birch
willows (withies), the pivot-joints of which are short
leather thongs; felt sides and roof pieces, bound in
on the exterior by two horizontal camel- or horse-
hair ropes and with a linen inner lining. Once, the
outside was plain felt but nowadays all but the
poorest Mongolians add a final outer layer of
canvas.

Interior layouts conform to a pattern, but are
always as different as only individuals' homes can
be. On entering through the often beautifully
ornate doorway, there will be boots, coats and

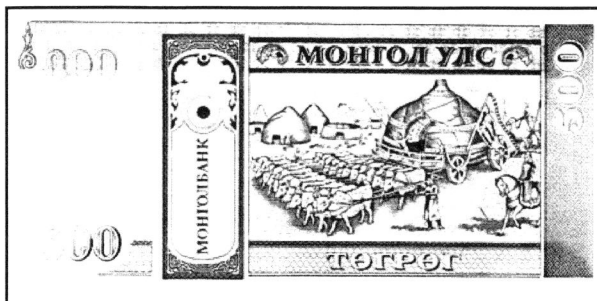
A Togrok or Yurta bank note

able. The oldest known example dates from the
13th century. A museum in Ulaanbaatar features a
kingly conservationist's nightmare version from the
early 20th century covered by 140 Snow Leopard
skins. The reverse sides of the Mongolian 500 and
1000 *togrok* banknotes feature an historic print of
a huge ger being pulled on a wide cart by 22 oxen,
the 10th century forerunner of the mobile home.
But the ordinary everyday-model ger is still home

guns on the left and perhaps a vat of milk in process of being churned. Beyond, usually towards the back on the left, will be a bed, then a chest of drawers, another bed; then, next the door on the right, a kist (a box or chest) for meal and a rack for dishes and implements. The rear half of the floor will be carpeted and perhaps even raised a little on wooden planks. The front, where the stove stands centrally, is left as plain grass or earth. On to this standard layout most Mongolians add decorative hangings, sometimes statues of Genghis Khan or the five animals of life: horse, cattle, camel, sheep and goat, family photographs, possibly Buddhist religious pictures, a radio and perhaps a solar- or wind-powered television. As you look around you begin to know a little about the family who live in any particular ger.

There are actually two Mongolias. To the south is the country referred to as Inner Mongolia: the Nei Monggol Autonomous Region under Chinese control which has a population of about 22.7 million. Then there is Mongolia – the People's Republic which is the size of France and Germany combined with a population of only about 2.7 million – yet, amazingly, every valley seemed to have a clutch of gers in it. Even more astonishing was our first sight of a Mongolian town. There

A typical Kazakh valley scene

were a few concrete buildings in the centre, mainly administrative offices, with possibly a block or two of flats in larger towns, but all the rest of the housing was comprised of gers! Each would be situated in its own fenced compound, with 'garden ground'. The impression from a distance was of a cluster of futuristic dwellings – or the eggs of some monstrous alien creature.

As an ecologist, I cannot think of any other extant culture that I have seen or read about, with the possible exception of some Amazonian Indian peoples, that is so perfectly adapted to the conditions in which it still exists. As we trundled slowly

Traceur pulling the caravan

across the plains in our little red caravan, towering peaks rising distantly to right and left, there was plenty of time to observe and to think. As for meeting people, the difficulty was rather in finding peace occasionally to be by ourselves.

There were no hotels in Mongolia and there are only a few now. Outside of the towns the traveller was traditionally dependent for hospitality on whomsoever he (or she) met. Riding up to a ger at lunchtime or towards sunset, you would shout 'Tie up your dogs!' If the occupants did, then you could dismount, unsaddle and hobble your horse and ducking through the small door, sit cross-legged on the carpet while a woman, wife or daughter probably, brewed up some salty tea – suuteichai – and put some mutton on to boil. If the occupants did not want to entertain you – perhaps because you were a known bad hat or maybe they had someone ill inside – then they just would not emerge and you would have to ride on, still seeking lunch or supper and a cosy bed.

To a large extent this system is still practised. Unfortunately, urban Mongols have begun to abuse it, driving out into the country for free weekends. However, we did not see much of that and were frequently invited to partake of hospitality.

If you arrive with an enormous horse, three times larger than the native breed, in a land where the horse is the foundation of existence and where there are few distractions from the hard round of daily chores, you can expect to become an attraction – and we did. The children, being children, were able to refuse the invariably proffered bowl of fermented mare's milk, but as an adult I could not escape without giving offence – especially if the giver had walked eight or ten kilometres to visit. Good *kumiss* is wonderful stuff, better than the best yoghurt, and I loved it. Unfortunately, it was not always good and the bowl not always clean… but I downed it anyway, for the sake of international

96

harmony. The woman's role in rural Mongolian society is frequently referred to as 'the caretaker of the milk'.

Next would come 'oohs' and 'aahs' at our horse Traceur's size, followed by gasps when some brave soul picked up a hoof and saw the size of his shoe. I would then get a lecture on how to look after our horse, because no Mongolian believes anyone who is not a Mongolian knows anything at all about equine care and management! To be fair, insofar as Mongolian horses go, probably few foreigners do know much. They live under a very different regime to that of Western horses and until one has acquired some knowledge of it, they can be difficult to handle and at least one well-known Western traveller allowed his horses to die, through ignorance. But it always amused me to be told that we knew nothing, after having survived for three and a half years on the road with Traceur. In fact the horse is so central to Mongolian culture that there are literally dozens of words used to describe the colour, age, size and gender of horse, for instance, a *ke'er* is a bay horse.

Catching horses the Mongol way

Several times we were invited into people's homes. Outside there would usually be a big stone atop a bag of curd, which was the cheese press and quite often a bag of milk with a froe-stick in it, to which passers-by inevitably gave a few strokes to aid the churning. A marmot or two are frequently hanging up out of dog-reach, awaiting the pot and there would certainly be trays of *kurt* drying in trays on the roof. Sometimes these had branches over them, to keep the snow-finches off. *Kurt* dries to the consistency of concrete and unless you have the wonderful dentition with which Mongolians are blessed, it is wiser not

A settlement of gers

to attempt to eat it as even a tentative gnawing puts fillings at hazard. Meat pieces are sometimes also put on the roof to dry.

On entering, especially if the door has been shut, the overwhelming odour of boiled mutton assails, no, assaults(!) your senses. It is a curious fact that the Mongols have never learned to roast meat. The early fires were open braziers, so roasting would have been difficult, but today everyone uses rectangular box stoves – but these also lack an oven. Sitting on the stove will be a big pan of milk, into which the hostess breaks off lumps of black tea from a brick about a foot long, nine inches wide and a couple of inches deep. To this is added salt and it cooks away for a bit before being ladled into mugs. It may sound revolting and it is an acquired taste but once you get used to it, it is very refreshing and sustaining. If you are lucky, the next thing on the stove will be fritters – at least, that is as near a description as I can get to the extremely tasty unleavened fried bread we were sometimes given.

Of course it may be that you will get neither because already occupying the heat is the still. A sloping but straight-sided barrel is fitted on to a large bowl of mare's milk that has inside it a collecting bowl, while at the top is a metal cone of cold water to condense the spirit. The end-product is *arkhi*. A single distillation gives an only mildly alcoholic drink, but the triple-distillate can knock your socks off. I well remember the first time I was offered it. It was a clear liquid with a rather odd taste – but as with *kumiss*, I did not want to offend and drank it off. It tasted rather like cough-mixture.

97

Fifteen minutes later, I thought my head was spinning into space and the rest of the day's drive passed in a warm glow on some distant planet....

Traditionally, only people over 40 were permitted to drink *arkhi.* I can see why.

We preferred being among the truly rural Mongolians, where the way of life has altered little in a couple of millennia and where the people retain their true character. We were to find that the urban Mongolians, especially the men, had all too often degenerated into drunkenness. This results from high unemployment, cheap liquor, but most of all from lack of purpose. Deprived of their proud traditions as stockmen, they need to find a new role that will restore their pride. Meantime, it is a modern tragedy that there are colossal social problems, most of which are alcohol-related.

Out in the country, one of our best experiences was in the west, where we were greeted by a galloping horde, that swirled around us and formed an escort back to their encampment. Although Mongolians are nomadic, moves are dictated by grazing and climate and are not made more often than necessary. In fact, their movements are often more akin to transhumance than nomadism. This camp, quite a big one, had been in place a while, sited by the banks of a stream. Our three children soon deprived local lads of their mounts and set off for a ride around, while I tried to explain in sign language and limited broken Russian, what we were doing and – of course – showing off Traceur. There were some splendid characters amongst these families, including one ancient patriarch who looked as though he might have served under Genghis himself.

A group of locals come to meet us

The traditional Mongolian saddle is made of wood. I suspect that that is why we so frequently saw riders standing in their stirrups.... A later model, introduced by the Russians, is more like a back-less car-seat and slightly less brutal on bony bums. But like all their kit, it would be hard to imagine how to improve on it. Plastic barrels have taken the place of skin bags for churning, braziers have been replaced by stoves – but it is still yak-

The caravan and an escort of cavalry

dung that fuels them – and enamelware has largely replaced traditional wooden jugs and bowls. Nevertheless, grazing regimes continue to follow age-old patterns (although overgrazing is becoming a problem in some places) and family life in the countryside, apart from the advent of some modern materials, cannot have changed a great deal over the centuries.

One of the neatest things I saw during our travel among the Mongolians was the way they milked goats. Forty to sixty nanny-goats would be lined up head to head, horns interlocking. A rope was run in and out between their necks and its ends tied together. The whole family from grannies to tod-

Another group of locals with their homes

dlers would then set to milking, using an assortment of pails, buckets and bowls, until every goat had yielded its milk. Then – undo the knot, pull the rope through and *voila!* all the goats were loose again.

The other really efficient practise (vegetarians may skip the rest of this paragraph) was the way sheep and no doubt other livestock, were slaughtered. A sheep was cast on to its back, outdoors. Swiftly, a sharp knife was used to make an incision into the body-cavity and immediately a hand was thrust in to sever the aorta (cardiac artery). It was done incredibly fast, taking maybe three or five seconds, so that the sheep hardly seemed to notice. Death was virtually instantaneous because of the rapid release of blood to the body cavity. The carcass was taken into the ger, skinned and, after the blood had been ladled into a bowl, butchered lying on the skin. It sounds terrible I know, but given the non-availability of stunners, I can honestly say that this method is almost pain-free. (If you have ever cut yourself badly with a sharp instrument, you'll know how, after the first stab of pain, you don't feel much for a bit. I believe it was like that for the sheep too). During the three and a half months it took us to cross from Tsaganuur to Ulaanbaatar we ate seven sheep – there was almost nothing else to eat because there are no shops in rural Mongolia. We should have starved without them and as I had no desire to retain the skin or the head, we bartered those for the butchering.

The final stage of a constructing a ger

I have tried to give some flavour of Mongolian country life as we saw it and to an extent shared it. I have not mentioned yak and mare milking, nor the fact that some people had motorbikes as well as horses and some tractors or trucks too. Nor have I described the way in which the horses, which run loose in their herds when not in use, are caught using very long poles with a noose in the end. Or that water has to be drawn from wells, sometimes a considerable distance from the camps. Or indeed many other things such as how wool is felted or the fact that suburban gers only differ in that they may have electricity laid on and in a few fortunate cases, running water. But if you really want to know more you must go and see for yourself.

It is a testament to the perfection of the ger as a dwelling that it is now freely available in Europe and America. Most of those offered for sale commercially adhere to the traditional shape but many use modern coverings for the exterior. Felt really is *not* the ideal material to use for tentage in our wetter western climates. But a couple of thousand quid will buy you spacious, weatherproof accommodation that will last for years.

A camp on the move

And if you want to move, all you need is a camel or two.....

Life in a truck
Julie Harvey

I've been living in our Dodge 100 for almost 9 years, a couple more for Dave, my partner. Dave bought the truck while he was working in Holland, from a clown in Zippo Circus. A cab with separate box on the back, it had originally been used by a baker, and then by Zippo to cart round trapeze equipment. Fast forward to the present and the box has been transformed into a comfortable home for us and our son.

Inside, the space is divided in two. A kitchen area and an everything else space. Dave being a wood worker has built a whole lot of nice wooden cupboards, bookshelves, windows and a seat. He has used scrap wood from skips, thick gnarled branches from woodland and more recently reclaimed timber. We have an old 1950s gas cooker, a generator and batteries for the radio, tv and lights, not the most environmentally sound we know, but an improvement on candles, especially with a child.

For me the decision to move into the truck was a romantic one. Being in love. I had caught up with Dave in London after an absence of two years when we had met as friends in Newcastle. He was moving around quite a bit, but had recently travelled down to Devon. So I spent a lot of weekends going to see him. It seemed pointless to keep on the flat in Hackney when I was far happier being with Dave, so I thought I'd give it a try, and I'm still with it now.

It was November when I moved in, the box was pretty sparse. Inside there was just the cooker, a sleeping platform and floorboards. The first weeks before we got the burner I can remember immersing myself in a sleeping bag to keep warm in the evening, watching the sunset, playing cards, reading.

I adjusted to the more physical nature of living on the road. Fetching water, chopping wood, doing all the usual cleaning up jobs that now took longer. Waiting for kettles to boil, making sure there was always water on the stove, ready for cups of tea and bathing. I spent a lot more time outside than I would do in a house. Nipping in and out to fetch a cup or spoon from the washboard outside, going for a piss.

The truck (our home!) at a woodland site

Inside we heat the truck with a multi fuel burner, it's pretty small but heats so effectively we can sit about in t shirts through winter. The woods nearby have provided us with a good supply of well seasoned oak, which bizarrely was all chopped down and replaced by firs about forty years ago. I don't do as much wooding as I used to as I'm picking up more paid work locally, book keeping and proof reading. I still love to walk through woods, enjoying the space and leafy smells.

When the weather gets warmer we make the most of the long evenings and spending time with friends. We have more campfires, hang up the solar shower, enjoy the end of the winter jobs.

We are now parked up at a free range chicken farm. Dave brings sawdust from the workshop for use as litter, and I deliver eggs to the local market town once a week. It is a small scale farm and there is no water on site. The farmer collects rain from the roofs and uses this for the fowls and himself. We fetch 20 litre water butts from one of the two local springs. At one there is a plunge pool where the water comes out a wide brick pipe. In summer we have braved the icy depths. In winter I'm not intrepid enough to go in, it's enough watching your hands turn blue as you hold the water butt under.

Our toilet is a choice between the woods and a composting toilet I have built from two tractor tyres. It seems to be working pretty well with the ash from the burner and wood shavings from the workshop. It has the advantage of being nearer than the woods, and I can dig it into the garden we've been working on for the last few years.

The garden is in a sheltered corner of the farm. Over the time we have been here, we have dug over the strips of prepared ground. The soil is clay and full of lumps of flint, but herbs and soft fruits seem to fare well in it. I've tried various techniques to discourage slugs and squirrels, who select their favourite crop and eat it before it's ripe. More recently some deer have managed to trample our recycled fence and eat everything down to stubble.

One of my first travels in the truck led us to a small village in the Conwy valley, in north Wales. We stayed a few months having found work locally. I couldn't drive at the time so I would catch the bus into town and walk back the 7 miles with a knapsack of essentials, taking in the mountain air and beauty of the countryside. Our only encounter with officialdom at that time was with the man who ran the village hall. We met him shortly after we had arrived, he was worried that we might leave used needles behind. What a distorted picture we have to deal with sometimes. We spent some time talking with him, and reassured him that we were not intravenous drug users. I think having work locally and having friends and family in the area helped assuage his concerns.

At the end of three months we had decided to travel abroad. The night before we left the village, we had our first police visit. An officer turned up in the evening and wondered if we knew when we were leaving, if we stayed much longer they would have to move us on. For us there was no problem as we were moving anyway. But later with the UK's 1994 Criminal Justice and Public Order Act, the police and local authorities were given powers to enforce more quickly *when* travellers left a site. This creates problems when you have organised work locally, and your kids are in the local school. It is great to be able to move around, but it is important to decide for yourself the time when you move on.

From Wales we went to Holland, got stuck in the freezing mud outside a fenced-in site right in the middle of Amsterdam. Dave had lived on this site a couple of years previously. So thankfully when we did get stuck, there was help nearby. Jazz was a huge help in persuading the man who had a small tractor on site to tow us off. At the time he seemed happier sitting in his trailer on methadone than helping pull a truck out of the freezing mud. Getting stuck there gave me my first encounter with the

Dutch police and vehicle inspectorate. They did not like us from the start. The site we were outside of had a bad reputation for drugs and violence. Their policy was that if we were not away within 36 hours they would impound the vehicle and squash it into a cube. We did at the 11th hour get out of the mud.

From there we ended up on a ghostly site in Diemen, still in Amsterdam. Being January I could understand the emptiness. It was bitterly cold, and the wood we were burning at the time was old

Fire juggling in Amsterdam

pallets. The pallets produced lots of heat, but no embers. On site there was glass and rubble all around from buildings which were being wrecked. Large pieces of iron and old factory equipment were scattered about. It looked better when it snowed. Inside one of the remaining buildings were a couple of caravans kitted out with TVs and game stuff. Around the back of this was a toilet which flushed with a bucket of water. It was a freezing and draughty place to go, but there was a great view of the canal and the birds. While we were in Holland we made the most of the cycle lanes and flatness to get about and visit friends, and ask after work. I met a lot of travellers who had been doing all sorts of interesting stuff. Great tales.

One night while we were still at Diemen a bus pulled in. The couple had come from Poland where they had been stuck, as the temperature fell to minus 40, and their gear oil froze. Unable to move, in the middle of Warsaw they became local celebrities and ended up on Polish television. Their plight highlighted, they were taken under the wing of the local community.

We returned to Britain, ever orbital. And shortly

101

Dave, Julie and a friend

after I had my first experience of British eviction. The owner of the strip of land was threatened with prosecution by the council if he failed to evict us. One morning a man turned up with a mallet and some notices. We, the 'persons unknown' went to court with 4 hours of green paper legal advice. The magistrate did not look up once during the hearing. We were given leave of possession for 6 months. The whole process was depressing.

More recently the truck has been pretty static. We have all put down roots locally, with work and school. Dave still travels widely with his work, Switzerland, the States and Wales have been some places his joinery skills have been put to use. He started up his own business about 3 years ago, and is moving more into specialist conservation work and sustainable dwellings. He shares a workshop in the area. Recently Dave built a gable end barn. It's a beautiful building, not unlike the kind of sustainable dwelling we are aiming to build for ourselves.

One of Dave's timber-framed buildings during construction

OAK
HOMES

Tel: +44 (0) 1297 489101   Mobile: +44 (0) 7771 860433
Fax: +44 (0) 1297 489101   Email: mortice80@hotmail.com

On the 'Cut': Narrowboat living in England
Alan Dearling

How it came about
Until the end of 1980s I'd always lived in 'normal' homes of one sort or another. Some had been fairly typical flat and house shares, with varying levels of communal and shared living, and in the eighties I'd had one long term relationship living with an Italian lady called Carla and her two children in London and then Scotland for about four years.

In 1988, I'd just finished ten years working for the Scottish Office (a government body) as their Publications and Training Officer for Scotland, in the area of community based work with young people. Of late I'd dabbled with a job share and self-employment working from my old fishing cottage at Burnmouth, on the rugged coast of Scotland's borders. I was just about scraping a living when Longman, part of the international Pearson publishing empire, invited me to move to Harlow new town in Essex as their Publisher for Social Welfare, Housing and Health titles. It was an enticing offer and I suddenly became pretty well paid, running a considerable commissioning and production, book and periodical publishing programme. I bought a flat on the outskirts of the town, at the edge of the common and woodland. It seemed a good place to feed my passion for cross-country running and be able to cycle on the bike tracks to and from Longman's offices in a town centre tower block. For the first year, I was reasonably content adapting to a heavily corporate, competitive and commercial environment, but I could see my income being rapidly eroded by the fast increasing mortgage interest rate. After two years working in Harlow, my mortgage outgoings represented nearly 90 per cent of my take home salary. I decided to abandon flat!

I sold the flat taking £10,000 sterling negative equity. While negotiating the sale I organised what the company referred to as the 'off-shoring' of my commissioning and production role. In future, I would work from my own base, and be paid a mix of percentage upfront on commissions agreed by the company, expenses, and a profit share in future income. It was a novel agreement and one which allowed me a lot more flexibility.

Creative of use of 'economic sustainability'
I had to choose somewhere cheap to live, but I wanted something that was more akin to an ecological lifestyle. My solution was arrived at, based upon the experience of half a dozen narrow boat holidays, and close friends, Ian and Pauline (known as 'I & P'), having their own narrow boat building and hire company, Starline Narrowboats. This was (and still is), based at Upton-upon-Severn in Worcestershire, a picture postcard village (apart from in times of flooding!) near the mystic and magical Malvern hills and the Welsh border. To prepare for this new adventure, I had to drastically down-size my belongings – not easy for someone addicted to books and music! Much of my belongings were stored with friends on a temporary basis (many still remain in their care after nearly 12 years!). But, amidst this boxing up of my belongings, I was symbolically looking forward to a new nomadic lifestyle. There are still over 2,000 miles of navigable inland waterways in England and Wales to travel around. In fact, did you know that Birmingham has more miles of canals than Venice!

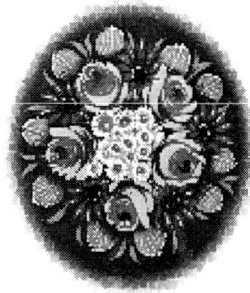

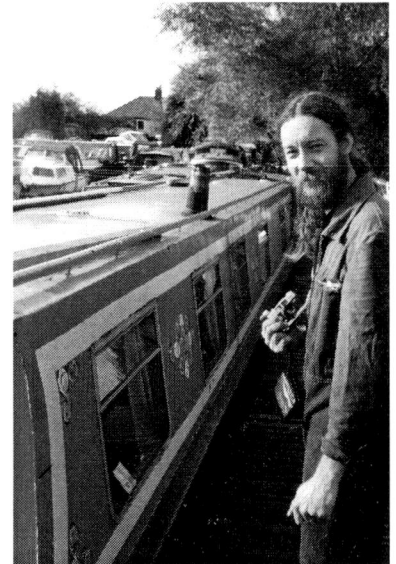

Ian with my new home

While searching for a suitable narrow boat to refit as my new home, I stayed at I & P's splendidly chaotic house in Malvern, often sharing bed and floor space with visiting rock bands, mime artists, Rastas, drag queens and their own two children, Ross and Ellie. Working for Longman, commissioning new authors and projects was a mite tricky in these circumstances, with only limited access to computer and phone. But, I had purchased a heavyweight mobile phone – back then they weighed the same as about two building bricks – and I started to get used to short economical phone calls…

Finally, Ian spotted a boat that was suitable – a derelict 68 foot steel-hulled 20 tonner, at the time semi-abandoned in Macclesfield – a two week trip by water from Upton. Making sure that a boat is for sale by its rightful owner, in good condition, and offers value for money is a professional task, especially with regard to the integrity of the hull. Ian had it surveyed and gave it a good looking over

The first voyage south from Macclesfield

himself, and the boat became ours. Immediately afterwards, myself and another friend, Alwyn, set off from Macclesfield in the week before Christmas. Our aim was to bring the boat back through the iced-covered canals, locks and rivers of Britain's waterway system, known affectionately as 'The Cut', I believe, because many of the canals were literally cut through cliffs, hillsides and rock faces. The boat itself was an unknown performer and internally very shabby, damp, mould-encrusted and without any heating system apart from an old stove.

It felt to be an epic adventure – the highlights or lowlights being the coping with the various little disasters that seemed to await us around every bend. It was bitterly cold, so part of my job in addition to sharing steering and lock opening duties, was to produce fuel supplies by sawing and axing my way through the internal furniture and any found wood from beside the towpath. Alwyn meanwhile had the engineer's role, keeping the recalcitrant boat moving forwards. During the trip, we collided with a sunken bath tub in an industrial section and ended up half way up the bank; got a length of barbed wire twisted around the propeller, which took hours to cut and ease off; and even more unpleasantly, we also picked up the rotting carcass of a dead dog around the prop.

On Christmas Eve, we lost control of the steering, ploughing our way from one side of a canal to the other and causing a rather irate fisherman to fall in the freezing water after we were tangled up in his line. A lump of metal

the size and shape of a fountain pen had broken off in the innards of the steering arm, and Alwyn spent the following two days cutting and filing a makeshift replacement part. That was our Christmas, huddled on the canalside outside of Alsager in the English midlands, sharing a selection of packets of crisps, that being the only food on sale at the festive pubs nearby! We had nothing to cook on for those two weeks afloat in the English heartland.

Anyway, you get the picture. It was an old boat and the refit couldn't happen a moment too soon!

Preparing the new home
Virtually everything had to be stripped out of the inside of the boat and replaced. The outside needed stripping down carefully and five coats of paint. Ian worked up the marine architectural plans in close consultation with me in terms of what I wanted to achieve.

Steve and Alan painting the hull

The refit starts in earnest

As well as using the boat as a home and as a base for my Longman publishing work, I also wanted to be able to continue writing and researching books, and to use the boat as a small scale training venue for 'teambuilding' courses. This meant that the boat had to be more than adequate as temporary dwelling for up to ten people. Inside, a narrow boat is only about six feet wide, so all the beds, seating and any bunks need to be fixed alongside the inside walls. Seating for meal times doubles as bed spaces at night, and everyone has to quickly realise that power for electricity is limited to what is stored up in the

One of the teambuilding courses

batteries; gas (for cooking) and any fuel for the multi-fuel stove and water has to be replenished, and the more you use the toilet, the quicker it starts to smell despite Elsen Blue, and the more frequently you have to pay for pump outs!

It was a big and expensive refit up to a high standard, with tongue and groove wood lining and insulation to keep the steel hull from excessive heat loss. There were two toilets, one shower, and a full galley with a double sink, a gas powered fridge, gas cooker and also a slow cooker and an occasionally used low wattage micro-wave cooker. Also on board were a TV and video set-up, complete with camera for use on courses, two music systems and my computer and printer. The

Upton was often under Severn, rather than upon it!

power for this number of electrical appliances came from running the engine, which charged two batteries for the boat's engine and four batteries for

the domestic supply, using a switching device and trickle charge system. The d.c. power from the domestic batteries was also routed through an inverter system, transferring the supply from 12 volts d.c. to 240 volts a.c.. Even when running the boat engine all day, the power supply was finite and people had to think before turning on a fifteenth light, but when I was on my own and moored up, I could get by for the whole day by running the engine for about 45 minutes at the beginning of each day. I chose to do this rather than use a generator.

Life afloat
A 20 ton boat is big by most standards and I could only just about handle it safely on my own, especially on long journeys. The difficulty comes when you are mooring up and moving through locks where the water

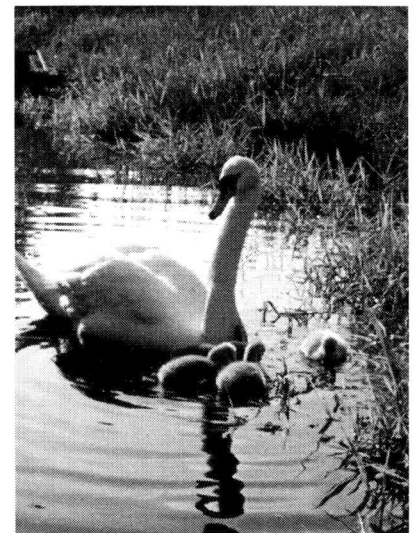
Neighbours

levels have to be adjusted by opening and closing paddles in the lock gates. The gates need to be opened, the boat moved into the lock and then closed again. It's manageable, but takes a lot longer on your own. To moor requires bringing the stern into the bank and jumping off with a stern line ready to tie off. Meanwhile, the bow can swing out into the watercourse in all sorts of alarming ways, often before you can walk, skip or hop the 68 feet along the outside of the boat to throw over the bow line!

So, in all honesty, I was 100 per cent waterborne, but about 50 per cent nomadic. I moved over longer distances when I had at least one other passenger, but kept close to Upton for much of the rest of the time. Waterway regulations require that you have a range of permits, including a cruising licence (or licences), a British Waterways (BW) Boat Safety Scheme (BSS) Certificate and insurance cover. Basically, you are supposed to have a permanent mooring registered – easy if you own waterfrontage from a house, or have a friend with the same, but expensive, if like me you had to register from a river marina base. Many water

Wintering in Upton marina

travellers have been disputing this by moving their boats a minimum number of times and distances up and down a towpath to keep just within the letter of the law, which states that you can only avoid having a permanent mooring if: *"you genuinely cruise continuously around the network, never staying anywhere for more than 14 days."* This is particularly true of boat dwellers who are on low incomes, or are students in a local town or city.

Day-to-day living and working found its own rhythm. I'd hand-fed a pair of magnificent swans and a larger array of ducks and moorhens, so most days I'd wake to the persistent pecking of the swan's beaks on the hull or window next to my bunk. They're clever, and like their breakfast on time! They even brought their new born cygnets to meet me, and scrounge a range of green veg, which the local vegetable shop gave me every couple of days.

Over the period of nearly three years that I was on the boat, I gradually accumulated a variety of water-borne and other travelling friends and colleagues. I never chose to live in communal groups, but we would often seek each other out and share a meal, or go to the pub together. Until you've lived for hours each and every day afloat, you haven't experienced the feeling of the bar and the floor moving even before you've had a drink! In early 1990s Britain, the nomads known as the new Travellers were being vilified in the media and in parliament. Some pubs saw me as one of them and refused to serve me as a member of an undesirable 'group'. From this stereotyping, I became increasingly good friends with a number of these so-called New Age Nomads.

Impact on the environment
If you are being careful about waste disposal while you are moored up, you have very little effect on the immediate environment. Floating dwellings could offer a cheap alternative for many of the world's homeless, and do so in many countries

and cultures. Most boats run on marine diesel, which is cheap, but not exactly pollution free, however, the pace of life on the Cut is slow and comparatively very relaxed, cruising at 4 and 6 miles per hour, but in reality a lot slower because of the frequent locks.

In terms of energy conservation, I reckon I used about a quarter of the power I needed in an apartment, by cost, and I often was able to use wood found at the waterside as a major source of fuel. At the time, wind and solar power sources were very expensive and bulky for use on boats, but now they would probably provide a useful back-up power source. As Ian Cundy from Starline Narrowboats recently told me: *"wind certainly now does save running the engine to charge the batteries, and boats are sprouting windmills everywhere."*

I lived amongst some of the most splendid country-side in England and Wales mostly travelling on the Shropshire Union, Staffs and Worcester, Worces-ter-Birmingham, Sharpness and Llangollen canals and Severn and Avon rivers. Even in urban areas, the canals are almost always quiet, semi-forgotten places, lurking at the backs of street and industrial life. Sometimes it's eerie and a bit creepy hearing the sound of a weir running at full spate, or the less ecological whoops and hollers of city drunks. At times, the extremes of the weather can seem a bit too 'real'. But, I do miss it, even though I continue to experience a semi-nomadic existence, travelling around the UK and the world for a large portion of each year.

Get on board the Narrenschip!
Alan Dearling

The context of this contribution is rather important. The 1990s witnessed attempts in parts of Europe, especially the UK, to criminalise travelling lifestyles. The 1994 Criminal Justice and Public Order Act was the tip of that particular iceberg. However, synchronicity demands that what goes round comes round again, and for something over two years a group of people in Belgium and the Netherlands has been active in trying to establish a network of stopping places and 'friends' of travellers. The network is based on self-help and is rather similar to the Willing Workers On Organic Farms (WWOOFers) which has become a worldwide movement and is perhaps the most sustainable form of eco-tourism!

NAR = Network Alternative Roadside Travellers (Reizigers) who describe themselves as being about freedom in coming and going and thinking!

I received two different copies of the newsletter of the NAR – 'T Narrenschip – from different Belgium and Dutch friends. They are neat little A5 booklets with a coloured cover and lots of individual articles and a number of black and white photos and line illustrations. The trouble for me was that all the words are in Dutch, which sadly I cannot read. Undaunted, I asked Thea Daleman, the Dutch mother of a friend, to try and translate some bits for me, so I could construct this article. I received a number of e-mails from Thea saying that she found it really interesting, and she eventually sent me some translations from one of the NAR magazines. It was only when I checked these out with another friend, Antwan, in Geldrop, Holland, that I realised that we'd put two and two together and made five!

The articles in the magazine are a fascinating mix of new and historical writings about travellers, Gypsies, nomads, festival goers, organic farmers, artists, protestors and permaculturists. In fact, the range is even broader. However, Thea had thought that this meant that the NAR Network had been in existence for nearly a hundred years – in fact it is very new, but sees its radical roots and ancestry in a whole range of environmental, travelling and protest cultures.

Antwan put us right, saying:
"The NAR Network is a group of people who live on the road and a network of people who live in communities, private places, eco farms, in park ups or in peaceful squats. Members (donation-supporters) pay in 2002 just £10 per year (£15 with 3x copies of 'T Narrenschip) to belong, and in return they receive a member's pass, maps and an address/contact list of all the places they can park up, work with farmers/ artists, or just stay for a few days.

We have two different kind of places:
MP = means you can stay there but you must work there.
VP = you can there stay but don't have to work.

The main thing is that that you must respect the communities, nature, neighbours and people who live there."

The NAR Network currently offers contacts in France, Belgium, Holland, Spain, Portugal, Wales and Turkey. The network consists of alternative travellers in both senses of the word, figuratively and literally. They say, *"To travel and be a real nomad, is to discover and experience."* The network first came into existence from a private initiative and has grown into a voluntary organisation that seeks to provide people with a renewed vision of life. They told me:

"The initiative is based on the following thoughts:
To prevent the extinction of creative spirit;
To see colour in the greyness;
To discover truth within the lie;
To wake from your dreams;
To discover that time is pressing;

To think, feel and want differently, and
To see nature as the universal truth and law to which we are all subject."

At a practical level it provides a network of friendly contacts and stopping places for travellers of all sorts: some have camper vans, waggons with horses, bicycles, tractors – a number even walk or hitchhike. The *Narrenschip* shares stories from the road back to members – but at present it is only available in Dutch. It also provides information about new intentional communities, alternative energy, self-sufficiency, organic farming, eco protests, arts and performance activities and upcoming events.

The NAR have purposefully taken a wide constituency for their focus and as such it should enable people to help themselves and to, as the *Narrenschip* claims: *"…pioneer new ways of life, which they feel expand their horizons. And share a common set of aims: to be pleasant, warm and helpful to each other, and share their knowledge and experiences."*

Antwan encouraged me to share information about the NAR: *"The Network is growing and it is getting a good group of nice people together. Maybe you can help us to connect to more like minded people and communities to help the NAR Network grow."*

The tracks are different for everybody
The NAR see their strongest roots in history. *NAR* in Dutch, for instance, means jester or the fool, and they have taken this wandering nomadic character as their logo/ symbol. But, more seriously, the organisers see that predecessors are the Gypsies. They told me:

"During the 2nd world war about 23,000 Sinti and Roma Gypsies were transported to Auschwitz. In recent times, the Roma and Gypsies organised an emotional reunion at Auschwitz to remember their holocaust dead. Other reizigers (travellers) owe the Gypsies a debt for their own history.

NOMAD THEATER

De jarenlange reis- en theaterervaring heeft ervoor gezorgd dat in 1999 en 2000 poppen- en straatfestivals zijn bezocht in Spanje, Frankrijk, België, Luxemburg, Duitsland en Nederland...

Today we are living in a time where every individual is expected to decide for themselves what makes life worthwhile. It is a reason for some to release themselves from society's constraints completely. For instance, some reizigers make an effort to reduce the amount they consume to preserve the earth. They advise people to live more sustainably:
• eat vegetarian food more often;
• put on an extra layer of clothes rather than turn up the heating;
• only use a washing machine when it is full;
• use your own shopping bag and refuse plastic carriers;
• repair your shoes, and give them a second life.

In the *Narrenschip* there have already been a number of accounts of NAR members, such as:

• 'Lion Van'. He returned to Holland from a tour on foot to Spain and found that he could hear his neighbours talking through the walls of his home! He then decided to actually 'go for it' – he did what he had been contemplating for years – he bought himself a caravan. It needed a lot doing to it, but he got to know many fellow caravan inhabitants through this activity. Many of his former friends also opted for caravans to live in after they had been evicted from their squats. After a year, his house on wheels was ready and he travelled all over UK and France. Miraculously, he said that he no longer needed medication for chronic bronchitis any more. Now he is enjoying his nomadic existence to the full, meeting friendly people all over Denmark and France.

• The UK's Rinky Dink collective with their cycle powered sound system and stage are good friends of the NAR network. In 2001 they visited Den Haag and Bonn to help set up a Critical Mass and Reclaim the Streets events at the Climate Conference. As Antwan told me they are very 'wicked people'!

• The NAR society also want to create an 'Inn', namely a farm with about 10 acres, so that all members can rest there. The leader of this potential scheme is presently applying for financial aid.

• Then there is the story of Chris. She recalls how every 100 kilometres, the scene can change completely. Her experiences commenced with a holiday for two people living in an 8 square metre space. It made her much more aware of the importance of

being considerate. In particular, how people must become much more aware of each other's needs, for instance, when one feels the cold, whilst the other thinks it is too hot in the van. Chris and her partner travel about in

The NAR headquarters

an old tractor pulling what they call their 'Gypsy-like caravan'. They have met all sorts of people, and have enjoyed the experience. they worked on a sheep farm with Liliane and Christian and helped with the milking and giving the bottle to the newborn little lambs. And then, a month later they found themselves in Auch, staying with a family who own a camping field and a lot of animals. Suddenly, their main job was sawing wood for next winter and putting up fencing for the black pigs.

They planted trees and shrubs and were invited to stay on, but as true reizigers, they wanted to travel on. They continued to find all sorts of jobs, met a variety of people, and even 'adopted' an American drummer, despite there not being much room in their caravan! Their travels then took them through France to the foot of the Pyrenees. They became street performers in various market towns, and met up with 12,000 Gypsies in Les Saintes Maries de la Mer. As well as being the shrine for Saint Sara, the black patron saint of the Roma, it is something of a new tourist ghetto, with pizza places, souvenir shops and a harbour.

• There is a peace village at Vea in Spain and many NAR people are trying settle in that area.

• Another reiziger moved to Antwerp and began to work there. He discovered via his neighbour that there was a small illegally built house currently deserted near the Antwerp docks. He moved there and now has chickens,

One NAR family

goats, sheep, donkeys and even a pony. He grows his own organic vegetables and hopes to develop his own little orchard as well. Initially, the dock authorities wanted him out, but recently he has persuaded them that his lifestyle is not a threat, and they have allowed him to stay. He even has gas and electricity now, and he welcomes all NAR travellers en route to stay with him, as long as they help out in return for their keep!

• Le Chevreuil commune in France is linked to the NAR. It has a 16 acre plot of land and rents a house, grows vegetables and herbs, and their meadows are grazed by the cows and sheep, with the remainder of the grass being turned into hay. They grow wheat for bread, and the acorns and straw is used as winter fuel. They say that their primary purpose is to better understand their natural surroundings and also themselves. They are happy for anybody interested in their way of life to visit or stay.

• The 'homeplace' (left) of the NAR is at farmer Ton's at the D'n Bobbel, Haghorst.

• Andre and Judith are, according to Antwan, 'real' NAR people. They've been travelling in their 'Petit Manoir' with two children and two dogs and their horses. They set out from the north of Holland and travelled to Spain. Currently they are on the border with France. The pictures at the bottom of this page are of them and their home in a forest squat in Gilze.

The NAR is run by volunteers, many of whom travel, so be a little patient if you want to join or get involved. Their post addresses are:

Karl Wouters (T' Narrenschip magazine)
NAR Redactie
De Willaert 34
2460 Tielen
Belgium
Tel: 00/32 (0) 14552147

Ton Lavrijssen (manages the membership and supporters of the NAR and has a book collection on Travellers)
NAR Redactie
Oirschotsedijk 4
5089 NA Haghorst
Netherlands
Tel: 00/31 (0) 135042702
Mobile: 00/31 0621220034
Web address: www.nar.yucom.be

110

My home in two parts
Ezmerelda

Part One: You're going home in the back of an ambulance

My home comes in two parts, one of which is more ecologically friendly than the other, but together I feel they provide me with a way of life which has many advantages over the average house-dweller. It has kept me happy, healthy and reasonably 'in tune' with nature for the last decade.

The ecologically-unsound part is an old

The site includes some natural areas

The blue ambulance

BMC ambulance, built in 1970 and still running beautifully on its original petrol engine, unfortunately guzzling petrol all the while and belching out fumes which destroy the atmosphere. Aware of this, I try to keep journeys to a minimum and usually walk into town when possible. There is plenty of room in the back, so when I do drive somewhere, more often than not I have a few passengers, empty water bottles to fill up, wood to collect or things to deliver, and combine several purposes in one journey.

The ambulance is my five-year-old daughter's bedroom and houses all her clothes and toys. It's painted pink inside, with fairies flying around the walls and a starry night sky on the ceiling, and there's something very comforting in the fact that this little scene is complete and unchanged wherever we might be.

With the ambulance I tow a seventeen foot caravan which is our main home (especially in the winter). It's large enough to contain all my essential belongings, including a huge selection of clothes and a lot of art equipment, as well as a small

kitchen, seating area and bed, but at the same time it's compact enough to be efficiently heated by a small wood-burning stove. It's a little older than the ambulance, and consequently quite solidly built with wooden cupboards and fittings, and it's decorated with the same pink and blue colour scheme.

The vehicles are parked at present on a disused railway yard quite near the centre of a town in Wales, but over the years we have lived in many different places all over Britain and further afield, as you'll read later on. We've shifted from city industrial estates to remote fields and forests – many of these park-ups have been on pieces of land owned by the local council, which have fallen into disuse and been forgotten about, or put up for sale to developers. Quite recently, I lived for two years at a gothic castle which was registered as a Grade One listed building, but no-one could afford to restore it to its former glory and no other changes were allowed by the authorities.

So, we move around between patches of no-man's land – pieces of waste land that have been shunned by the house-builders; where the ownership is unclear or in dispute; old commons and disused railway tracks. Sometimes we visit friends, trying to tuck the vehicles out of sight from nosey neighbours, or travel to festivals where we are actually given a parking space (and sometimes expenses!)

I can't recommend my way of living as completely ecologically sound and sustainable, and I don't think everyone should 'take to the road' and live in a trailer. But living this way has taught me to consider a different range of priorities from the average house-dweller, and perhaps this change of attitude is the basis for living a more eco-friendly life. Before we can make great changes, we need to be aware of what we are consuming, what waste and pollution we are producing, how we are using our space and resources.

As already mentioned, my heating consists of a small wood-burner. It has a long chimney which radiates heat. While I sometimes resort to using coal on cold winter nights, wood has the benefit of being 'thrice warming': the collecting and cutting of it burning up those extra calories. And, of course, it's free! The firebox is tiny, so a few sticks cut into short lengths will last all night.

For cooking I use bottled gas, and sometimes an outside fire in the summer. A bottle of gas costs £8.50 and generally lasts three or four weeks. We light candles at night and don't have electricity, except a car battery which powers the radio. My son has solar panels outside his caravan, so we use these to recharge the battery when it's flat.

Water is carried back from the local garage in five gallon butts and stored outside. Because there's a limited supply, it is used carefully and rarely wasted. We don't have a fridge and storage is limited in the kitchen so we tend to eat fresh rather than pre-packaged food, buying only for a few days at a time, although there are always a few 'standby' tins at the back of the cupboard.

A flat top on site

Work and play overlap every day

nowhere nearly as damaging to the environment as the average street of houses. Rubbish is generally burned, tin cans and bottles buried or recycled, vegetable waste is fed to the animals or composted. The lack of 'bathroom facilities' shocks some people, but digging a hole in the earth and filling it in afterwards is a very real way to start getting to grips with the whole idea of waste and pollution, ecological impact, personal responsibility, soil, regeneration...you see what I mean. Flushing a toilet is an act that prompts one to think that, *"it's nothing to do with me anymore,"* whereas going for a shit in the woods demands an attitude of, *"I produced it – I have to deal with it,"* which is probably a good starting point for an eco-friendly life.

I think many travellers in the UK were forced to become conscious of ecological issues because of the lack of services (no rubbish collection, no toilets, no constant running water or electricity). There were no 'basic ameni-

My daughter and I both have an enormous collection of clothes and spend hours picking through bargain rails and charity shops, but this our only foray into 'consumerism' really. Our means are quite limited, but I don't want that to limit our quality of life, so a small but beautiful, memorable space that uses very little resources to run is a practical choice, which gives us a lot of freedom.

So, ecologically, we have become extremely aware of what we are using up, and keep it to a minimum. What about the waste and pollution we produce? Again, while not a perfect solution, our small site is probably

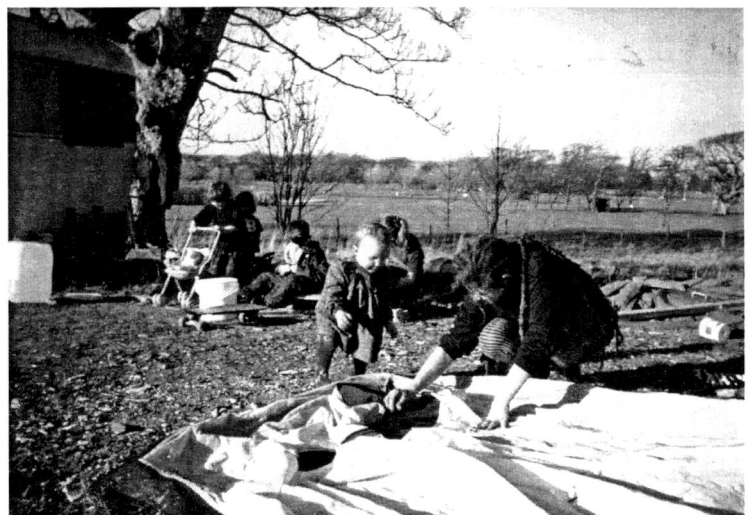

Fixing a tent – no throwing away

ties' to take for granted, and we had to think about everything from scratch and work out a better way of doing things. We had to be careful how we used our meagre resources and we had to keep waste to a minimum. So we learned to be responsible and fend for ourselves,

Lots of activities are part of site life

Some travellers took to the road because of their love of nature and a desire to live in some sort of harmony with the earth, while others encountered the elements for the first time, by collecting wood, lighting fires outside, digging trenches when the doorstep got flooded and so on. There's a lot of direct, basic contact with the forces of nature which is denied to people in 'residential' areas. It may not

and taught our children to be responsible and fend for themselves too. Instead of 'two hours of telly before bed', we tend to have lots of art equipment and musical instruments, and toys, and the children are encouraged to make their own social visits and mingle freely with neighbours on site.

Space is another central issue in most travellers' lives. Even the largest vehicle cannot possibly accommodate 'all the trappings' (interesting phrase!) of say, a suburban semi or even a bachelor flat, so one has to be choosy with possessions. Practicality is of the essence and everything has to 'earn its keep' or it will be discarded (and probably be recycled by someone else!) A leather three-piece suite with matching reclining armchair may cost more than a truck (£1,500?), but it's no use to us except as garden furniture. On the other hand, we need somewhere to sit down, preferably with some storage space underneath. Polished slate kitchen worktops might be 'all the rage' (another interesting phrase) this year in *Home and Garden* magazine, but I wouldn't want to tow them down the road. Rather than striving towards an environment that mirrors my 'success' in the world, by being fashionable or expensive, I am always looking out for small practical objects which will fit in with the very real and limited world I already possess. I think it's a much healthier mental attitude.

Because the trailer is small, and usually parked on what could loosely be termed a 'field', a lot of life takes place outside – especially in the summer. And even on the coldest winter night when we are tucked up in our quilts with the burner glowing and no intention of stepping out the door, it's hard to ignore the fact that Nature is out there, on the other side of the wall.

be at a 'flick of the switch', but it's very satisfying to struggle to light a fire on a damp day and finally succeed, or to battle with the wind to set up a waterproof awning, or to carry a heavy container of cool, refreshing water across a bumpy field in the sweltering heat of midsummer. These are not 'inconveniences' to be removed from our lives by modern technology, and money. These are acts of empowerment, whereby we remind ourselves that we are not in control of everything, but we can always do something to improve our lot if we are prepared to give out some energy too. We cannot expect everything for nothing, but our efforts can make a difference.

And then there's MOVEMENT: One of the distinguishing characteristics of animal life. What makes us different to plants and trees. We are not rooted to one spot on the earth. We can change our environment by moving around. We can extend our horizons, refresh our minds, go in search of what will fulfil and interest us – and this can change and evolve as we travel. We encounter places and people different to those we know already, and our view of the world is enlarged.

Rent and mortgages are a double rip-off, since they limit not only your financial resources, but your ability to see what the rest of the world is doing too. In buying-in to security, you have to give up freedom of movement, one of the basic human attributes! Security was an issue which bothered me, my parents and my friends when I first moved 'on the road'. How would the children have any security when we were always moving around, everything was always changing? But ten or more years down the line I know that security is a feeling inside yourself, and doesn't need to depend on familiar routines or surroundings, possessions or 'status symbols'. In fact, these things can and do sometimes get 'snatched away' even from those who have worked hard and sacrificed much to attain them.

My sons are capable and adaptable young men, now having survived their unorthodox upbringing and had many adventures of their own. My daughter is supremely confident at five and has no conception of 'missing out' – in fact she is used to being the centre of attention at all kinds of social gatherings in different places. She doesn't live in a 'safe and secure little world' where everything is perfect, unchanging, and revolving around her; she understands that there's a whole wide world of possibilities out there, many of them inviting and easily accomplished.

Balloon animals outside Strasburg cathedral

In 1998, we stored the ambulance and caravan at a farm called 'Paradise' and travelled around Europe with a friend in his bus. Busking, playing music and doing circus shows we went around Holland, Germany, Denmark, Belgium and more. In France, we ran a tequila bar at a huge festival and made balloon animals in the street outside Strasbourg Cathedral. I learned to juggle and ride a unicycle.

In the winter we went to Thailand and lived on the 'perfect' beach in a truly ecological beach-hut made of woven coconut palms. In a climate like that, possessions become even more of an unnecessary encumbrance (except the essential hammock, mosquito net, sarong and sunscreen). Life on Koh Pha Ngan had many similarities with life on site – it was simple and basic, healthy, plenty of contact with nature, much ingenious use of

The hut in Thailand

the few bits and pieces of 'technology' that were available. And because they are all Buddhists, the Thais have the same basic conception that we are all linked in some way, all part of a family. The belief that my profit or happiness will not benefit me if it causes you pain. We are all in this together, and we have to be 'saved'; all together or not at all. There's no room for amassing personal wealth or salvation in the human race towards enlightenment.

The Year 2000 seemed like some sort of milestone in my life and I decided I'd like to put my 'ten years of travelling' on show at some of the festivals. I'd also developed a keen interest in gardening, transforming a disused slaughter-house yard where we lived at that time into a thriving garden full of herbs

Nature's child

and flowers; so I contrived of the idea of a *Living and Working with Nature* travelling garden and demonstration space, which I volunteered to exhibit in the Green Crafts field at Glastonbury festival. Together with some friends, I grew plant displays and made wooden furniture and woven fences, and even constructed a giant 'goddess head' out of woven willow and hazel canes. This was crowned with summer flowers and had a face built up out of moss and clay, with green ears of corn for eyelashes (which gradually turned golden as they dried out in the sun, matching the golden flowers which wilted over as they grew taller in the head-dress crown, trailing down the sides of the 'face'). Out of the open mouth cascaded a 'waterfall' of tiny blue flowers and foliage, falling into a make-

114

shift blue-lined 'pond' surrounded by sea shells and crystals. It seemed to speak to people without the need for any explanation, and I was pleased with the result.

We also made an air garden full of fairies, where people could make a wish – we kept a fire going where they could get a warm, and we demonstrated simple skills like glass painting, making natural incense and herbal prod-

Corn dolly

ucts, carving wood and stone and modelling clay. We dressed up, played music, sang, told stories, and generally tried to show a way of living in harmony with nature, organically, adapting to circumstances and opportunities that came up. It was lots of fun and lots of work. Later in the summer we did the *Living and Working with Nature* garden again at the Northern Green Gathering in Yorkshire, this time incorporating a giant corn-dolly, a haystack and a spiral earthwork sown with cress (i.e. the seeds were sown, the cress spouted up during the festival, and we ate it in sandwiches on the last day!). It was nice to talk to ordinary people who don't usually consider these kinds of issues, and say, *"You can do this if you want to. It's easy."*

Although, as I've said before, I'm not a crusader who thinks everyone should live in the way that I do. I don't think I've got all the answers, but at least I have considered some of the questions. And, for the time-being, I feel I've found a happy medium. A fairly eco-friendly lifestyle, which gives me a freedom of movement as well as basic security, which is cheap and low-impact, but full of possibilities, which fits in with a world of ever-changing cycles instead of trying to impose some rigid linear order on a world which, for the most part, obeys the laws of chaos!

Part Two: All change!

On 19th April 2001, which coincidentally is Holocaust Remembrance Day and the anniversary of the bloody ending of the Waco siege in America, I was towing my son's caravan to a site in Corby where a few long-lost friends are parked up. The driver behind me dozed off, or at least lost his concentration for a moment. He was working a night shift, and his scheduled rest break was coming up in a few miles. He wasn't going too fast, just plodding along at about 50 mph. But he was driving a 38 ton articulated truck, and his moment's lapse completely destroyed my son's home and all his possessions, my daughter's bedroom and all her toys and clothes, and my beloved method of transport. We were hurled onto the central reservation but miraculously we were not injured, and even managed to pick through the wreckage and rescue some belongings before the road was cleared by emergency services. By a bizarre coincidence, one of the motorway maintenance crew knew one of our friends at Corby, and within a few hours we were installed in a new, much more beautiful caravan, sipping brandy coffee and surrounded by familiar faces.

We were shocked and bruised, of course, and we were saddened by the loss of many treasured possessions (although curiously, the truly irreplaceable little things all seemed to survive and get rescued). But we were still 'on site', and still laughing. We wondered how irrevocably the lorry-driver's life had changed? His moment of tiredness, of inattention, had quite likely cost him his job, maybe his house. All that security he thought he had was gone in a flash and probably he felt devastated. And we were huddled together under an oil-stained blanket, laughing, looking at the trees out of the window, and the other vehicles on site, and wondering what sort to get next?

Ez

Tribal Travellers
Alan Dearling

The DJ known as 'Dope on Wax' is a member of the UK's legendary – some would say infamous – **Spiral Tribe** collective. They say of themselves: *"Spiral Tribe have travelled the world and met fellow thinkers in every place we have stopped, but we have returned to England. Perhaps it's our love of the mythical past that has brought us back, or perhaps we feel that real change can only be effected in the place you most understand – home…We are not Spiral Tribe, you are all Spiral Tribe, it's you that makes the party happen."*

Spirals in action (Vinca Petersen)

Some readers may feel that is hardly appropriate to include a contribution from an international sound system, designed primarily to run parties across the globe. However, it is in groups like this that many young people begin to understand cultural diversity, and start to think more deeply about their temporary place on the fragile surface of the planet Earth.

Spiral Tribe are part of an increasingly complex and anarchic, global network of travelling sound systems, DJs, techno shaman, international squats and new age type travellers. In the last twelve or thirteen years, the Spiral Tribe, originally 23 in number (*"…the number of chaos…"* they say) have played at parties across Britain, and teknivals in Europe, including the one in 1992 at Castlemoreton Common. Originally charged with 'conspiracy to cause a public nuisance', the charges against 15 of their

number were dropped in the UK by 1995. Alongside groups such as Bedlam, the Mutoid Waste company, Total Resistance posse, Alien Pulse, Tibetan Ukranian Mountain Troupe, LA Full Moon Tribe, Oms not Bombs, the Spiral Tribe and United Systems, have turned the party scene and raves into a lifestyle revolution. The heart of that revolution is the fact that all of these groups have adopted a nomadic way of life. Many of them are now working together under the name: International Conspiracy for a Global Sound. They say: *"At our core is a sound system. It feeds us, nourishes our talents, brings adventure and keeps us together. Sound systems are multiplying and the tribes that establish each one are becoming wiser and stronger."*

"…expect the unexpected…" Their party culture has even been exported to America. In a 1997 article for *'xlr8r'* web zine, Ralph Perring wrote of the Tribe, *"Their goal: to maintain the diminishing civil liberties in the Western world, the right to free assembly, the right to free expression, the right to lead an alternative lifestyle and, of course, the right to party!"* And, paradoxically major parts of their lifestyle are not fundamentally about 24 hours-a-day music and repetitive beats, although dance is certainly central. For instance, much of the Spiral's philosophy comes from the Hare Krishna movement and alternative technology sources. In one of their booklets, *Talks from the Hare Krishna and Spiral Tribe,* they suggest that: *"Krishna is called Bagvan, but what is this meaning of a Bagvan? Bagvan means one who posses all wealth, all strength, all beauty, all knowledge, all fame, and at the same time, he doesn't care for any of it – renunciation."* Loosely translated into the lives of the Tribe, what they call 'techno terra' – non-stop dancing, is seen as a ritual way of reconnecting humanity with the primordial energy of the earth.

Doug, from the Tribe says they are part of the underground, *"…a seed-bed for new ideas, an instigator of progression. It is a point which is central to the ethos of our tribe."* Their parties incorporate performance arts, fire, computer animation and circus. At a Spiral Tribe party, you are told to expect the unexpected!

Vinca Petersen wrote about her travels with them in her 1999 book, *No System*. She said of the community that exists within the sound system followers:
"People from all walks of life come together, on an equal level, giving no space for prejudice…it's unnerving to strip the world around you back to simplicity, perspectives change, priorities shift, like switching on a harsh headlight when you've been using a torch."

"…new age techno traveller…"
Jim, aka Dope on Wax, takes up his part in their history:
"I arrived at the decision to convert a Transit into a habitable dwelling because the vehicle came along at the right time, and at the right price. It was something I had wanted to do for some time. I love travelling, and you can park somewhere beautiful and be at one with nature. Since I was introduced to photovoltaic panels (solar energy) I've wanted to run my vehicle's electrics, lights etc. by harnessing energy from the current bun."

Interestingly, and unlike myself, Jim and many of the Tribe see the likes of Shell and BP as the 'good guys' in a conflict with global governments: from *Get the perspective:*
"There are noble companies such as BP that are waiting in the wings, with clean, renewable energy. Electric cars, communities harvesting their own electrical needs. The way ahead! (but) BP and Shell are slaves to the regime just like the rest of us." See www.bpsolar.com

Another environmental and sustainability development organisation the Spirals and the International Conspiracy for a Global Sound support is the Green University, established in 1999 at Woollas Hall, Bredon Hill, near Pershore, Worcestershire WR10 3DN, UK. Together they are attempting to establish an *"area for the production of electronic/studio produced music."*

Jim continues, *"My lifestyle could be described as nomadic: a new age techno traveller. I really do believe a new golden age is awaiting us. Basically I've tried to create a space that I'm happy and content with. I do not like static buildings – 99 per cent of buildings are out of tune with how mother earth would like us to live. The cooking arrangements are simple, I use a stove similar to*

a Coleman's. When on my own, I eat fruit, vegetables, and cereal produce. My way of living is part of an extended family. Many people live like this, we often cook around a fire. Cooking on a fire for a group of people, is an art form in itself.

The inside of the vehicle is insulated and carpeted. I've chosen shades of green and lilac. I was fortunate to be living with friends who own a pine workshop. So while there I designed a unique storage system using pine-wood. This gets most of my kit organised, and creates a good balance throughout.

We utilise lots of surplus things, much of what we use may once have been close to death's door. To recognise the value of an object, and bring it back to its original splendid condition, whether it be an engine, a vehicle, a plant, or whatever, is an enviromental statement in itself.

My sleeping arrangements are simple: I use an army sleeping bag. I love army kit, it's designed and built to a high standard. My clothing lives in my web set; all these things are ultra compact. I do not have space for beds or cupboards. Most of my food and kit resides in ammo crates. I earn money from my love of electronic music, and also art. I hang backdrops at dance events and also DJ. I'm not motivated by money, but petrol in the UK isn't cheap; as long as I have enough wedge to cover costs and save a little, I'm happy.

"…my vehicle as a potential studio…"
A slight problem, is that my records are cumbersome and take up space. However, times are moving on and heavy black vinyl is becoming redundant, thanks to the sheer volume of music becoming available on the world-wide web. I look forward to the day when laptop computers have built into them, a Telecom Internet satellite link. I do not believe turntables will ever become completely redundant, they will just take a lesser role as we expand into new ways of obtaining and delivering music. Turntables really won't become a thing of

the past, you only have to watch the DMC mixing championships to be assured of that. But the DJ arena is slowly evolving. DJ's in the future will plug their 'slim line' computers into the mixing desk, and the tracks will come out of their computers, not their record bags. Musicians will be able to obtain, trade, and network music by utilising a more evolved world-wide web. So at the same time, I like to think of my vehicle as a potential studio, as well as my home-base.

It's good living close to nature. Summer time is best; winter is a time of contemplation, a little more rest, and hot water bottles! A vehicle given love, and plenty of care, will serve you well. I am not mechanically minded, so I always have RAC/AA cover, which on occasion can be a Godsend. I'd like to stress how easy it is for people to become independent, if they wish. Initially it can be difficult adjusting to a new way of living, as it's unlikely you'll have everything you need in one go. But owning a vehicle doesn't mean that you don't live in a house; you can utilise the best of both worlds.

Also, it is a myth that spare parts for vehicles are expensive. There are so many vans, trucks, and buses in breakers' yards, and the parts off them are peanuts, in comparison to trade, or dealership prices. Many are almost brand new, and are only being broken up after having been wrapped around a lamp-post. Breakers' yards are the pure essence of re-cycling. And guaranteed, you'll always come out with some nice extras or choice fitting you didn't know existed. It was at a breakers I obtained the roof rack, rear ladder, and tow bar. (I still owe Pete twenty quid for the tow bar!)

My plans for the future are to keep travelling to free festivals, and checking out basslines and beats that stab! To stop at various communities mixing with people that are making it happen. The motto that I follow is: Free Party, Free People, Free Future."

Here are some......Words to live by
Many people will walk in and out of your life, but only true friends will leave footprints in your heart.

To handle yourself, use your head,
To handle others, use your heart.

Anger is only one letter short of danger.
If someone betrays you once, it's his fault.

SPIRAL TRIBE

If he betrays you twice, it's YOUR fault.

Great minds discuss IDEAS;
Average minds discuss events;
Small minds discuss people.

God gives every bird its food, but
He does not throw it into its nest.

He who loses money, loses much;
He who loses a friend, loses more;
He who loses faith, loses all.

Beautiful young people are acts of nature,
But beautiful old people are works of art.

Learn from the mistakes of others.
You can't live long enough to make them all yourself.

The tongue weighs practically nothing,
but there are so few people who can hold it.

Spiral Tribe say:
"We will make you paranoid, but then so you should be. Our existence has a wider cosmic significance in a world that is losing touch with its arcane ancestry. We are the self-styled shamans of the new age. We're here to alert you to something that's going very wrong out there."

The photographs and much of the research material for this contribution was provided by INVISIBLE_SP@hotmail.com – they say thanks and respect to Vinca Petersen.

References
Petersen, V. (1999) *No system.* Steidl
Perring, R. *Spiral Tribe in the area,* at www.xlr8r.com/archive/26/
Spiral Tribe, *Tales from the Hare Krishna and Spiral Tribe.* SP23, Spiral Tribe mailing.
Spiral Tribe, *Get the perspective,* SP23, Spiral Tribe mailing.
Spiral Tribe, *United Systems.* SP23, Spiral Tribe mailing.

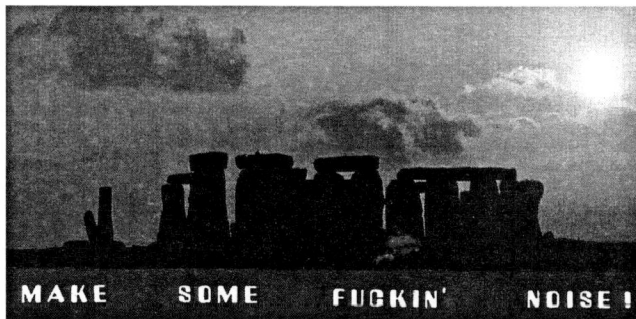

MAKE SOME FUCKIN' NOISE!

Part Two:
Collectives: extended families, communities and tribes

Eco Building for Community Development
Peter Cock and Bob Rich

Imagine that you are standing on the edge of a grassy plateau, the almost flat top of a mountain, behind you the lofty eucalypt forest, facing you is the starscape; the glittering millions of lights which

Horticultural common

are the reflections of life in the streets of Melbourne, fifty miles to the west.

You are at Moora Moora, one of the oldest surviving Australian intentional communities. The 245 hectare property was bought in 1974 by the founders of the co-operative. Since then, 26 houses in 6 clusters of up to 5 houses have been

A mudbrick house

built, with a community/education centre located at the hub of the community. The land, which is a mixture of natural forest and bush and farm land shaped by humans, is held in common while the solar powered houses are privately owned. Even though a visitor's first impression is shaped by seeing the farm, two-thirds of the land is bushland, much of it kept as a nature reserve.

The houses are mostly built of natural materials: earth, stone, timber, with personal labour from community members and some help from outside the community. Moora Moora is a place which demonstrates that building your own dwellings is one way of building community, and love of place.

The importance of place
The place where you are building your home is important in shaping what you build. Instead of imposing our building on to the site we spent time becoming attuned to its micro climate and designed so as to be responsive to the slope of the land, pre-existing features and the elemental attributes.

The decision to take advantage of the wonderful view or to choose the best position to harness the natural energy of the sun created tension for many. Some people chose the disadvantages of a westerly aspect for the spectacular view. Others didn't want to look over the city, but chose selective views in order to reduce heat transfer through windows. Choosing a site below the top of the hill was wise as it offered natural protection from the predominant winds. Given the location on a mountain top, with occasional snow in winter, the main challenge was to maintain a comfortable temperature all year round with minimal human and technological intervention.

A view or natural energy?

Building a new community meant having to do everything at once, but the building of our houses had the highest priority. For many this was an education, a sport and a consuming hobby.

Our co-operative was a collection of people with one thing in common: dissatisfaction with the environmentally damaging, socially alienating and soul-sapping life of a suburbanite, commuting wage slave. Safety, and the creation of a stimulating environment for our children was a major impetus for the change.

Co-operative building as a life saver

The community was a key to making the experience achievable and pleasurable . Most of us knew something we could contribute to building, but none of us knew it all. So we formed the first Moora Moora building group. This was simply seven home builders agreeing to work together once a week. Each week we rotated whose house we were working on. It was up to each home builder to organise the tasks and allocate the work force. We would meet for coffee in the morning and review what was to be done. The host of the day provided lunch and drinks. Over time we developed a system of credits and debits so that individuals were free to come without anyone feeling that they were missing out. We very quickly came to learn each other's strengths. As a group we found useful ways of employing each other and learnt to become comfortable with different levels of skill, standards of care and levels of courage to have a go.

It is amazing how mistakes can add character to buildings, or can be hidden and not matter. We each in our own way all wore a design or building

A building group in action

handicap. For Bob it was doing everything by hand, for Mark using stone work, for Peter and Sandra it was building an overly complex building that would sustain their interest and pleasure for a life time – so far it has.

The first group consisted of seven members: three couples and a single mum. We were in the 25-35 age bracket. We worked together for over four years. Because of our success another building group was formed that worked together on another day of the week. The group stopped when most of the work was done and our houses were livable. After that, building co-operation was on a person to

person, largely barter basis. This gradually gave way to monetary payments.

The building group provided the support structure to keep going and to not become overwhelmed. We all learned new skills through trial and error and were freed from having to do it all ourselves. Even so, some also employed some outside labour.

Becoming an owner builder – Peter's story

Like our community plans, our house design tended towards the grandiose. Of course mine had to be an autonomous house design, the first Victorian house with solar central heating. Our home has multiple levels, and the original plans had no right angles. Sandra, my partner, was a life saver in her dogged determination to keep going. I suffered from my ideas being so far ahead of my hands. Thank God for the blindness and arrogance of youth. When building our home I had never built a house before and had trouble hammering in a nail without bending. I was scared. Luckily I was able to work as a labourer and as an organiser of materials, and draw on the skills and experiences of other community members.

House building involves so many tasks and different domains of design and construction; from energy systems, landscaping, concrete pours, woodworking to stone wall construction, hunting second hand materials, best deals and more. Building your own home always takes longer than your worst fears. Our home cost $40,000 to build and took seven years to finish. We dearly love our home and have just now completed a burst of renovations and corrections of some of our original mistakes, such as replacing my mother-in-law's forty year old kitchen sink cupboard. It is a big challenge to design and build a home to last you a lifetime so it can accommodate the expansion and

Peter in his greenhouse, which is part of the home

contraction of family, the increasing needs for comfort while aging and changing roles. An example is the conversion of a bedroom into an office.

Bob's story of building his place

My wife Jolanda and I wanted to change the world, not liking the future facing our young children. We knew that the first step was to change our own lives, a need that led us to Moora Moora. Like Peter, I was an academic, with a strong belief in my lack of practical competence, but also the determination to learn. In my case, in time this led to a new field of expertise: for twenty-five years, I taught people how to build houses with their own hands, and I am the author (with Keith Smith) of a highly successful book on the subject.

This is typical of many who make a major change towards a more self-reliant lifestyle that is in touch with nature. A varied, challenging way of living brings out creativity and often leads to a new and more satisfying direction. Designing and building my house was the vehicle that took me into a life of contentment and continuous growth.

My principle of design is diametrically opposite to Peter's: KISS – 'Keep It Simple, Stupid'. Any building can be made beautiful, however simple it is, but if you design for aesthetics only, you are not going to accidentally stumble into a house that is functional, cheap to build and easy to maintain. I built a house that uses the sun for winter warmth without getting too hot in the summer, that is resistant to bushfires and is out of the winter storms, and that was cheap enough for me to build without having to borrow. From footings to the move into the first stage was twenty-two months. The total cost of the sixteen square struc-

Bob and Jolanda inspecting a solar panel

ture was $10,000 (about one-sixth of what the commercial cost would have been), though since then we have spent on add-ons like solar panels and space heaters.

There is nothing like helping to build your own house for it to engender an attachment as home. Those who have built stay longer than those who haven't. There is something special about walking around the property visiting houses you helped build, they are now part of me and I am a part of them, the land, community and self joined in the process and celebrated in the end result. It is amazing what we can do when we do it together. Doing it all yourself asks too much. When self reliance is without community interdependence then owner builders risk the paradox of losing their marriage/family while making their home.

Owner building is a life style issue

The sheer energy involved, the strain as well as delight of building, means that it is no wonder most people get others to build their houses and spend their lifetime paying for it. Most owner builders say that the key to success is to approach building your home as a way of living.

While middle-aged and even older people have done it, mostly it's for the young. Progress slows down once you move into the first stage, and can halt once you are comfortable. After twenty years, long-waiting projects might get completed during renovation that has become necessary by then. And sometimes a building only gets completed when it is being readied for sale. A change of ownership usually results in improvements or at least major modifications. Internal walls are removed or added, solar-electric systems enlarged, kitchens refurbished, and so on.

The difficulties with staging

After making houses livable there is then the slower developmental process. For example

Living on a building site

122

houses were built usually in either formal discrete stages or informal ones which involved constructing a shell, then fitting it out with core living areas and then bedrooms. The final phase, the never to be completed finishing touches, is usually done much later and often in tandem with updating.

While staging saves money and gets you shelter while you are building, the cost is in terms of comfort, pressure on relationships because of living in cramped, uncomfortable, temporary premises. This is especially difficult in our cold climate in winter. One of our older members is now suffering because he wasn't able to achieve the 'lock up' stage before this winter. As a consequence some Members have agreed to help him get in before next winter.

Buses – then and now

Another way of staging is to live in a bus or caravan alongside your building site. One advantage is

Buses can be homes and then stores

that at least living space is separated from the building work, and yet it is close at hand. We have a policy of one bus per cluster site. Buses have been used for a variety of purposes although now largely for storage.

Building with earth

We have used all kinds of ways of earth building: mud brick, rammed earth, rammed blocks and earth pour. The last is a more recent technique as we have found it to be the most labour efficient and can be used in all seasons. Twenty five houses later what we have built is a terrific variety of earth, timber and stone constructions. Some are large and complex, others small and simple.

Renewable energy systems

Many of the houses are passive solar designed. All are powered with solar electricity and built at less than half the cost of conventional buildings. As Moora Moora is not connected to the power grid, the developmental process also applied to energy

systems. Houses often began with a few gas lights, one solar panel and then gradually upgraded the number of solar panels. We have tried a number of wind generators, which, but for one, have been very troublesome. Even with six panels our use of power is approximately one quarter of normal domestic use. With

A cluster's solar and wind power supply

new inverters, more efficient and cheaper panels, solar power is much easier and more reliable than it was thirty years ago when we started to experiment.

Trade offs

There is a tension between:
- time and money,
- the monetary and environmental benefits of recycling versus a shorter life span and increased needs for maintenance, and
- the requirement for a lasting, solid structure despite lack of knowledge and resources.

The results are not always completely satisfactory, for example, a recycled corrugated iron roof led to later problems (see below).

The core of this house is the first to have been completed. It was of rammed earth and all recycled components. Later it was extended, a much better built mudbrick teenagers' wing on one side, and the attached extra single-person unit (visible in the photo, and made of poured earth).

Since the community is strongly conservationist in

A recycled corrugated roof

123

A large poured earth house (left) and a small and simple house built from recycled railway sleepers and field stone (below)

There are awkward questions: when is a house a house? Here is a studio (below), legally 'attached' to another dwelling, without a bathroom or a toilet. Is it a house?

orientation, it was important for us to keep the ecological cost of buildings down, but some builders opted for large houses that made a bigger footprint.

There is an ongoing struggle between individual freedom and accountability to the community. Should the builder be allowed to cut down mature trees in order to improve solar access to the house? Should solar-efficient (passive solar) design be obligatory? Should there be a list of permissible materials? At Moora Moora we have mostly opted for freedom. Legally and on paper, every building project needs Co-op approval. However, in practice other members advise, but will rarely if ever veto a plan.

Conclusion
Moora Moora Co-operative Community began with a clean slate, without a history, traditions or resources. It was intentional, having to be designed, decided, built and gradually evolved.

Building our houses was an initial tool for building our village community and a very physical way of growing your roots and falling in love with our place.

Now twenty-seven years into our co-operative experience, stable patterns have been established – members can relax, breathe and enjoy the present. The time for deferred gratification is over. We are not perfect but we have made it through over a generation, while most haven't. As one original member said, *"we have created an organic culture that has a life of its own."* Now that the community is established the next generation can draw on this supportive context and participate in taking us forward into new fields.

Krakers, squatting and an arts community called Ruigoord

Alan Dearling with lots of help from the Amsterdam Balloon Company, Stichting Landjuweel, Squall magazine, Orryelle Defenestrate, Antwan, Montje and others

The case for squatting in the Netherlands and elsewhere

In the 1970s and 80s squatting was virtually a 'way of life' in the Netherlands. The *krakers* – the squatters and the *kraakpanden* – the squats. And it wasn't just the homeless who chose to squat empty properties in the Dutch cities and towns. Frequently it was people who wanted to make a political and lifestyle statement by liberating an unused building and not paying a rent to what were frequently characterised as money grabbing, capitalist landlords. Or even just young(ish) people like my now partner, Christine, who lived in Holland for over ten years, for much of the time in squatted apartments which were 'legalised' and quite luxurious!

The rather tenuous link between 'homelessness' and 'squatting' also exists elsewhere in the world as well, since the organisational effort involved in moving from rough sleeping to squatting a building is just too great for many homeless people. The action of squatting, the buzz, the being part of a 'scene' and a social movement all characterise the krakers, who have spent more than thirty years playing a cat and mouse game with the Dutch authorities and the police. Sam Beale in *Squall* magazine explains this politicised lifestyle:
"...along with the on-the-edge, radical squatters' life comes a taste for the on-the-edge radical squatters' life."

Part of this radicalisation relates to how 'housing' is perceived. In most of the developed countries of the world, there is an abundance of houses, flats, commercial properties: warehouses, stores, cinemas, pubs and the like that are conspicuously empty and unused. Meanwhile, most of these same countries have an expanding underclass, especially amongst young people and ethnic minorities who cannot afford to rent or buy in the

![Kalenderpanden in Amsterdam]

Kalenderpanden in Amsterdam

'housing market-place'. The proactive process of putting these people into the active squatting role can allow some a positive experience of empowerment – and a much needed roof over their heads! Some readers may disagree that this constitutes the provision of eco-dwellings, but in a harsh urban reality, the continuing presence of property left empty as means for speculation and profit does appear to be greater evil.

A bit of kraker history

There are at least two very Dutch peculiarities in their squatting movement. The first, has in the past, been the willingness for many authorities to 'legalise' squats, even allowing the squatters to buy their 'homes', such as the upstairs living accommodation of Amsterdam's Vrankryk. These squats have often been large by the standards of squats in the UK and other European countries; up to 50 people lived permanently in the old tax office, the Blauwe Aanslag (Blue Attack) in the Dutch government capital of Den Haag, with another 200 a day using the arts and social facilities. In Amsterdam, the Binnenpret is 'home' to over a dozen different groups and organisations with activities including children's theatre, band rehearsal space, bicycle workshop, sauna, and a restaurant and coffee shop. The Amsterdam Do Maatschappjj (ADM – Amsterdam Do Society), The Silo, the Vrieshuis Amerika, Hotel Bosch in Arnhem, and the Kalenderpanden in Entrepotdok, Amsterdam are other long-standing squats and arts/info centres which have fought long legal battles culminating in eviction.

During the last twenty years many of the larger squats have developed almost iconic status in their local communities, uniting the social rebels and dissidents, and alienating some of their neighbours and increasingly hard-line authorities, who have pledged to 'clean up' the cities of the krakers. These evictions have often been very well organised battle-lines, for instance at Kalenderpanden at the end of 2001, over 1,000 squatters built barricades and faced tear gas and water cannons. The second quirky feature in Dutch squatting is the existence of 'anti-squatters' – people who are sometimes paid by absentee landlords or who live cheaply or rent free in the landlord's properties to prevent squatters gaining access. These anti-krakers are recruited through private bureaux much like estate agents, but it costs them in terms of frequent house-moves.

'Success' in squatting terms has only been achieved by some krakers through making sure that they have a thorough understanding of the legal apparatus. Since 1994 in the Netherlands, this has meant working within Article 429, which stipulates that only buildings that have not been in use in the previous twelve months can be legally squatted. Quite a difficult condition to confirm or deny. For the krakers, this requires research and use of detailed information concerning owners, landlords and building plans. There is even a network of Kraakspreekuren – squatters' information centres, which assist would-be krakers to locate potential homes.

The Amsterdam Balloon Company (ABC) and Ruigoord

I personally became acquainted with the history of Ruigoord after I met Antwan, a Dutch self-proclaimed 'activist'. Our paths had first crossed at one of the UK's Big Green Gatherings (sort of a green festival, with no electricity or generator power, but plenty of musicians, performance, talks and alternative energy). Antwan took some of my books on counter culture in the UK and Australia back to the Netherlands and he sent me a book , *Ruigoord – Amsterdam's Ballongezelschap 1972-1998.* It's a colourful, A4 production, full of living history of celebration and protest. An English translation forms the basis for much of the next part of this article.

The book kicks off describing its focus: Ruigoord as, *"...one of the freest places on Earth, an autonomous cultural zone, where nature can create herself."* And the main players in the action that took place there and around all four corners of the world over the next thirty plus years are the Amsterdam Balloon Company. Their slogan is: *Fortuna Favet Fatuis – Fortune Favours Fools.* And the events in their communal life have certainly been colour-and-eventful!

This is the sign of the coming time
the symbol of the androgyne

The male and the female will unite
to put an end to the old fight.
Look, so you may recognise old spirits in new disguise.
The three teeth on top form a Yoni perfect,
the stick and balls are penis erect.
Together they make up the Greek letter Psi,
in honour of grandmother psi-locybe,
the dear little mushroom that helps us see
the lemniscate of eternity beyond the veil of reality.
The trident of Shiva, the Devil, Neptune
nesting on the reclining moon.
And all the while the cosmic smile....

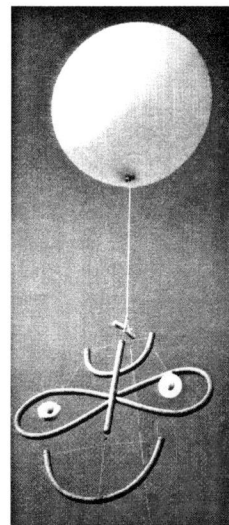

The letter Psi

The 'Balloonists' as they call themselves made Ruigoord their cause célebrè. Ruigoord (the rough place) is a former island, reclaimed in the polder-dykes, formerly the estuary of Ij. For about one hundred years the village had prospered with a population of about 500, but by 1972 when members of the balloon collective came upon it, there were only twenty houses and the church remaining, all under threat from the Amsterdam city developers. The very few members of the community that remained were happy to have the support of the artistic balloonists, and in particular, the elderly priest of St Geertruida Church, who handed over the church keys to the balloonists and their friends and it became the cultural centre of a new Ruigoord community. Writer, Henry Mulish said at the time,

"Religion gives way to advancing technology, but art lies in wait to jump into the gap between the two. Thus we begin to practise our country life: we mow,

The almost deserted village of Ruigoord

126

reap, prune, plant and harvest – we write, sculpt and paint, while trying to widen the gap between the onslaught of industrialisation and wild nature."

The new Ruigoorders squatted the deserted houses, built new ones, and it seems worked together with the small indigenous community to fight against the forced encroachment of Amsterdam's industrial network into the rural landscape.

The ABC in England 2002

The balloonists described their community as a 'post-apocalyptic oasis'. Children were born into the community and the natural habitat was nurtured, with rare and threatened species of plants and animals gradually becoming more abundant. The Balloon Company also engaged in a variety of local, national and international arts endeavours. Ruigoord remained its home community, its heartland, but its travelling wing started to export theatre (Why not theatre?), ballooning, art, performance and eco-protest around the globe. From 1979 through the 1980s the Magic Bus and its multi-coloured inhabitants travelled to Tibet, India and as they say, from, *"Belgrade to Bombay, Berlin to Budapest and Bergen to Baikal."* And indeed to England, where I met Antwan again, in the summer of 2002 and one of the founders of the Dutch psychedelic movement and the Ruigoord community, Hans Plomp.

The ABC activities
The balloonists said that they were, *"artists working together against abuses such as racism, exploitation and the destruction of nature and war…we no longer use our talents for a successful individual career in the rat race, but have joined forces to work on a change of awareness to enhance a change in society."* They also adopted the 1925 manifesto of the Surrealists: *"…the aim…is not to change the physical reality, but to establish a movement of spirits. This revolution has to do with*

the mystery schools and alchemy and wants to create a new imagination. We are on the side of the lunatics, the ecstatics, children, tramps, Gypsies, and the suppressed people of the world. We are for love, wisdom, freedom, humour and generosity."

Inside the church

Ruigoord was used as a site for many local Amsterdam festivals (annual 'landjuweels' – open air festivals – a concept borrowed from earlier 15th and 16th century events). They also celebrated indigenous cultures from around the world, and formed strong bonds at a number of these events with Aborigines from Australia (Dreamtime Awakening, 1993), Native Americans (the Stomping Ground (1992), people from Mongolia and Baikal (Baikal Cultural Express, 1990), and Gypsies (the art route of the Gypsies – art without borders in 1995). They also took a number of displays and shows into the heart of Amsterdam, including a Volksopera (folk-opera at the famous alternative venue, the Paradiso).

However, by 1997, Ruigoord was under physical threat once more, with the Amsterdam authorities having been granted permission to 'develop' the site for industrial use. Dozens of tree houses were built, tunnels were dug, even a fort was constructed, and the Green Front co-ordinated an international team of eco-protestors in trying to save the community. It became the focus of much international attention, but not enough to prevent 850 members of a special police force removing protestors from the wild fields around the village. But the spirit of Ruigoord lives on and the balloonists created a memorable event to welcome the new millennium in 2000 with their Tower of Babel. My Australian alternative arts friend, Orryelle Defenestrate was there. He wrote:

"I am still in the Netherlands and loving it. I've been staying in Ruigoord in a large wooden 'Tower of

127

Babel' construction nearing completion for burning on nu year's eve. Created by the bohemian theatre group The Balloon Company – who've been squatting the beautiful old church in the middle of the Ruigoord village for 30 years. The Tower of Babel they are building is an amazing ramshackle structure which creaks and sways in the gales – like being on a pirate ship.

The fort at the protest

I felt elated as I and thousands of others watched this looming symbol of humankind´s inherent arrogance and of miscommunications – the historical Tower of Babel crumbled because people living on the higher levels stopped communicating with those below them – was destroyed in glorious flames! And we were all united as one, the panglobal mongrel hybrid crosscultural diversity of the Thirteenth Tribe, returning to the Dreamtime as Marduk´s Temple toppled, and the stress and pressures of anticipation and preparation for the moment of midnight year 2000 Gregorian calendar went up in smoke. What a huge fucking inferno. The heat it gave off was intense. Once the blaze picked up people were recoiling from the edge of the moat with roasted faces. The flames roared stronger on one side, and we watched the structure crumble and topple piece by piece quite slowly and gracefully. I knelt on the sandy banks of the moat, caduceus-dancing with my arms (apparently I was on Dutch national news doing so), following the flickering dance of the leaping firesnakes."

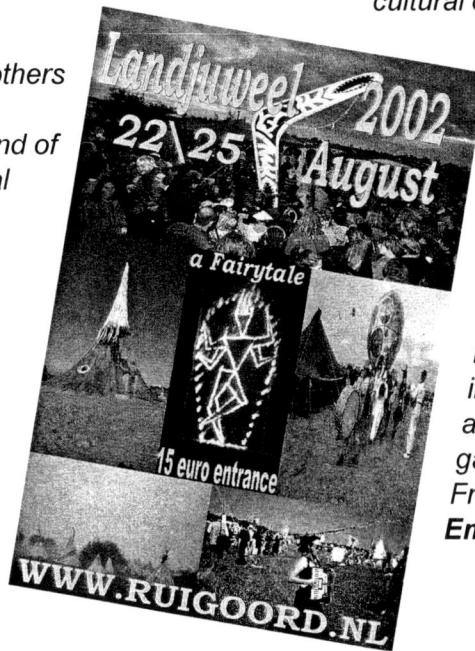

The Ruigoord community and of course the Amsterdam Balloon Company are still going strong. In 2002 they organised the Landjuweel-festival. Their web presence is considerable, with an increasing amount available in English. They are at: www.ruigoord.nl

Recently, as proof of that future, they wrote:
"The arts community Ruigoord is approaching a new future as an international cultural heart within the harbour – an industrial area of capital Amsterdam. In this period of transition the friends of Ruigoord are striving to give the renowned Freeport a new élan as a cultural oasis with a unique identity built up through the years. More than ever we will lay the accent on the theatrical, musical, visual, poetic and last but not least, magical aspects…Nation made war on other nation, but artists from different cultures kept on co-operating and drawing inspiration from each other. It is in the spirit on the interface of ancient traditions and avant-garde experimentation that the Freeport Ruigoord stands open. **Empower the imagination!"**

Tower of Babel

N Street Cohousing
Kevin Wolf

Perhaps it was being raised with six brothers and sisters in a newly-built California suburb with fifty other kids running from house to house. Or perhaps it was living in the dorms at UC Davis. Whatever it was, something in my past had prepared me to be strongly attracted to living in community the first time I was introduced to a co-operative house. The six person, co-ed student co-operative on N Street had an immediate pull on me. It changed my life.

It took two years before I moved into the co-op, and another seven years before the fences between that co-op and the neighboring house was torn down. And another fifteen years before the N Street Cohousing Community had grown to the 17 houses, 37 adult and 18 kid members it is today. But that first visit, the first time I was exposed to a real example of people living in community was all I needed to know what I wanted.

This is the story of the evolution of that student co-op, how it became the premier example of a growing movement termed 'retrofit' cohousing, and how it evolves into an environmentally sounder community. This is also a collection of some wisdom and truths that may be useful to others attempting to create sustainable communities.

That first potluck at the N Street student co-operative convinced me I didn't want to live in an apartment with three of my male dorm mates. The co-op was co-ed with the residents sharing meals. There was a garden in back. But why would that be more attractive than hanging with the guys finding parties in some modern apartment complex? Somewhere in the recesses of my 20-year old brain, a part of my primordial self wanted to be part of a tribe and not part of the group of male bachelors living the wild life of the unwanted.

The N Street co-op didn't have room for me after I left the dorms so I joined another co-operative house – all male but with important similarities.

The main one was that we took turns cooking and cleaning for each other. Thus the truth of my parents linked to a truth I carry today. If you want to foster a true sense of family and create community, take turns serving each other dinner and cleaning up for each other.

It was also in this first co-op house that I became friends and housemates with Guy Baldwin. I didn't know it then but it was Guy who would leave the permacultural and sustainability stamp, first on our co-op yard, and now, 20 plus years later on almost every house in the cohousing community. And he hasn't lived here since 1983.

Starting the community
Today when people ask me about starting a retrofit cohousing community, I tell them to find a block of houses they like, rent or buy two and share meals at least once a week. Most importantly, invite friends and other prospective members to those meals. By sharing food and dreams, a community grows.

In 1979, two years after I moved from the UC Davis dorms, the N Street co-op had a major turnover, and my household, now a co-ed co-op moved in. Dave, the only remaining resident of 716 N Street joined the Hari Khrisna that summer so we had the house all to ourselves. It was this lucky opportunity that helped formulate one of the truths I hold most strongly about community. With Dave's departure, the five bedroom N Street co-op had a room open. The four of us knew how we wanted the house to run, and we told the applicants the groundrules. The vast majority of people, when they know and commit to following rules and policies beforehand follow through on their commitment.

It is easier to maintain existing values, principles, processes and goals than to create them anew among people who don't know each other well.

For the next seven years we had almost every kind of person imaginable as housemates – a fraternity brother, a Brooklyn-born Rastafarian, Ph.D. students and undergrads, single moms and river guides, professional gardeners, political activists, gays and straights, Catholic, Protestant, and Jew, younger and older

Amalgamated back yards

(some housemates were even in their 30s!) and more. If they didn't know how to cook before moving in, they certainly did by the time they left. And just about every single one accepted and followed our basic house rules and honored our values and processes.

Two homes in one

Community. We made decisions by consensus then and do so today. To change an existing groundrule requires everyone's agreement. Regularly scheduled meetings work best. In the co-op we had short, after-dinner discussions using the phone logbook to see what item we had written about that previous week. House cleaning and social activities were the items we most dealt with. Both of these helped craft truisms that held after the co-op became cohousing. Now as a 15 year old cohousing community, we meet once a month for 1-2 hours. We don't have as many tough issues and we are, like many tribal people, becoming more 'conservative' in terms of changing the status quo – because for the most part it works quite well.

Five nights a week one of us cooked for the others. This simple practice was critical to binding us together as a household. Meals at N Street were fun. The conversations were memorably irreverent and stimulating. One of the major ways we selected among prospective new housemates was to invite them to dinner to meet them and see how they fared in a typical meal conversation.

Tribal communities from time immemorial have solidified the bonds between their members by sharing food and eating together. Every successful cohousing community I know of shares cooking and eating together.

A common value that the student co-op had which N Street Cohousing retains is a strong commitment to the environment. Then and now this commitment, like love, is shown through action. For example I learned composting from Guy and my basic biology classes at UCD. (Bacteria and the four basic ingredients of life – air, water, nitrogen and carbon – turn leftover kitchen waste, grass clippings, leaves and almost anything else organic into rich humus from which a plants thrive, soil life is built and water is saved.) Acting on a commitment to environmental values means households recycle. People are conscious about riding bikes and avoiding car use (though of course only a few keep from being lazy about this on a regular basis). Houses are insulated (though we haven't been completely successful in getting the landlords to insulate the rental units). Energy use is low.

Another example of our common values is that only one person out of the 200 plus who have lived here was a Republican.

Decision-making was another important aspect of the N Street Co-op and of the N Street Cohousing

Tearing down the fences
Between 1986 and early 1989 we had linked up four contiguous backyards and had three great 'fence tearing down' parties. In August 1988 my wife Linda Cloud read *Cohousing* by Kathryn McCamant and Charles Durrett. When she finished it, she said she knew what we should become, a cohousing community! We needed to start cooking dinner for each other, and ultimately we needed a common house for these meals and other activities. Potlucks, as we had been having since the first two houses joined were still stressful for everyone because one either had to make something for the meal or feel guilty about showing up with nothing. McCamant and Durrett reported that in the cohousing communities in Europe, teams of members cooked for one another. For us, this initially meant that each house hosted the meal while everyone brought their own utensils and plates. It made for crowded conditions in our small (1100 square feet) homes, but it was an immediate improvement over potlucks. Wow, just show up for dinner at 6:30, pay the cooks for your meal, and wash your dish afterwards. That more than made up for cooking for everyone else once a month.

As N Street Cohousing grew, it became clear we needed a common house. The logical home to convert was the original co-op at which I no longer lived. I had moved next door to live with my wife and her housemates. The co-op didn't oppose the creation of a cohousing community, but didn't feel the need for it as they continued to successfully share their own nightly meals and cooperate amongst themselves. But none of the co-op residents were planning on staying long in Davis. Thus, after some very intensive meetings, we worked out a two-year transition whereby the community would use their garage as our eating area until September 1990.

(Another of the most important of these early decisions was that every renter had equal rights as homeowners. For example, after three meetings and three months in residence, the newest member could block consensus just like everyone else.)

After the two years, all the co-op residents had graduated and moved on. We remodeled the house to make the kitchen and dining area big enough for a constantly expanding community. (And now, with twice as many households, we are actively working on how to finance another major expansion.)

Common chores and the size of a community are linked. One of my fondest memories living in the student co-op was the six month period during which we never had a meeting about chores nor a discussion about them because we all saw each other doing the needed work. This utopian situation fell apart when we brought in a new housemate who didn't pitch in. It didn't take long after realizing he was freeloading on our efforts before the rest of us stopped doing our share of cleaning chores. This crisis led to the creation of chore wheels, weekly time commitments and house meetings dedicated to ensuring that everyone was working equally to keep the house functioning properly.

As a co-op, we believed that to be an egalitarian community required the sharing of work to each one's ability by all its members. Yet it is difficult to find a group of people all able to assist with the same amount of effort during the same time period, especially if they are all expected to share the types of work equally. When we were a five-six person co-op, we used a job chart and weekly meetings. When we became a cohousing community, we embraced the honor system, in large part because we did not want to be policing each other. This is where size of the community becomes important.

The smaller the community, the more important a high percentage of participation becomes. The larger community, the easier it is to absorb members, who do not put in an equal amount of time, if

there is a core level of involvement. Europe's experience that 25-30 houses in a community are best probably comes from the need for about 12-15 strongly committed households or the equivalent in partially involved households.

We certainly noticed the importance of a minimum level of involvement in the 'work' of living together. A few years ago, our community meal level dropped to 1-2 per week. As the number of meals shrank, more of those who cooked felt the return in the number of meals at which they only had to show up, pay, and wash their dish and utensils wasn't worth the effort they put into cooking for 20-40 people once a month. As they stopped cooking, the negative loop intensified into crisis, confrontation and admission of vulnerability.

As a result, we organized a community retreat to better understand what was occurring in our lives and community that caused the number of meals to decrease. As M. Scott Peck describes in his book on community *The Different Drum*, when a crisis leads to sharing of vulnerability and weakness, community is strengthened. Some weren't cooking because they felt the other cooks weren't caring about their dietary needs. Others were in their own crises and didn't have the time. Others admitted to laziness. Others felt awkward asking people to cook with them to make a team. From this airing of the personal, came changes in our practices, a resolve by most everyone to try harder to make room in their lives to cook for the community once a month, and other solutions. Our meals sometimes drop below 12 per month but it now triggers informal discussions on what needs to be done.

Sometimes our reluctance to change how we do things has led to a shaking of our collective heads at our foolishness when we finally did end up improving something we thought we had become part of our routine. For example, for years we cleaned the common house by rotating the chore monthly house by house. When it was your home's month, your family/housemates would spend 3-4 hours checking off the cleaning list and doing the best they could to do as much as possible in that time. We all hated the chore. It was a major stress that one month out of 15 when your house had to 'do its duty' and scrub away.

The change? Now, when your house's turn comes up, you 'host' the cleaning, provide refreshments, advertise the cleanup beforehand and work with whoever shows up for a couple of hours. Everyone in the community is expected (though not required)

131

to spend a couple hours a quarter doing common house clean up. It is so much more fun cleaning with a crew of others, talking, laughing, playing music, catching up on life, than doing this with your spouse and child, or your roommates who all wish that they could be spending the time cleaning their own house.

Outdoor work

Outdoor work is not done much in our community now. Before he left in 1984, Guy Baldwin had converted 716 N Street to a model of urban permaculture, a term invented by Bill Mollison from Australia. Grapes on our side yard shaded the blazing summer heat. The chickens ate our kitchen waste, the dropped grapes and 'harvested' weeds. Guy scattered the seeds of edible plants across the entire lot. Plants would come up, some would be thinned, mulch would be added, harvest would occur but always, some plants were allowed to go to seed.

As a result Miner's lettuce is harvested all winter. Chard is steamed all year round. Magenta-headed amaranth provides summer greens and beauty all the summer. Cherry tomatoes come up any and everywhere as kids graze, spill and smash their sweet fruits as they wander through the yards. Potatoes never are completely harvested and continue to pop up year after year. Garlic heads are forgotten, and sprout by the fist full. When the soil is moist, it is easy to transplant them all over, and then forget where a few are placed for next year's starts.

Permacultural principles ended up guiding our community as it grew. Don't rip out plants until you know what will replace them. Think integration – thus the chicken yard moved under the fruiting mulberry. Observe. Observe. Observe. Then act to make permanent pathways, meeting nodes, play structures, clotheslines, etc. Evolve over time. Don't waste one's time creating the perfect master plan or one will end up redoing a lot of work. Have fun and make natural beauty a harvest for your eyes.

Our desire to expand the small permacultural garden at 716 was an initial stimulus for joining 724 and 716 N Streets together. (Other stimulus included: getting rid of the rock and roll band that played nightly on the back porch, stopping their dogs from biting the mail carrier and thus getting our mail delivered again, not wanting to listen to fighting step kids and yelling parents, and destroying the marauding snails which escaped back behind the fence into their yard.)

Children's play structures

Using overlapping sheets of cardboard on which we piled six inches of leaves, grass clippings, compost, hay and other organic material, we buried the worst weed known to gardens with clay soil – the hellish Bermuda Grass. In this permaculture 'instant garden' we placed potatoes and kept adding green waste and mulch as we found it. At the end of the year, we started purposely spreading seed heads of plants we wanted to see become established. In about one and a half years, the Bermuda Grass was gone and a self-replicating garden (with a lot more flowers – poppies, larkspur, calendula, hollyhock and more) was established.

Unfortunately it has taken a lot longer for the houses that came in after this first one to decide that permaculture was the better way to 'do' yard work. In our community (as with most cohousing communities) whoever owns or rents a house controls the yard that comes with it (and can do with it as they please so long as they don't harm their neighbor by, for example, planting a tree that shades their garden). This unwillingness to adopt permaculture could be expected. Most people are taught the 'control' method of good landscaping – not the let-it-wild version. Some of the early, 'every plant in their place' gardeners moved on and over time others saw how beautiful the permacultural gardens were almost all year round without a great deal of work being invested. So even this year, another house covered their Bermuda Grass with cardboard and mulch and surprised themselves with how prolific that space became with very little work once it was covered.

So our community now requires little communal outdoor work. We help each other on big projects like digging French drains and swales and building berms to hold the water on our properties. (Like most subdivisions, the highest elevation is in the middle of the back yard and all land slopes to the street and storm drains. By holding water on property we reduce downstream flooding, recharge groundwater and improve water quality.) We communally take care of the chickens (rotating monthly from house to house with the traditional rubber chicken left on your back door to remind you your month has begun). We make a lot of compost (utilizing 30-50 gallons of kitchen waste a week). We share each other's over-producng fruits and vegetables. And we help each other move from house to house as it usually takes living in 2-4 houses before a person finds their permanent home (either by buying it or becoming the senior tenant).

Christmas celebrations

And it is much better being of service to each other in these ways than in having to share in the 'chore' of maintaining the communal landscape that comes with traditional lawns, hedges, and the like.

Renters and the vision
The last cohousing community lesson I will cover that builds on what I learned living in the N Street Co-op involves renters. Renters were the heart and soul of the co-op (with me being the only owner who ever lived in the co-op after I bought in from our landlord in 1985). Renters are a vital part of N Street Cohousing. Eight of the 17 units in the community are rentals. A former community renter bought almost every owner-occupied home. Every year we have a turnover of around 4-5 renters in the community with the new ones almost always adding a wonderful addition of energy to our meals, work, social life, discussions and fun.

Having rental units as part of the community allows for new people to live with us and learn first hand about our values, principles, processes, and expectations. Most fit in great. Some make us glad that their lease allows them to leave sooner than later. In cohousing communities without rentals, when houses are sold, they are often bought by outsiders who know little of what the community is really like and vice versa. At N Street, when houses come up for sale, nine of the last ten house sales have been to community members who rent. No one who has a long term stable living arrangement in the community (renter or owner) is not a cared

for member of the community (even though some of them may not put in as much energy and time as others). This is not the case for many cohousing communities that experience house sales and member turnover.

There are a lot of other of other characteristics, practices, lessons and truisms I could write about from my 22 years of living at N Street. Our many failures on the path to flyless composting. The difficulties of and lessons learned from taking on the huge task of installing 18 tons of flagstone rock and building our community path system. The differences between children born into the community versus those who come here later in life. Our wonderful traditions like the Christmas gift exchange and Thanksgiving. And much more.

Instead, I will end this contribution by encouraging the reader to create 'community' wherever they are. In your work, through your schools, within your church or organizations, but most importantly, if you can, where you live. Community can grow in a house of strangers renting rooms together. It can flourish on a block or in an apartment complex with a couple of people who truly 'love thy neighbors' and show it through action. A couple of 'burning souls' can grow any place into another N Street Cohousing. They just need to make a long-term commitment, learn the skills of consensus facilitation, be generous, patient, sincere, fun, and somewhat humble. And have a vision they keep alive by sharing and growing it as others join in.

And over time, one can create a community that will flourish as long as those of tribal people who lived in hospitable lands. To advance this sustainability N Street recently changed the zoning of our community from Residential-1 to Planned Development. To change it back would take a huge change in our community. We believe we have in place the legal, social, familial, and cultural components that will allow N Street Cohousing to flourish as long as Davis is a city in the Sacramento Valley of Northern California.

Make the journey the destination, have a lot of fun, experience and learn much, and share the wonders of community with others whom you will grow to love and appreciate.

Becoming a communard: an interview with long term intentional community dweller, Graham Meltzer

Alan Dearling

Alan first met Graham while he was compiling his book with Mook Bahloo, 'Alternative Australia: celebrating cultural diversity' (2000)[1]. Graham was kind enough to drive Alan around most of the Rainbow Region (roughly described by a triangle from Byron Bay and Bangalow to Lismore and back to Mullumbimby) in northern New South Wales. At the heart of this region lies the famous or infamous, depending upon your point of view, township of Nimbin, the original home of the 1973 Aquarius Festival. It remains a hippy Mecca.

Living deep in the mystical hills around Nimbin are many forest dwellers, including some who built their individual versions of Eden in the early 1970s. There are also a number of intentional communities including Bhodi Farm and Tuntable Falls. Graham has intimate knowledge of all of these communities and in the years before he qualified as an architect, he helped build a number of homes in them, living himself for many years at Tuntable. This interview offers one man's view of why he and others chose communality and some glimpses of the challenges involved in living in an intentional community.

AD: Graham, I believe that your first experiences of intentional communities were in a kibbutz in Israel. Can you tell me a bit about that time and your background?

GM: I was born and grew up in Auckland, New Zealand, enjoying a comfortable, middle class existence amongst loving family and personable friends. Given such a background, my early interest in communalism was as much a surprise to me as to my somewhat conservative family and friends. I had learnt of kibbutz through my involvement in a Jewish youth group and become politicised in the process, adopting a 'way-left' socio-political world view that has never left me. In 1972, after three years at university involving limited study, considerable card-playing and continual protest action against

Vietnam and apartheid in particular, I left for Israel and life on kibbutz. I immediately fell in love with the lifestyle – the agricultural work, the rich social life and the lived ideals of equity and mutual support that seemed like a modern-day, village or tribal reality. I would still be there but for the requirement after three years to undergo military service and subsequently, fight wars indefinitely into the future. Israel in the seventies – there was no place for conscientious objectors, so sadly, I had to leave.

AD: And after the kibbutz what did you want to do?

GM: I spent a couple of years in London, enjoying both its mainstream and alternative offerings. I lived in shared houses, worked on building sites and in factories, took lots of drugs and generally had a great time. Eventually, in 1976, I returned to Sydney where my family then lived and started to think about the next phase of my life. I desperately wanted to live communally. Something within me drove a desire for, and fascination with, what I now understand to be a deeply tribal instinct melded with a progressive socio-political orientation. For me, this is a kind of communalism.

AD: So, when did you first hear about or visit the Rainbow Region? Did you know people there?

GM: In the process of seeking an intentional community to join, I attended a 'Down to Earth' festival in Canberra where I knew there would be a strong current of discussion about communal alternatives. It was there that I met my wife to be, Jane. She too, had dropped out after university and was looking for a community to join. We decided to travel for a while, checking out the possibilities. In

The view from the bedroom at Tuntable

early 1977 we visited friends of Jane's at Tuntable Falls, near Nimbin in northern NSW. I can still remember waking up on the first morning (having arrived late at night) to a breath-taking view of a mystical, mist shrouded landscape. It took little time to fall in love with the people and the place. They seemed like a lively, diverse community with a strong idealistic dream, few rules or restrictions, a beautiful valley in which to live and, most importantly since we were broke, a joining fee of just $250.

AD: And so you decided to stay?

GM: Yes. We negotiated to join Numenadi, one of the 'hamlets' of like-minded folk living in a cluster of dwellings, sharing gardens and some facilities. At the time, Coordination Cooperative, as it was legally constituted, comprised about 150 adults and kids, living in some 10 hamlets on approximately 1,000 acres. We decided to return to Sydney for a few months to make the money needed to build ourselves a modest home. We were soon married, Jane was pregnant and very excited about the future. We spent the weekends scouring the demolition yards for second-hand building materials. A Holden EH 'ute' we bought for $35 was invaluable for the purpose. It also enabled me to work on disparate building sites, contract cleaning brickwork with acid – probably the worst job I ever had. Ultimately, I was ripped off by two successive bosses who 'disappeared' with $1,000 of my wages, as if I needed any more convincing of the evils of capitalism! Still, we managed to save some money and accumulate a great collection of stained-glass doors and windows that we acquired for $5 or $10 a piece. In July, we headed north again with the ute so laden with building materials that it caused its demise, though not before we had driven within 20 km of our destination. We arrived at Tuntable three or four months before our baby was due and immediately set about building our home in the hope that it would be ready for the birth…which we always knew was to be a homebirth .

AD: Had you any building or architectural qualifications at that time?
GM: Hell no! I can remember being shown how to

drive a nail without bending it. Whilst I built alone most of the time, there was always help on hand and plenty of advice and inspiration available from more established residents. I also learnt from books and, of course, from making mistakes. I guess too, that I'd spent a lot of time on building sites over the years, always as a labourer, but in the process had subconsciously absorbed an understanding of how buildings go together. The 'design', though not drawn at the time, was a consequence of the site conditions (steeply sloped) and the building materials we gathered. Jane's dad gave us some wonderful 7 x 6 inch and 9 x 4 inch timbers that became columns and floor beams, respectively. Salvaged from a recently demolished road bridge, they were of ironbark that had been perfectly maintained for about a hundred years. An old L-shaped piece of flooring determined the footprint of the building and the stained-glass doors and windows more-or-less dictated the configuration of openings. It was a simple and modest dwelling, unlined internally, but with some beautiful qualities thanks particularly to the stained glass. We moved in just a few days before the baby was born.

The 'Nest' completed

AD: Was your relationship at the time very much a part of your move into communal living or did you have different aspirations?

GM: Sure. We were very much in love and definitely had the nesting instinct. It was mid-winter, so living in a tent with only the crudest of amenities, was certainly challenging. We used a pit latrine and washed with a hose. Yet none of that seemed at all difficult. We were driven to create an environment that would be wholesome and nurturing for our child. Being part of an extended family was paramount. We wanted our kids to have more than just a nuclear family as their primary social source. There were many more ideals in the ether. It was the late seventies which, in Australia, was that halcyon period of greatest 'new-age' idealism. At the time, Nimbin was at the epicentre of the dream. We were going to change the world by our example…of an environmentally responsible community of communities, as self-sufficient as possible, materially, culturally, socially and economically. And for a time there, we were on track!

AD: So what did you hope to get out of joining an intentional community, and what did you think you could offer?

GM: I think I've already alluded to my principle motivation. I fervently, ideologically, believe that a nurturing extended family is the ideal social grouping for the human species. A genuinely socially cohesive group of individuals (some related by blood but most, probably not) has the potential to be a profound milieu for the socialisation of both children and adults. An appropriately sized group, thus socialised into caring for and supporting one another, has the opportunity to create a truly civilised and civil society. I see it as our best chance to fulfil our individual and collective potential for creativity, generosity, compassion, love and all those other wonderful human attributes that, for the most part, remain unfulfilled.

That's it in a nutshell! I first had this insight whilst on kibbutz and, interestingly, I was there at a time when the kibbutz movement was beginning to lose sight of its communal principles. I could see where it had been, what it then was, and what it was likely to become. That the reality of kibbutz today is but a shadow of the dream does not negate or diminish its social, cultural and economic achievements. That kibbutz remained true to its communal underpinning for fifty or sixty years, indeed, validates the dream. And there are plenty of other examples throughout history of successful, long-lived communal societies that have achieved as much.

To answer the second part of your question, I'm not sure what I thought I could personally contribute. I/we were coming from a position of hope, faith and uncertainty. Most of us were carrying a lot of emotional and cerebral baggage that, even in the best of circumstances, requires decades of working through. At Tuntable, we had no charismatic or spiritual leader to provide us with a formula. It

was all so experimental.

AD: Tell me about the early days at Tuntable.

GM: Well, we arrived a few years after it began, so I can only relate the early history second-hand. The myth/legend goes something like this. Following the 1973 Aquarius Festival in Nimbin, (which I suppose, was Australia's Woodstock) many who attended wanted to stay on in the area – the Rainbow Region, as it became known. The festival had enabled a critical mass of hippies to get together to experience, dream and rave about the possibility of actually living alternative lifestyles, together, as a community of communities. The countryside was gorgeous – Middle Earth like in its topography of valleys, rivers, mountains, rocky crags and with tiny villages scattered all about. The climate was sub-tropical and the rich volcanic soil well suited to subsistence farming. It seemed as though the time and place were perfect for the birth of something profound. So, a group of dedicated entrepreneurial hippies spent some months raising enough capital to place a deposit on 700 acres of land about 10 km outside of Nimbin. Effectively, 'they passed the hat around' selling $200 shares in a cooperative which was to legally take possession of the land. Many of the shareholders never intended living there, but saw their contribution as a donation to help make it happen. The land was spectacular. It comprised a whole valley, lined on both sides with dense forest, but with plenty of arable land, a decent creek running through it and, at one end in the mist shrouded distance, a most magnificent high waterfall. This was a powerful place, a legendary place, and a sacred place.

AD: What sort of people were attracted to the community?

GM: All sorts! One of the greatest things about Tuntable (and for that matter, Nimbin and the whole Rainbow Region) is its rich human diversity. It was diverse back then, as it still is today. This has always been Tuntable's most laudable accomplishment and, of

Entry to the house via a covered pergola

course, its greatest challenge. Because the shares were only $200 anybody could join. So, according to one newspaper article, there were *"professionals, philosophers, gurus, freaks, misfits, ex-Vietnam officers, craftsmen, bushies, nihilists, adventurers, mixed-up kids of wealthy parents and political figures, numerous single parents, feminists, environmentalists, peaceniks, and save-the-planet missionaries."*[2] I'm sure there were many more shades of humanity than this, but you get the idea. The first residents moved onto the land early 1974.

AD: I gather that the original main community was based in 'hamlets' – how did these work?

GM: That's true, but therein lies another story. There were two habitable buildings on the property. One was ceded to Sam the previous owner to occupy for his remaining years. The other was a white weather board house, perched on the creek bank, roughly in the centre of the property. Imaginatively named, the White House, it became the one and only means of shelter for the original residents when, shortly after they moved in, the wettest 'wet season' for 90 years began. Apparently, it didn't stop raining for three months. Estimates of the number of occupants at that time vary between 40 and 80. It must have been an extraordinary, wonderful, difficult, but life-changing experience. Can you imagine what it must have been like for that diversity of people to be holed up in basic, way over-crowded accommodation, cut off from civilisation by floodwater, low on food, high on drugs….it's the stuff of legends. When the rain eventually stopped, they took off to all corners of the property, probably to get as far away from each other as possible. Subgroups of more-or-less like-minded individuals formed hamlets to colonise the ridges that run down from the forest to the creek. They cleared Lantana, pitched tents, built crude humpies, started gardens and began the next phase of the dream. Over the next few years, during which Jane and I arrived, the hamlets became established. At first they comprised 'exploded dwellings' of modest private shelters sharing some manner of community building containing cooking, eating and ablution facilities. Over time, most of the dwellings became self contained but the communal spaces remained and continued to serve a useful social purpose.

AD: Once the main sites in the valley were all taken, new people had to occupy sites which were hidden away up in the forest-clad hillsides; it was called the Wild West, I think. Can you tell me a bit about those people?

The kitchen and dining area

GM: This is news to me. It's true that finding a building site became more difficult over time, but that took at least 10 years or so. Some people certainly did live in the forest, but by choice. The whole place seemed like the Wild West to me. The social dynamics of the time were fascinating. Whilst there was social cohesion within the hamlets, there was often tension between them over land-use, building proposals, drug usage, animal grazing etc. As I mentioned, the hamlets were populated by like-minded folk. There were hamlets of pioneers working from dawn 'till dusk, hamlets of dope-growing hippies, hamlets of dedicated organic gardeners, a hamlet or two of ambitious engineers and builders, a hamlet of transsexuals and so on. There was a suitable hamlet for everyone…and there were very some individualistic folk who just did their own thing.

AD: What sort of personal skills and attitudes do you think those early communards needed to survive and prosper?

GM: Courage, vision and resourcefulness at a personal level, but perhaps more importantly, the will and the requisite social skills to work with others, to build a common or communal reality.

AD: What were the good parts of the lifestyle?

GM: Oh, there were many. At an abstract level, I'd say the freedom…the freedom from constraints…the opportunity to wake up each morning and decide what it was we would do that day. The camaraderie, friendship and bond we felt as pioneers, setting out together to create a profoundly new reality. The excitement, unpredictability, fun, personal growth and discovery…all of these things. On a day to day level, I enjoyed the work, loved building and establishing gardens and orchards. We took long walks, went swimming, played and listened to music, raved, partied and hung-out. It was paradise.

AD: Do you see an intentional community as being a good place for nuclear families and long-standing couples to move into?

GM: Of course. Why not? In fact, intentional community can provide a very nurturing and supportive context for the intimacies of family partnership, which in different circumstances, might become isolated and self-referential.

AD: What was it like for the young people growing up there?

GM: The best! Our two daughters had the best possible life at Tuntable. Firstly, they were born at home, a home that we had made for and because of them. Their births were both magical, serene and deeply moving…overseen by a midwife and shared with close friends. They grew up amongst an extended family of loving neighbours, in a beautiful natural setting, with complete freedom, a fine community school, organic produce to eat…I could go on, but I think you get the picture. Of all the 'positives' we enjoyed at Tuntable, there is no doubt in my mind that the socialisation of our kids was the greatest gift bestowed upon us and them.

AD: And did Tuntable really operate as a community?

GM: Yes and no. The hamlets were pretty communal, but as I saw it, the community as a whole was not. But, don't get me wrong. Tuntable was, and still is, a unique experiment. I know of no other hippie commune (anywhere in the world) that has lasted as long, with a population as diverse and a property as vast to steward. To achieve all that Tuntable has without the guidance of a charismatic leader or spiritual belief system is an amazing thing. But yes, it could have been more successful in terms of harnessing the collective potential of all those people. However, that was not Tuntable's thing…and that's just fine.

Graham on the outskirts of Nimbin

AD: What shared facilities were there?

GM: The pre-existing buildings, apart from the White House, included a few farm buildings which at different times were used as community space or private rental accommodation. The White House itself became the community school, and it was fantastic! There was an old mill. It took about 15 years before a community hall was built, but there was always a small shop and sometimes a café.

AD: There's also common land and forest land, some of it rainforest, isn't there?

GM: All the land is common, with usage by negotiation. One or two adjacent properties were purchased to take the total area to over 1,000 acres, with vast areas of State forest beyond it. Most is covered in dense bush including some sub-tropical rainforest. There is also plenty of cleared land for agriculture.

AD: What are some of the community rules?

GM: There were very few. No cats and dogs, and no firearms were the two that were most cited, although a few individuals insisted on transgressing even those. Such was the anarchic spirit of the place. We determined to have as little governance as possible. There was a monthly 'tribal meeting' which made decisions by consensus and an AGM…because we had to, as a registered cooperative. There was a loose process for gaining permission to build, involving raising a flag on the site to the height of the proposed dwelling. There was an attempt to keep buildings below the ridge lines to reduce their visual impact and blend them with the landscape.

AD: Did many people leave quite quickly?

GM: I guess so. Some would have decided it wasn't for them. Others probably found the going too hard.

AD: What were the chief sources of conflict?

GM: Those people who transgressed the pets and firearms rules copped shit from the rest of us. As mentioned, there was friction over building sites, but these were always resolved one way or another. Some brave individuals took to raiding other's orchards, which was tolerated to an extent. Others more crazy, took to raiding other's dope crops, which was not tolerated at all and led to considerable grief.

AD: I believe that the question of tenure and ownership of only the building rather than the land, was always a problem in the community – it's called MO: multi-occupancy – can you tell me a bit about it?

GM: In fact, at Tuntable, we didn't even own the buildings. Legally, the co-op owned dwellings built by members, who then had exclusive right of occupancy. There was no legal tenure, as such. Other MOs have different arrangements.

AD: Was it a problem for you personally?

GM: Only when we came to leave. Because there is no individual title to the dwellings, the market is limited, even though one can sell the right of occupancy for a fair price. We ended up having to let our place at first and eventually sold it for way less than a fair price.

AD: Can you describe the circumstances and feelings you had when you finally decided to leave Tuntable?

GM: Our decision to leave was multi-factorial. The kids were growing up and needed some more serious schooling, we had finished the nesting/pioneering thing (building the house, garden and orchard etc.), I was looking for new challenges in terms of a vocation, Nimbin itself had passed through its halcyon days into a more difficult period…there were lots of reasons. My feelings were accordingly mixed. It was very difficult leaving the home we built, the hamlet and our good friends on the property and in the wider community. But a new phase beckoned and that seemed exciting. I had enrolled to study architecture in Brisbane. Jane and the kids felt differently. I'm sure it was more of a wrench for them.

AD: So, in retrospect, what were the pluses and minuses of life at Tuntable do you feel?

GM: Pluses: family, friends, love, joy, freedom, organic food, music, creative work, lots of recreation. In short, an integrated and fulfilling lifestyle. Minuses: not many.

AD: As the largest of the intentional communities in the region and Australia, did you ever feel that you were acting as some kind of ambassador?

GM: Not really. I don't think Tuntable is a very generalisable model. It's fantastic in many respects, but of its time and unique circumstances.

AD: And what was your involvement with the other communities in the area around Nimbin?

GM: We had very good friends on a number of other communities. We used to visit a lot and hang out. Jane was more involved with the communities beyond Tuntable because she was a member of the homebirth team and so visited numerous and made enduring friendships that way.

AD: Finally, Graham, I believe that you are now contemplating a move back into 'community', after a spell in academic life in the big city of Brisbane. What are you looking for this time around?

GM: Good question to finish. Since leaving Tuntable I've lived an urban and not very communal existence but maintained my interest in communalism through academic research and consulting as an architect. In the last 10 years I've been lucky enough to visit intentional communities in Denmark, Germany, the Netherlands, Portugal, Britain, Canada, the US and Japan. My research has focussed on cohousing, a relatively new, mainstream but communal housing type, popular in Northern Europe and North America. There are some Australian examples.

Personally, I deeply desire and fully expect to return to communal life in the future. All my experience and a considerable amount of thinking and writing about communalism has left me in a very good position to know what I want and where I might find it. I'm only interested, now, in communities that deliberately seek social cohesion through building open, authentic and supportive interpersonal relationships. My ideal community is also politically way-left, secular and democratic. There are a few around the world that have all these ingredients.

AD: Thanks for your time and honesty in sharing some of your experiences.

Notes
1. Dearling, A. with Hanley, B. 2000, *Alternative Australia: celebrating cultural diversity.* Enabler Publications, Dorset.
2. Hawley, J., 'Nimbin Ten Years On' The Age, Melbourne, Nov 13, 1982. Quoted in the book by Margaret Munro-Clark, *Communes in Rural Australia: The movement since 1970*, Hale & Ironmonger, Sydney.

The Floating Neutrinos
Captain Betsy

It was just before Christmas 1975 that I arrived in New Orleans and stumbled across a funky looking, 38' barrel raft tied up almost right next to the

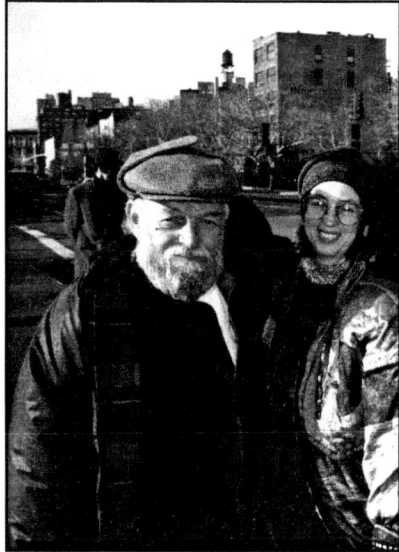
Poppa Neutrino and Captain Betsy

Natchez, a big paddlewheel tourist excursion boat. The contrast was huge – here at the end of the dock, within sight of the tourists boarding the old-style riverboat, under the tune of the wavering off-key notes of the steam calliope which welcomed them aboard several times a day, was this conglomeration of used plywood and driftwood, something more akin to Huckleberry Finn than the modern French Quarter. In some sense it seemed to me more authentic than the Natchez itself. This raft, the *Ms. Leslie*, had been built from scrap and recycled materials in Sioux City, Iowa, and had floated all the way here by way of the Missouri and Mississippi Rivers. It wasn't long before I joined the group onboard, led by Poppa Neutrino, then known as David Pearlman. This was the beginning of what would be an odyssey of 26 years, (and still continuing) – building scrap rafts, travelling the rivers and the Gulf and Atlantic Intracoastal Waterways of the US, eventually taking the first scrap-built raft across the North Atlantic Ocean to Ireland and then France. To date 9 rafts have been built, and a 10th is soon to be launched.

Each of the rafts has been built almost entirely of salvaged and recycled materials. Each has been designed for the environment and waters upon which it was to be used. In date order they were:

Ms Leslie
A 38' barrel raft, built on top of discarded, 700 gallon, fertilizer barrels; after arriving in New Orleans, she was converted to a paddlewheeler using recycled parts from cars and assorted old machinery, and travelled as far east as Mobile Bay. From this raft we learned the value of foam over barrels: barrels eventually start to take on water.

Nancy Jane
A 48' wooden catamaran pontoon boat built in Lafitte, Louisiana, the first raft in which we combined chunks of salvaged polyurethane foam with poured, 2-part liquid foam, providing a solid flotation hull. Travelled the Gulf and Atlantic intracoastal waterways for 2 years, most of that time running on paddlewheels.

Stone Soup
A 50' framed monohull, with foam in the bottom one foot of the hull, this design was similar to the *Son Of Town Hall*, though not nearly as strong. She travelled from Freeport, Texas, to Miami, Florida, and it was on board the *Stone Soup* that we conceived the idea of taking a raft around the world.

Town Hall

Town Hall (left)
Built atop a condemned steel barge which had started to sink; we filled the barge with foam taken out of discarded dock floats, and used the wood from the same floats to build housing, a stage, and paddlewheels. Travelled from Provincetown to New York City, where she remained anchored in the shadow of the World Trade Towers for 9 years.

Child of Amazon
Built in New York City by Rodger Doncaster, one of the crew of the Atlantic crossing, using wood from a night club which had closed on the pier, this raft served for a number of years as home to artists and musicians, tied up next to the *Town Hall*.

Dragonfly's Banquet (next page)
Built and decorated by artists and now part of an artists' colony in a wildlife refuge in New York City, this scrap-built raft sailed successfully from Provincetown, Mass., to Martha's Vineyard, and on to New York City. Although we consider every Neutrino raft to be an artpiece, *Dragonfly's Banquet* is proof that Neutrino Rafts can also be beautiful in the more conventional sense.

Son of Town Hall

Now in southern France, this raft was built with scrap from the streets and waterfront of New York City, and made the North Atlantic crossing to demonstrate that it was possible to build a perfectly safe, ocean-going vessel out of scrap and recycled materials – a vessel which did not look like anything else ever to cross an ocean, yet with purpose and reason behind every element of its design. This was the prototype which was to prove the feasibility of such a raft, so that our future Orphanage Raft could be designed and built using the same principles.

When we decided to attempt the North Atlantic Crossing, we spent years designing, building, testing, and redesigning the raft so that every possible problem at sea was handled in advance. The raft that ultimately made the crossing was self-righting, self-steering under sail, and capable of self-steering dead downwind in a storm, thus keeping itself continually aligned at a right angle to the waves and avoiding the danger of broaching and rolling.

Dragonfly's Banquet

Vilma B, the future Orphanage Raft. Built at the headwaters of the Mississippi, initially a wooden pontoon

Vilma B

catamaran, ultimately to be transformed along lines similar to the *Son of Town Hall*, but twice as long, twice as wide, and twice as high, to be the travelling home and school for up to 25 street orphans from third world countries such as Brazil and India, their teachers and crew. After coming downriver to New Orleans, the *Vilma B* travelled west to the southermost tip of the intracoastal waterway – Port Isabel, Texas, only a few miles from the Mexican border. Here she is presently undergoing reconstruction, and will continue to travel and slowly transform toward her eventual seagoing form.

June's Barn

Built in Dows, Iowa, (a landlocked town surrounded by corn fields), using wood from a 100 year old barn that was being torn down, this raft joined the *Vilma B* on the Mississippi River and travels alongside, acting as a pushboat and providing additional public interactive space.

Absolute Absolution

Ed Garry, one of four who made the Atlantic crossing, is building a sailing catamaran with a more traditional style hull, but also filled with flotation, and using recycled materials. This vessel, soon to be launched in Corpus Christi, Texas, will serve as a training vessel, teaching people how to build scrap rafts and sail them.

Nomads at heart

Poppa Neutrino and I are Nomads at heart; we feel fully alive only when freely moving from place to place. Over the years we have supported ourselves, our children and our many students through jewelry making, sign lettering, music, writing, art, and video documentary making. We took a vow to each other years ago, never to work for another person, and we have taken a vow of poverty to the Universe. We vowed never to have for ourselves one thing more than what we need for our basic necessities and to carry on our teaching work, and always to pass on whatever came into our possession beyond this level. We have given away whole rafts, loaded with equipment, motors and shore boats, because it was time to move on to the next step, and the material objects had ceased to assist our progress and had become an impediment.

From the time I first joined Poppa Neutrino on the *Ms. Leslie*, it was apparent to me that there was more going on than was evident to a casual outside viewer. Not only was the mode of life unusually primitive – for example, there was no electricity on board, and no running water – not even water tanks, but buckets and one gallon containers which had to be filled and carried, sometimes from quite a distance. No shower – you just dipped from a bucket and poured the water over your head, and knowing how far you might have to carry that water, you were naturally as conservative as possible with this valuable resource. In fact, almost everything that I, in my middle class background, had taken for granted, took on new meaning – either extreme value, or a realization of how dispensable it was. Later I would come to understand that, unlike accepted standards of living in the US, most of the world lived in conditions equal to or more primitive than these.

Dragon's Banquet, Child of Amazon and Town   Hall in New York

There was a continually changing flow of crew members coming and going – people from all walks of life were attracted to these strange floating, travelling craft. There are incredible healing powers in nature, and in being out on the water, away from the direct influences of cities and highways. Poppa always made it the first order of business to teach every new person an independent method of earning a living. Having a trade which allows you to earn a living without relinquishing your own timing has a tremendously freeing effect. And in learning to build and to sailor a vessel, you gain a sense of competence, resulting in an automatic raising of self-esteem. Since many of those who came along were drifters or down-and-out types with few skills and often with problems with addictions or having been on the wrong side of the law, these basic beginnings were essential steps toward recovery.

But aside from these simple and very basic healing and empowering factors, this was an ongoing experiment through trial and error, to discover basic psychological tools that would work for anyone, to free yourself from whatever bonds, inner and outer, were holding you captive; and then to find ways to make these tools available in every medium on the planet, so that anyone searching could find some simple starting points with which to move toward finding a path. We believe each individual's path is different, even those who choose to follow a well-defined path or a specific teacher. But what we have discovered and distilled are some very simple psychological tools, so rudimentary that even children can grasp and utilize them, and be better able to find or forge their

own individual path toward self-realization as a result. What follows is a distillation of 26 years of psychological struggle, study, and interaction.

Triads
Thinking with triads has to do with the three elements involved in the manifestation of any force, or the three possibilities which exist in any situation. For example, the three elements necessary for a vessel to function on the water are: it must FLOAT, GO, and STOP. The three possibiities which exist in any situation for everyone are: PARTICIPATE, REDIRECT, or LEAVE.

Seven levels
The seven levels are seven parts of yourself, corresponding to the seven chakras in Eastern philosophy. They are the:

♦   **INSTINCTIVE, which has to do with physical nurturing and well-being;**
♦   **SEXUAL,**
♦   **IMITATIVE, which consists of everything which has been learned through imitation, from talking and writing to high finance;**
♦   **EMOTIONAL,**
♦   **INTELLECTUAL, which is a different type of thinking than most people do, having to with describing, comparing, and evaluating;**
♦   **HIGHER EMOTIONAL, which is your spiritual part; and**
♦   **HIGHER INTELLECTUAL, which has to do with cosmic consciousness.**

Through a simple monitoring of these 7 parts, comparing your present condition in each part to the highest you personally have ever experienced, it is possible to make a more conscious and more complete assessment of how your life is going.

Types of timing
The three types of timing are:

•   LINEAR, which is time determined by appointments and schedules, followed in a straight line;
•   EXISTENTIAL, which is living moment to moment, in the present only, without commitments, past or future; and
•   CIRCULAR, which is living in your own personal sense of time based on your circulation by choice through your own seven levels, from which it is possible to connect with an existential experience, but also possible to maintain linear contacts and make intersections with them, then step back

142

into your own circulation.

Once understanding what types of activities fall into each of these categories, you are free to choose how much of your time you wish to spend in each one.

Reprograming your inner software

The basic premise of this idea is that from the time you are born, you are being constantly programmed by outside forces – your parents, teachers, friends and relatives, and the society and culture you live in, through the media and the demands of school, work and laws. Most of these outside forces are acting on you in a mechanical way, giving pretty much the same programming to everybody. The programs of society, for example, are designed for the preservation of the society itself, not for individual self-fulfillment. All these programs form the basis of your inner software, that unconscious part of yourself from which most of your driving forces come. The difficulty of making a conscious decision to do something different or individual and then carrying it out in day to day life is apparent to anyone who has ever tried to break a habit or start a new pattern of behavior. We have devised a simple system through which you feed new information into your inner program level, automatically erasing and overriding the old programs over time. It is very much like replacing an obsolete piece of software inside your computer with a new and updated program. You do this by using a specific question and answer process through which you give yourself information about your own three deepest desires (by asking yourself what you would do if you could only do one thing before you die, then a second, and finally a third thing), and your own evaluation of how each of your seven levels are functioning now, (on a scale of 1-10, using your own personally experienced 'best ever' as the 10).

All through the years, our focus has been, with all the individuals who have chosen to join us, whether short or long term, first economic empowerment, then psychological empowerment, leading to the freedom of choice to find the necessary moves to each person's own self- fulfillment. Our only demand was that each person teach what they learned to others, pass on what they had gained. We were, and are, engaged in the business of recycling not only material objects, but the

Son of Town Hall on the epic crossing of the Atlantic

human psyche as well. The rafts serve as a moving, changing, organic platform upon which to work this human transformation; the physical transformation of scrap into functional vessels is a symbol of this process, which acts on the psyches of all who see the rafts, whether or not they are consciously aware of it. Our hope is that through future raft projects – whether small, individual, inland-water rafts, world-travelling sail/ training rafts or the Orphanage Raft – that these psychological principles and tools will spread and become known and available world-wide to anyone seeking a way out of the mechanical wheel of life.

www.FloatingNeutrinos.com

Update: August 2002

On July 13th 2002, Ed Garry's *Absolute Absolution* after a year and a half of preparation, left Port Isabel working southwards along the Mexican

Absolute Absolution on her maiden voyage

coast. Captain Betsy's log reads:
"We were so elated to be on the move at last, and the cheers and waves from fishermen on the shrimp boats lifted our spirits even more. She handled better than we could have possibly imagined. She tracked beautifully through the water and steering her was a breeze. In spite of the wave action 'Absolute Absolution' was rock solid – not a creak or groan of protest from her structure. We arrived at the port of Mesuital – arriving at dawn – the people were incredibly friendly. I don't think they'd ever seen anything like our vessel before, and were intrigued that we were not merely tourists. The construction project itself is serving as a raft building school."

The Harmonic Healing Foundation (HHF) in Spain
Alan Dearling with Laurence and Brigitte Burton

Nestling amidst the panoramic mountainous scenery of Almeria in an area of Southern Spain known as El Desterio de Tabernas, the HHF has

Mountains of Almeria

been established to rejeuvenate and heal the land, and as a site for eco-festivals and holidays. The 120 acres of neglected farmland, set in canyons and on mountain sides, 25 kilometres from the sea, were discovered by Laurence and Brigitte Burton in 1999. In the 1980s it had been a renowned wine growing farm but it suffered from the vagaries of EEC farming policies and grants, and the vines were replaced by almond and olive trees. In the 1990s, a severe flood destroyed the irrigation system and by the end of the decade the farm was sadly decayed. Their aim was and is to establish themselves as land guardians, rather than land owners. To date they have paid part of the purchase price for the land and have registered it as an organic farm school and ecological camp site.

Brigitte and Laurence were in touch with me by e-mail. They were seeking more supporters and 'guardians' and wanted to spread the word of their existence and plans for eco-festivals and more. I explained the book I was putting together and the rest of this contribution is a result of that dialogue. However, even in the age of the electronic information highway, it can still prove tricky to keep in touch. You'll get the picture through what Laurence wrote to me recently:

"I am sure you will understand the long delay in writing to you when I explain that for the last three years we have been living in a desert canyon with no basic facilities such as running water, electricity, phone lines or any of the fundamentals that a modern individual could expect. Just living in these conditions eats time like a hungry wolf. Please do not consider these words as complaint, because the peace, tranquility, open spaces and the challenge of survival are themselves the just rewards. A friend has lent us an invertor to run off our one solar light system and at last I can put my fingers on a computer in the luxury of my own home, avoiding the dreaded night times in the Spanish internet cafes, where I have made no less than three attempts at this communication, each time running into the street tearing out lumps of hair from my head and turning the air blue with expletives."

At the heart of the Harmonic Healing Foundation are two complementary notions. The first is the guardianship and nurturing of the land. The second is living in re-locatable dwellings. The HHF has set out to purchase the land as a trust organised by a group of people called land guardians, as opposed to land owners, with the understanding that the land may never be sold again. This will entail:
• A deep and abiding commitment to the integrity of the land.
• Support for their interdependent community on issues of alternative power sources and other green issues.
• A balanced approach to farming for small target markets and specific micro-environments that minimise damage to the existing eco-systems.

HHF maintain that each guardian should attend to these details in their will so that their inheritors will assume this mantel of responsibility. They believe that once our attitude to the earth becomes more harmonious with universal principles, we in response will become more whole again.

The meaning of guardianship

Roof of a yurt

By definition, guardians choose to believe in a dream, and have the personal discipline to carry it through. HHF define this sort of person as, *"seeking solutions to ecological issues"*, and within this context, each pays 2,000 pounds sterling to secure the land without fences for the future of all the children. In return, each guardian has the right to live at the site for the rest of their life in re-locatable housing, e.g. geodesic domes, teepees and yurts etc., and by agreement, build ecological and streamlined structures, with planning permissions where appropriate.

Building up the resources at HHF
Andalucia, as this larger area of Southern Spain is known, is one of immense historical importance, having been the centre of the Moorish civilisation. It includes Granada, Seville, Cadiz and Malaga – but in recent times, the coastal strip has become some sort of never ending holiday-resort from hell! Luckily, those holiday-makers rarely spend much time inland, and the HHF-ers have spent much more time building relations with the local population, and trying to identify and use the natural landscape to provide a memorable eco-space for visitors and residents. This inland area of Southern Spain has also become something of a haven for hippies and the UK's Travellers, with other notable sites at Orgiva and Castellar de la Frontera.

When Brigitte and Laurence arrived, the farm had four dwellings in various states of repair, a well filled with silt and two large redeemable reservoirs. Brigitte and Laurence say,

"During the last two years, our assessment of this area of Spain inclines us to operate within a philosophy of low impact on the environment. We know that drastic changes would generate ecological instability. We understand that this land, as well as much of Andalucia was forested with majestic trees and although there is much empathy with the concept of re-forestation, realistically we may be able to implement the groundwork, but it will be the guardians of the future who will see the results. Because this is a social project for growing people, we are concentrating on making things viable for the people who have come here to help us in this undertaking.

We have built two depositos for fresh drinking water (12 tonnes), ecological drop toilets, showers, a sauna, kitchen with facilities, repaired one of the reservoirs, a carpenter workshop (for which we are collecting tools), two of the cottages are now available for rent as self-catering holiday cottages, which provides a little income towards for the farm and of course building materials. The work of tree pruning continues as a sound method of saving those still living. Many of the dead trees are to be used in furniture making, *again to provide a little revenue.*

This area of Spain has a wealth of connection with the traditional hinterland, very low population density which means that the local people are keen to find ways to encourage the young people back onto the land."

They now organise a number of linked projects which they hope will bring like-minded visitors to their version of paradise. These include:
• A cheap camp site with clean drinking water, showers, eco-loos, café and sauna. The local facilities include horse trails in Velifique mountains, the local hot spring baths in the Alhamilla mountains, the 12 kilometres of the Sorbas caves, and a 45 minute walk to the traditional Spanish village life of Tabernas.
• An organic farm school where visitors can 'volunteer' to help with ecological projects including chumba (an indigenous cactus) and aloe vera planting, dry stone walling, tree planting, hydroponics, and growing plants such as milk thistle, lavender, thyme, and carduus benedicta which can be utilised in homeopathic tinctures.
• Workshops and an ongoing learning programme about alternative energies and re-locatable housing.

Ecological Oriented Construction (Konstruction) – EOK
Brigitte and Laurence have been looking at alternative structures and covered spaces for many years. Establishing HHF on its 120 acre farm has provided them with an abundance of space which allows much experimentation to occur. As well as their yurts and domes and other re-locatable structures, they have been building permanent structures into the surrounding mountains with an attempt to minimise the impact on the surrounding beauty, through utilising as much natural stone and local materials as possible.

A mix of permanent and temporary structures

The EOK concept concerns large-scale, portable structures, which could save lives and provide shelter in areas such as flood plains. Laurence in particular is currently working on designs for large scale gyroscopic dwelling-structures.

Laurence says, *"We first conceived of the EOK house as an emergency structure to cater to the needs of mass homeless people often gathered in areas of limited, or even no infrastructure including roads. With this in mind no section of the EOK is too large to be flown on site. Quite obviously the sheer size of the structure will require a seriously large budget to build just one. But it is, of course, my greatest ambition that these structures would be mass produced along similar lines to cars or aircraft. As well as emergency needs this would also make the cost of house building affordable to many more people globally, as well accessing the flood plane, earthquake regions and other usually inappropriate land spaces, or even shallow coastal waters. I feel that once we have learned to live comfortably in places we have until now considered hostile, to human well being, far from being overpopulated, this planet could probably handle several more times the numbers here at present."*

Life at HHF
Laurence and Brigitte write:

"Rainmakers, chanters and cloud callers have passed this way, with shamanic magic in their spirit bags and eyes on mother earth and her little needs. Odd, that the meteorological office here, has declared that we are in danger of losing our semi-desert status. We have experienced three unusual years, with

Laurence and Brigitte

much more rain and humidity than recorded in the last decade. We all know that the climate is undergoing a process of change. The wind,. butterflies and birds, and all other connected strands, collude, and we are in a state of responding and listening to our planet. There is abundance (A BUN DANCE), of water here but the wealth of this land just passes through, taking the top soil with it. The deluge that shared the opening of our festival dampened the fire dragon dance, just a little. However. It did provoke almost libertine release from the tension of atmospheric build up and arrival. The colour of the lightning strikes was amethyst, Patricia led the mad caprice with every muscle and sinew devoted to dance. Woman inspired and inspiring.

For us down here in the Spanish winter sun, the year 2002 had a more balanced and accommodating feel. This is the time of anchoring and establishing for our nine committed guardians and we have two more waiting in the wings who we are happy to say are taking their time to make the decision that becoming part of a social and ecological experiment is something they would willingly elect to do!

Tabernas, the local town over the mountain, have accepted our presence and the constant stream of colorful ESTRANGEROS (strangers). They are interested in our project and are inclined to support ethical tourism. Just for the birds, we intend to have one of the landing stages for happy travellers on their migration pattern down South. Our club HHF has a necessary upper limit of 2,000, making sure that the facilities and capacities of this fragile ecosystem are not over-taxed. From the club members we already have a plethora of potential alternative health and related disciplines. THERE ARE MANY ethical and social questions that would warrant guided conferences and workshops. THERE is minimum electrical stimulus here, and the delight of this wild place is the time it gives you just to experience being, with accentuated weather sensitivity. (Please leave message for Bri at: www.harmonic-healing.com if you are interested in running workshops or want to get in touch with us.)"

In the future it is hoped to continue to encourage and support ideas that are in step with making this a viable community. Events for the whole family are planned including a mummers' play, music and arts festivals and children's activities. After each outdoor event participants are invited to stay on and help with the building of the community either through picking olives, planting seedlings or whatever.

They are planning to have an annual festival probably around September each year. Check out the HHF website for details. They are keen to invite people who would like to run craft stalls, small stands and develop fun ideas. Their festivals are based upon acoustic sounds, not what they call, *"electrical dominance".* They say: *"We are offering sound around the mountains for drummers, didgerido players, guitarists, inventive musicians, shy singers and all the other members of the cast. We aim to inspire each other under the stars as full moon lights the natural drama of this beautiful wildness. A superlative backdrop! Remember to send love and light to us here down in the canyon, we need your continued support. Lighten up the dark spaces."*

Living Small and in Community in Tasmania
Mary Jenkins

Since realising how happy I can be in a tent, my homes have been small but always with a view to the outside that keeps my spirits up. I learnt about a sense of place and happiness being in wild environments – as they seemed to me – when I was a child camping in English bluebell and rhododendron woods where once I experienced a magpie resting on my hand. I am still most content when I am in the bush, living outside as much as possible, and boiling the billy. Now I mostly spend relaxing times around a 5 x 4 metre timber shack that I own with friends. It is hidden amongst eucalypts and diverse understorey in 80 acres of wild life sanctuary, close to the sea and buffering others in the small community, called Cascade Housing, who have purchased land without intentions of logging or major development.

But there's a urban side to the moulding of my character. I was born in London. Half my life has been spent in Europe, mainly in London, but also in Sweden, France, Switzerland and Spain, and the latter half of my life in Australia: Sydney, Brisbane and Tasmania. When I first moved to Tasmania my Sydney friends thought it far too parochial a place for me. Of course it is not, but my response was: 'why not Hobart – Paris?'. And Paris (and other parts of France) is where I have been for several weeks, enjoying architecture that continues to amaze me, squares so well suited to human

Mary at her front door

interactions; churches as places of spirituality, peace and art; and poetry and music – music everywhere. I was swept up with a crowd on the night of summer solstice into Le Palais de Justice (law courts). In every salon there was music and, during the interval, a spectacular event, all of which made me forget how tired I was after walking all day enjoying the museum that is Paris. In the square of St Sulpice there was lively weeklong poetry and a book fair; and in the town hall, cafes and bars around the square there was an English-French poetry festival. Yes, culture, free and for everyone.

Now I'm back to a wintry Hobart, enjoying the mountain with its tentative sprinkles of snow, and nature more than culture, but I have just seen a film that was running concurrently with

Cascade's passive solar homes

147

those advertised in Paris: *Moulin Rouge.* Literally fantastic but still reminding me of Paris and my time in an apartment lent to me for a night in Ville-Paris, just around the corner from the jaded old art of Montmartre, and the churches of Sacre Coeur and St. Pierre with its Salvador Dali windows.

Cohousing in Hobart
What a change to be in my Hobart home, part of a cohousing venture of fourteen houses – strata title houses around a common house – a property that I share with close to thirty adults and children. An essential for the site choice was that it had to be within cycling distance from the city centre. There is an excellent bus service and a bus-stop outside our

Cascade cohousing with Mount Wellington above

entrance. A little under half of our land has been left for regrowth (and bandicoot habitat), orchard, community gardens, chickens and cubby house.Planning started about eleven years ago with houses built in stages. The choice of building materials was difficult for us all. Building is not an ecological process. All one can do is try to make it the least damaging possible. We all had to make our own decisions but generally opted for smaller than usual houses and to use materials and finishes that were the least damaging biologically. We are a diverse group with no dominant ideology but I think its safe to say that we have ecological leanings.

Many of our practices have become ecological habits as we re-use, recycle, and reduce by sharing clothes, cars and equipment. We garden 'organically' and endeavour to use non-toxic substances – for example, bi-carbonate of soda and

vinegar for our cleaning.

Many of our houses are built with aerated concrete (Hebel blocks) which are perfect for limewashing and rendered finishes and complementary with the timbers we have used. The lime washing of my interior Hebel block walls – with lime and yellow ochre dug from the site – cost less than $30.00 for three coats. The interior walls 'breathe', while the outside rendered walls have a small amount of Bondcrete added for weatherproofing, so there is never mould or dampness in the house. I notice colours, textures and patina and have always enjoyed the warm toned ochres and limewashes of Europe as well as the ancient stones of buildings and the patterned cobbles of streets. So when we were about to build I collected leaves, bark and stones so that we could plan textures and colours that would blend with our bushy environment.

Now the last house is about to be built. For the early cohousing dwellers the mud and building site environment has not been easy but we are now settled in, enjoying the relationships that have developed and mellowed over the years. We try to make up for the loss of traditional social community by sharing time and chores with each other as well as cars and dreary objects like washing machines and lawnmowers. To give you an example of interactions: one of our families is about to depart for two years. We're sad they are going. I will miss them, including the children. I have been involved with their growing up. You need help to pack up a house and to move. Help has been available, baby sitting as well as packing; and the use of the common house for the week they are without home and goods. Many of the things they are not taking are stored under one of the other houses. A cohouser's friend, who has already shared meals and other times with us, is renting their home. Another friend, who stays with us at times, is supplying energy and his truck so that removal costs are reduced.

Living small
My neighbour and I shared our finances and energies to build together on one site and, for me, it was a most rewarding and learning experience. My

50m² home is classified as an 'auxiliary dwelling'. There is a mezzanine bedroom – officially storage because of the steep narrow ladderlike stairs – a small downstairs bedroom-study with adjoining bathroom, and French windows which open onto a small deck which has enough space for an outdoor table and benches. My livingroom-kitchen also has French windows which open onto an outdoor sitting area and garden. Views from all of my windows show native vegetation or fruit trees. A skylight in the mezzanine gives me much valued extra light and a view of trees, sky and stars. Because I have built such a small home storage is limited. Sometimes I think of adding storage space but then I remind myself of the third 'R', 'reducing', which is more difficult than 'reusing' and 'recycling' – and a clearout starts again.

I appreciate the ease of housekeeping a small home and the warmth of my well insulated passive solar house but my floor-heating failed. After a three year long battle I was compensated for the 'one in a million' failure. I bought cosy slippers, added another layer of curtains to improve insulation and decided not to bother with replacing electric floor heating. I have a small (1k) electric heater which is adequate. Hobart, like most cities, has air pollution problems, so most of us decided against woodheaters with a compromise plan for one in the Common House. This hasn't happened and perhaps never will as there are now moves in Tasmania against the use of woodheaters. Hebel blocks are efficient insulators but a single layer does not entirely buffer noises from my neighbour. This may be a problem for others but I find the sounds comforting rather than annoying.

Valuing friendship

When I look at all the work that has been done on site it is satisfying yet there is always more needing care and winter shows what summer growth conceals.

Soon, though, trees in my small private garden – some grown from kernels – will be blossoming and fruiting, and I will look across to my neighbours gardens and trees, including walnut, cherry, nectarine, apple and pear – and that's a joy. I wonder why it is that I have never planted fruit trees before. Planning and sharing the communal gardens, as well as the working 'Bs', increase my knowledge as well as my outside activities. When I was away this was what I thought about the most. I wanted to prepare for Spring. One of the reasons I am in Tasmania is the pleasure of the seasons: the time for darkness and introspection and the gradual coming of the light that we are experiencing just now, post winter solstice.

It's always interesting for me to return from a trip – glad that, always, someone is prepared to do the airport run, to take care of plants, and to feel so secure about my home and friends, knowing that I can get all the privacy and peace that I need. There are fresh eggs in the pantry and stores that will keep me going until I shop, as well as dinners in the common house three nights of the week which I can share if I wish. I'm single now, the oldest member of the group and value friendship above all.So, for this traveller, Hobart is home. It's important for me to put roots down after such an itinerant life. If I were to give myself a title it would be as an ecologist. I try to work towards the good health of animals – including people – and planet. I just want to keep on growing without the use of toxic herbicides and pesticides and to support those who also try to work organically. I want to continue trying to do what I can with others to stop the loss of forest in an endeavour to maintain diverse habitats for creatures that are fast losing their places in the world.

A community meal outside the Common House

149

Women's Land Wales: sojourn in an eco-feminist utopia
Rachel Auckland

I came to Women's Land by a winding road: In my early teens I fled a 'nice' but violent home, and survived in squats until my daughter could crawl. I gradually progressed via council temporary accommodation and a short-life, hard to let inner city flat to reasonably stable, decent, subsidised social housing in South London. Still I faced stigma and prejudice as a single parent which prevented me from finding work. I endured repeated threats of eviction each time my life changed and interrupted my housing benefit claim, for example when I took a lodger, studied for my degree – whenever I attempted to improve my lot.

Despite environmental reservations, getting a van proved extremely empowering, allowing me to trade junk from yuppies' skips at car boot sales and to travel to festivals. How very 80s! Indeed, this was the Thatcher era in Britain, the time of coal disputes and Greenham Common Women's Peace Camp. Unemployed youngsters and homeless families were taking to the road in droves. I adopted a semi-itinerant lifestyle, sublet my substandard flat and 'worked my ticket' round a circuit of alternative camps by providing child care and home-education support to other nomads.

After a heady couple of summers of apparent freedom I began to question the libertarianism of a scene which seemed unable to genuinely deal with its own sexism, ageism and homophobia. Everywhere women were struggling to create safe spaces. Throughout the 1990s I was involved in organising accessible camps for women and children.

I seem to remember women raising money in London to buy land. The idea of women's land was so charged with potent political and spiritual symbolism. The moment someone gave me directions I struck out.

On the first visit I hitch hiked with my 11 year old daughter to West Wales. It was a long, hard ride. At that time, if you wanted to escape the drug problems plaguing inner cities, you'd retreat to places like this to set up your utopian alternative. We arrived to find the streets of the little market town thronging with other seekers and settlers.

After a long walk alongside a snaking river the ground rises sharply, the road becomes a track into woodland and eventually brings you to the place – marked by a triangular metal letter box embossed with rusting Celtic knot work and perched on the stump of a tree the path to Womynsland.*

The main house

Probably the tiniest corner of this Earth ever to declare UDI, this feminist nation spans an acre and a half of hillside so green it's called blue in the local dialect. At any given time the population may surge up to a dozen or more, especially in the warmer months, but in all, by now Womynsland probably has about a thousand ex-pats scattered round about, women who have come, stayed a while, moved on.

The long, rutted driveway is lined with hazel, holly and blackthorn which form a kind of processional arch. In season the hedge banks are carpeted with snowdrops, primroses, violets, wild strawberries, bluebells and so on. A squat stone farm house appears, with a run of barns and outbuildings resourcefully converted to provide rudimentary dwellings.

Idyllic, but life seemed impossibly hard there to begin with – stealing as much unseasoned pine as we could carry from the nearby forestry plantation; trying to light the Rayburn range, which soon became clogged with resinous soot. If you got a fire going, having to burn loo paper because otherwise the cess pit would block – you couldn't dig a shit pit since the water table is so high, the lawn is virtually a bog.

Fetching whole food from the fabulous, funky hippy-run Post Office in the village entailed a ten minute walk there and half an hour's climb back up a steep, muddy footpath. Cooking took place in a cauldron in the massive fireplace. Food was shared with all comers. There was, for a long time, a jam jar in the kitchen for womyn to make their

Some of the outbuildings

pound a day contribution, but the system was never fool-proof.

I admired the hardiness and commitment of those who stayed, but questioned some of the more extreme political views which formed in the hot-house of this absolutely female-only space.

On my next visit I came in a transit van. I helped a friend to move down from London to live. I shall never forget that journey. We slept the first night (myself, my daughter, my friend and her two large dogs) on top of all her worldly goods in the back of the van on a garage forecourt in the Cotswolds, in sub-zero temperatures, awaiting delivery of a replacement water pump. We were lucky to make it to Wales before snow closed the roads. On arrival we slept – or rather tried to sleep – in one of the barns, on a mattress on a palette, under a mountain of freezing bedding. Hot water bottles and dogs' breath only melted the ice on our blankets making them less stiff but more wet.

In the morning we got a fire going in an oil drum, which went some way to driving out the cold and damp, but it was never what I'd call comfortable. My transit van was put to good use hauling a winter's supply of logs out of the forest; stocking up on sacks of spuds and flour; taking the dogs to the vet.

Later that year women rigged up electricity to the barns and to a large caravan, in which another friend made her home for three

Images of women's creativity

years. This has gone a long way to improving the quality of life here, but is used with immense discretion, so that bills never represent more than a tiny fraction of household outgoings.

My third visit took place in the summertime. After a Spiral women's camp, temporary structures were dismantled and brought here for maintenance and storage. We found a tidy, well stocked tool shed available for use. We set to work in the sunshine, fixing and painting dome poles. By now, there was a bustling atmosphere with many women in residence in an assortment of barns, tents and mobile homes. There was a beautiful, cosy bender on the lawn. One couple occupied a tipi in the lovingly tended vegetable garden. Another had tucked their library bus home alongside the hedge. Outbuildings had a homely look about them, reminiscent of Doris Day's log cabin in Calamity Jane, with cotton print curtains and cast iron stove pipes.

Everywhere were vivid images of the power and magic of women's creativity, given space to flourish – sculpture, painting, horticulture, writing, music. In the evening women and girls gathered on the front porch to eat and sing together. After sun down a fire was lit beneath the outdoor bath tub, filled from an ancient well. There is nothing can compare to the enchantment of bathing under the stars. I cannot overemphasise the importance for women and girls of the right to safe, affordable accommodation and freedom of access to the land, free from the fear of male dominance and oppression.

Over the years, this women's land has been the resort of Traveller women from many countries as well as a refuge for homeless women and those fleeing domestic violence. It has also served as a retreat for Pagan women and a haven for lesbian women. Goddess energy is palpable in the artefacts littering the site, and in the woman-nature linkage which permeates the discourse around 'the land', as it's sometimes known.

When my daughter took her first young baby (a girl, significantly) to live there, I must admit I worried. They lived in a room in the house – a sort of mezzanine loft above the communal bathroom and kitchen. Accessed by climbing through a cupboard type door 3 feet high, half way up the stairs, this space was just wide enough for a mattress on the floor, with scant headroom, storage comprising plastic bags in the tapering gap under the rafters. She laughed grimly as she described to me on the phone how the terry nappies hung to dry in the Dutch barn had literally frozen stiff. But at least she had fresh air and some emotional support.

Again I came to question the ideology underpinning this eco-feminist utopia. Is this place primitive by design or due to lack of resources? The answer is in fact that it's a bit of both. Use of organic, locally produced and at times home grown food, low impact dwelling design and renewable sources of fuel may well contribute to sustainability whilst also keeping costs down – no problem there. But does it need to be so downright uncomfortable? There is an attitude among many of its supporters to say, well yes, it does. To retain its ideal and remain fully inclusive, *open* women's land, great store is set by a kind of underclass politics which makes a virtue of necessity, promoting the move away from materialism. However, beginning to feel the effects to my health after nearly two decades of such self denial, I was starting to break out in a different direction.

By this time I had established reasonably secure accommodation for myself in London. I had graduated and formed a committed relationship. Before long my daughter also resumed her studies. It then transpired that she had a second and then a third daughter. After several moves she eventually rented a lovely but tiny cottage near the Welsh speaking village school and enrolled the eldest. The middle girl was registered in nursery. My partner and I agreed to stay in

Bathing under the stars (Sue Jacob)

Wales for a time, to help with baby care. But there was no way we could fit in that little house. Neither could we afford to rent a place of our own. So we came up with a plan. We became home owners.

For £1,800 we bought a beautifully converted 1967 Austin truck from a young couple who had toured in it for a summer, then settled in the area. Before them it was owned by a Hippy circus performer who had fitted it out with an ex Army workshop box insulated with wood panelled walls; a bed above the cab embellished with Romany style fretwork; perspex windows; a cast iron pot bellied wood burning stove with tiled surround; and a fitted kitchen! Before that I understand it worked as a crane on a scrap yard.

We worked on the truck, got it legal, took it around the circuit of women's camps for the summer, then parked up at women's land, where that mobile library used to stand.

The beautiful truck

Now it has been suggested that vehicles do not constitute ecodwellings, by virtue of the pollution they cause, but I would respond by pointing out that we covered about 500 miles in 2 years, at a top speed of 40 mph, using only a couple of tanks of diesel. In all we used only a fraction of the resources consumed by the average household; and we re-used / recycled much besides.

Julia's mum lent us the folding table her family had used when caravanning throughout Scandinavia. We bought a cloth wardrobe from a catalogue, and a trunk which doubled as storage and seating. For our bed we piled up layers of carpet, foam, sheepskins and cotton quilts. I selected un-breakable kitchenware, and packed a small armful of books to keep me going through the winter. All the rest of our stuff went into storage. It wasn't missed – we had all we needed.

Julia worked hard throughout the autumn to raise the truck up on blocks and weather-proof the porch with rough timber paint and heavy duty polythene side panels. We fixed chicken wire to a palette by way of a back step. We invested in a spare 12 volt battery and charger to run a small fluorescent strip light; plus a quantity of paraffin lamps and candle lanterns. The cooking stove runs off a big cylinder of propane. We decided to buy in a load of wood for the burner, rather than keep trying to rip it off from the forest.

Water came the short distance from the outside tap in polythene butts by wheel barrow. I convinced Julia not to use the drainage pipe from the sink, for fear of it blocking or over-flowing, but to chuck washing up water out into the hedge. We had a nice old enamel bowl and jug for body washing. We peed on the grass in the orchard in the day and our piss pot was emptied with the compost and ash each morning. We still had to use the loo in the house for no.2, but otherwise were entirely independent.

Julia

This very hands-on lifestyle evoked strong feelings of environ-mental embeddedness, self determination and deep joy. I felt more secure than ever I had in former, more communal times. In this sense I thrived.

Some of the residents

However, the economy is pretty depressed in rural West Wales and the nearest work I could find was in the city 50 miles away. So I lodged there three nights a week and returned to spend long week-ends helping with the kids and staying in the truck with Julia.

She resigned her lucrative job as a computer programmer in a finance company and took a year off to fulfil her lifelong ambi-tion and walk – alone and carrying all her own kit – from John O'Groats to Land's End. All through the winter, between reading stories and changing nappies, she studied maps and trained, carrying camping gear up the moun-tains and walking, walking everywhere.

It was a hard winter, terribly cold with fierce winds. The two women who had lived for many years in a static caravan at the end of the paddock gave up and moved into a house in the village, leaving just us, and one other rather anti-social woman who lived in the house. There were very few visitors. It gave J and I the chance to grow very close. I signed up for Welsh language classes at the village school, which also afforded an insight into the life of the farming community.

In the spring we invited a few women to come for a working weekend building a geodesic dome from hazel poles, connected with moulded alcathene pipe and coach bolts. (One prime advantage of women's space is the freedom to develop techni-cal skills without the well-intentioned interventions of men.) Although the event was a success in that the structure was completed and has since been used as a workshop space at women's camps, problems arose over the policy of allowing no boy children on the land.

Then a visitor came down from London offering to organise some Women in Manual Trades trainees to repair the barn door destroyed in the gales. But again the no boys rule proved too divisive at this time when so many lesbians and single women are raising sons as well as daughters. It still remains to be mended.

This seems a great pity when we recall the incred-ible potential of the site to provide a resource for the women's community locally and further afield. It's so perplexing when the local women's group can't find a suitable venue, and at the same time this fantastic space is going to rack and ruin.

I have heard stories of women's lands in other

The truck at Womynsland

countries – France, Denmark, New Zealand, Australia – which are more sustainable because they are more appropriately structured and funded. I reckon we could do that here given the chance.

There is a glimmer of hope: One zealously separatist disabled woman has bought a few acres of cheap, ex-forestry land on a nearby mountainside and is painstakingly clearing it of the debris of 30 years monoculture, donating firewood to Womynsland (still pine, but at least it's seasoned) and replacing it with a mixture of indigenous trees. She lives in a small van which she shunts between the two sites, but is amassing materials to put up a 'shed' – i.e. a structure with no foundations, for which one doesn't need planning permission, and which is not for habitation as such, but can help with providing precious extra space for work and storage.

Inspired by this, another idealistic novice Traveller woman, who has been parked here for a year, has started raising 250 oaks from acorns and is hoping to raise enough money to buy a neighbouring field, to extend Women's Land, reforest the hillside and pay off her lifetime's carbon debt.

A further recent addition to the community, a practical lass from Northern England, spent last Autumn attempting to build a straw bale house in the paddock but was defeated by the unrelenting Welsh rain. However, undeterred, she is now trying instead to erect a wooden framed roundhouse using reclaimed timber (the omnipresent palette!).

And the rock-steady Asian woman who joined during the Winter has organised a stall at the town's fair, selling vegan crocheted hats, bags, socks and mobile phone holders (!) to raise funds for expanded metal to line the sides of the planned compost toilet.

Between them this group have reclaimed the house as communal space for residents and visitors, and begun to re-establish the organic vegetable garden. They also put on a Landyke gathering this summer, attracting some 20 odd women from around Ireland, England and a couple from a women's commune in the Outer Hebrides. As well as cooking and eating together and helping with general gardening and maintenance chores, the women offered workshops such as drumming, shiatsu, and tools sharpening. They brought news of women's self-build projects on the Gower, woodland skills courses on the coast; and crafts to trade – candles and hammocks for example.

This 'experiment in living' as it has been described, may not be so technologically impressive as some of its male-led counterparts. There are no expensive solar panels or exciting new materials to be found here. But I think this project is significant none the less because of the opportunities it creates for women to participate in sustainable development. The value of this is summed up in the beautiful, gentle campfire song:

by our hearts be we women
and by our lives be we spirit
and by our eyes be we open
and by our hands be we home

Meanwhile Julia and I have bought a little house near the city, with spare bedrooms for the kids and some mod cons including a working Rayburn. We intend to establish an eco-friendly lifestyle here, involving teleworking, gardening, cycling and recycling, but one which is free from the worst rigours of communal living.

For the time being the truck still stands at women's land, packed full of women's camp equipment and ready to move once a new site emerges. I'm unsure what will become of it. I don't want to part with it if I can help it, as it's become a home from home and means so very much to me; but it will need to earn its keep somehow – maybe by taking temporary women's space to Green Gatherings?

I don't know what the future holds for Wimminsland either, but I do know that I'd like to retain some kind of a connection to that tiny corner of Wales, and everything it represents.

*There is no received spelling of the term; rather, feminists use various spellings to uncouple the word 'women' from 'men' and to emphasise political and spiritual linkages between wimmin (etc.) and the land.

Living the Cohousing Lifestyle
Gerry Kilganon

"I'll come and get my plant, now", says Jean, as she heads for the lower atrium to get a small handcart. "I really appreciate you looking after it while I was away." When she returns to my place, we load up her miniature tree and trundle it off to the south wing of our building to her place. Jean and her husband Ray are retired now and spend two months every winter in sunny California in their 5th wheel trailer and are just now getting settled back into life here at Windsong Cohousing. Several people are sitting around in the alcove across from Jean's place sharing dessert after dinner.

"Come and have a bowl of strawberries" invites Leah, as I leave Jean's place. So I join my neighbors and catch up a bit on what's happening in their daily lives. Some of their children come and go as we visit. Michael comes by and we all welcome him home after a two week absence. "I think Teresa might like you to stop by. She's working on the accounting and I think has a few questions for you", says Leah. I have recently passed on the book-keeping responsibilities to Teresa after having been the community's volunteer book-keeper for the past 6 years (during

Gerry in her garden

construction and since we moved in July 15th, 1996). I walk down the atrium and join Teresa who is sitting in front of her neighbor Kevin's computer entering data. The accounting is kept on Kevin's computer because Teresa's children use theirs so much, she has a hard time getting to use it. We work on the few questions she has and I leave her to return to the quiet of my own place to read for awhile, take a relaxing hot bath and go to bed.

This kind of neighborly interaction is typical of life here at Windsong Cohousing located in the suburb of Langley, near Vancouver, British Columbia, Canada.

Who are we? We are just over 60 adults and around 45 dependent children; some of whom are young adults who come and go a bit. We have people living here ranging in age from 1 year to almost 80. All adults and occasionally some of the children contribute to the decision making and the maintaining of the community. Each person contributes in some way. We have no staff, so everything is done by our residents except jobs requiring expertise which we don't have, For example. we don't have a plumber among our people, but we do have an electrician. We are each responsible for our own home maintenance, but we help each other in many ways.

We are able to help each other through temporary illnesses or disabilities, such as the flu or broken ankles, etc. We have had two babies born here and each time, people organized meal preparation for a couple of weeks after the births.

Windsong Cohousing, like most cohousing in North America, is legally a condominium, which means that each private unit is owned by a person or persons and the common areas are owned by what is known here in B.C. as a

The atrium at Windsong

Strata Corporation. The Strata Corporation is owned by all the unit owners. The original members of our community worked with the architects and builders to design the building and the landscaping. Most of us have been living here since July 1996.

Our community has 34 units, made up of 8 x 1 bedroom and den units, 19 x 3-bedroom units and 7 x 4-bedroom units The units are located in two equal size wings with a 5,000 sq. ft common area in between. The units face each other with a 16 foot glass covered street in between the units in each wing. This row housing design, with the units having common walls saves on the use of energy for heating. Everyone furnishes and decorates the front of their unit as they choose. So there is an interesting variety of furnishings and plants and trees in pots along the street. The streets allow us to go anywhere in the development under cover. This is a great feature in this rainy climate. Also it facilitates interaction among the residents.

Inside the glass covered street

Seeing Alan walking by in the atrium. I stick my head out the door and call to him. "Thanks for reminding me about that meeting we coordinators need to have. You say you want to have it before you leave on your camping trip? Is it the end of this month that you leave? OK how about Sunday night, for you. "That's fine for me," Says Alan. "Let's meet in the lounge off the dining room. I'll see if the others are available at that time." I say.

Here comes Julia with Nancy's big white dog on a leash. Nancy is away for a few days and eleven year old Julia, who is unable to have a dog of her own (Her family has 2 cats) is conscientiously and lovingly looking after Sparky. Her best friend Lani has been away all weekend, so Julia has had Sparky with her almost all the time.

Our common area consists of the two covered streets and a common house which is a storey and a half. It totals approximately 5000 sq. ft. The upper floor has a guest room and a multi-purpose room that is used for exercising, small meetings, workshops, kids parties or whatever. The main floor has a large entrance area we call 'The Square'. Off of it is a dining room and kitchen, craft room, teen room, laundry, playroom, office and 3 bathrooms (one for the exclusive use of people using the guest room and one in the playroom) The main floor has wheelchair ramps. We have one young woman who has cerebral palsy and can only get around in a wheelchair.

Our building sits in one corner of 6 acres, most of which is wetlands. A small creek runs through this swampy area. Because the wetland area is officially designated as fish habitat it is protected by a covenant which restricts any human encroachment. We just enjoy the sight of all the greenery, the sounds of the birds and the smells of nature.

Some units have small yards. Some have none. We have a lawn and community garden behind the building. as well as individual plots for those people who want to have their own gardens. The community garden and all the landscaping is cared for by our two outdoor teams made up of both adults and children who have chosen this as their contribution to the community's upkeep. We use no chemical pesticides or fertilizer anywhere on the property, indoor or outdoor. Living together on this common property as we do, eliminates the need for every family to have a lawn mower, as is the case in most suburbs.

We have both underground and surface parking. Everyone has a car, with many families having two and sometimes more. We are located in a suburb of Vancouver and like most North American metropolitan areas was built to accommodate cars. Our public transit system is very inconvenient and not efficient, which is a source of much frustration by us who care about the environment. Some of us do car sharing, rather than have 2 cars and several of our residents work from home.

Allan has set up a committee to look at the parking problem here. He is in the process of soliciting creative suggestions from all the members of the community. He is using our Internet Service, Communi-Link to start a discussion on this issue. Ken, one of our residents built the service to help us communicate with each other and provide access to the community information we all need, such as meeting minutes, policies and instructions about everything and anything.

When I arrived home today, I found Marj, who is on Allan's committee, out in the parking lot pacing out spaces for more parking. She thinks we may have to cut down a couple of old trees to make way for the cars. The trees are in very bad shape anyway. This kind of decision will have to be approved at a community meeting.

Community meetings are held monthly. Proposals, such as recommendations for solving the parking problem are presented to everyone in the community by various means (our internet service: Communi-Link, telephone voice mail, bulletin boards and at a previous meeting for clarification and input) so everyone knows what is being proposed. Decisions are then made by consensus, after much discussion. The type of consensus decision making we use is one in which everyone does not have to wholeheartedly support the decision. They must, however, at least support it enough to not block it. We very rarely have everyone attending meetings, so we operate on the assumption that everyone has been informed of the upcoming proposals and therefore if they do not express objections, they must support the decisions being made by those attending the meetings. Of course that is not always the case.

We explain to potential buyers that they are buying a lifestyle. We tell them they are buying a share in a community, not just a dwelling; that we manage the community ourselves and the expectation

is that all residents will contribute in some way. For me, the biggest advantage to living here is a having a perfect balance between privacy and community. I say perfect, because I can determine the balance myself. I have my own space in which to spend as much time as I want and right outside my door is a variety of people to be with. We have the evening meal prepared once or twice a week by volunteer residents, for which we pay our share of the cost of ingredients. Otherwise we can choose to prepare our own meal or participate in a pot luck meal every other day or just take our own prepared dinner to the dining room and be in the company of others. We do many things together, such as gardening, cleaning the building, discussing books or other topics, going off-site to plays or concerts. We have our own concerts here occasionally. They generally involve both children and adults. Great fun!!! One of our residents is an excellent pianist, so we have many impromptu sing-songs after dinner.

None of my children or grand children live near-by, so this community acts as an extended family for me. I can have as much interaction with the children as I want. That goes for all of us. All the children know us by our first names. One of our young couples who has a 1 year old has been able to arrange child care right in the community when they need it. There is quite a bit of child care sharing and car pooling to school or swimming lessons, and other activities among the families of young children.

I feel safe here. I hardly ever lock my door. My feeling of safety comes from knowing everyone who lives here. We lock all the outside doors of the building at night and some during the day. One volunteer job is to go around and check all the doors and windows every evening. One of the people doing that right now is our oldest resident, a woman, 78 years old. We have had some thefts, but I do not feel personally in any danger.

In summary, I cannot imagine being happy with any other lifestyle at this time in my life. The biggest benefits for me are being able to have my own space, contribute to decisions about how the community will function, participate in social opportunities and be part of a very supportive community.

A community meal in the common house

Not an ending
but a beginning

Not an ending, but a beginning
Alan Dearling

"...buildings to become extensions of their environments..."
Frank Lloyd Wright

"...dwellings which become extensions of ourselves and our lifestyles..."
Alan Dearling

At the end of the process which has produced this book, I realise just how much I've learned from trying to engage with the diverse range of people, ideas and ideals encountered on the journey. It's been part of a highly personal journey – one which hasn't ended yet! I don't know who said it first, but there aren't really any answers, just a longer list of questions! Having said that, I hope that the examples of dwellings, lifestyles, communities and individual quests presented here, even when relaying somewhat contradictory messages, have enthused and energised. Maybe they've even offered some sense of hope amidst the challenges.

What has certainly become a lot clearer for me, if it's not a non-sequitur, is that 'eco-dwelling' as a chosen activity isn't something 'out there' in splendid isolation. At a practical level, we can all do it, to a greater or lesser extent. We can actively choose to make our dwellings become extensions of ourselves and our lifestyles. If we want to live more sustainably, placing a smaller footprint on the earth, our dwellings can

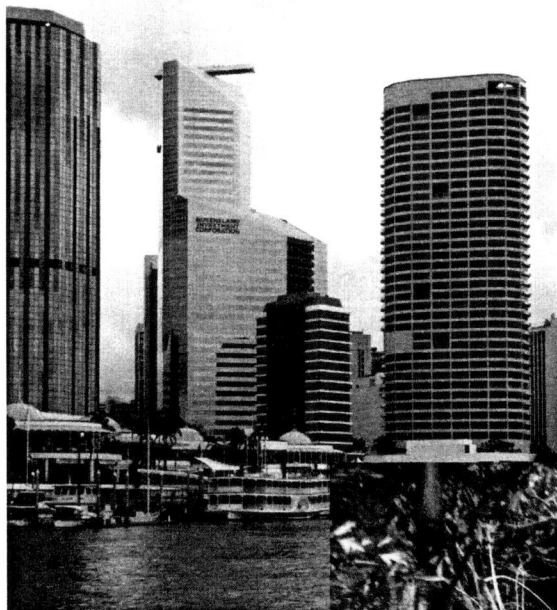

Which sort of dwelling for our futures?

become an integral part of our lifestyle. At a more abstract level, it's a part and parcel of the first law of ecology, namely that is, the law of integrated systems, what Arne Naess has called 'ecosophy', with its philosophy of ecological harmony and integration. Without

too great an effort, it can become an essential part of all our lives, whether we are considering an issue such as where exactly to live, what to live in, recycling, public transport or thermal insulation, be it in the Blue Mountains of New South Wales, Australia; Eugene in Oregon, a mobile home in the South of France or an apartment in London.

Without moves towards sustainability in many of the ways we've read about, the whole built environment remains what James Wines says is: *"more a part of the problem than the solution"* or in the words of Le Corbusier, the earth is a *"machine for living in"* – but handle her with extreme care!

When we set out to create this book, at that time both based at Queensland University of Technology in Brisbane, Australia, Graham Meltzer and myself had a 'wish list' for what lives and dwellings would be represented in Part Two. Here's what we wrote:

Free spirits: Gypsies, Travellers and nomads
From traditional tribal dwellings such as tipis, benders and yurts to modern nomadic structures including geodesic domes, converted vehicles, caravans and boats.

Pioneers: innovators, artists and craftspeople
Shelter as a lifestyle statement. Examples of building with natural materials in both rural and urban settings. Experiments with unconventional building materials and styles including: mudbrick, straw bale, underground shelters, bamboo and more. Designs for the new millennium using energy efficient and appropriate technologies.

Collectives: extended families, communities and tribes

Real life stories and examples of collaborative housing and communal living including communes, cohousing, squats, intentional communities and sustainable regeneration.

We had always aimed to try and share something important about their lifestyles and dwellings. A year and a half later, and a bit wiser, I find myself finishing this book largely on my own. For a variety of reasons, Graham, having successfully been awarded his doctorate, has temporarily or permanently, abandoned academia. I wish him well. I think that the selection that has ultimately been assembled does offer a window into some very different worlds. In addition to a Cook's Tour through the byways and green lanes of environmentalism, a fair amount of commentary and information about the need for active partnerships between the 'professionals' of the building world: architects, planners and developers and the residents and potential residents has been introduced and some debate about eco-tourism.

Then, in the 'heart' of the book: Part Two, we have collated the experiences of a number of *free spirits, pioneers* and *collectives.* These include indigenous people of Mongolia, newer nomads of the UK and Europe and traditional Romany Gypsies; through to the pioneers and innovators of the long-distance scrap raft: the Floating Neutrinos; the Vales' autonomous house and the return to underground shelters in China; forest eco-tourism operators in Australia and Turkey; and then finally the communards such as Peter Cock and Bob Rich, the co-housing collective of Windsong in Canada and Ruigoord experiment in the Netherlands.

A building workshop

The personal choices of the people we've met, both for dwellings and lifestyles, encompass a style-preference range from 'luddite' to 'techie'. For most people, their own choice will be somewhere in between a return to peasant society, joining an intentional community, or life in a future sci-tech movie-drome. But it is great that we can learn from the experimenters and pioneers of the eco-dwelling world!

Neither this book nor our lives exist in a time capsule. The way people are choosing to live in society is experiencing a sea change. Thomas Schmitz-Günther hasn't needed a particularly prescient crystal ball to be able to

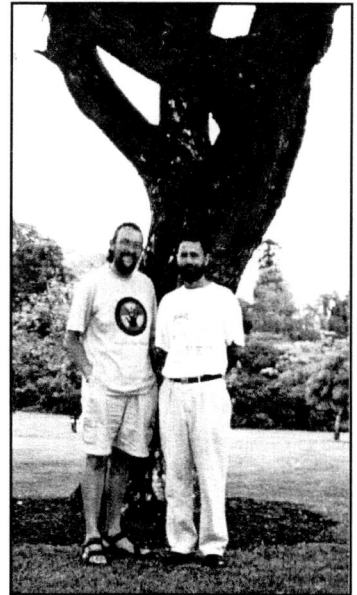
Alan with Graham in the Botanic Gardens in Brisbane

note: *"...households are also becoming smaller and less 'conventional' in terms of make-up. The nuclear family is no longer the norm...there is a trend towards living in groups."* (Günther, 1999)

And alongside this, there are also increasing demands for dwelling spaces for single people of all ages, but particularly young and old, and single parents and their offspring. People are also increasingly working from home, which can save on transport-related environmental degradation, but may increase isolation. Therefore, a major consideration when looking at what is required in 'eco-dwellings' in the widest sense, is how they can help combat social isolation, provide positive aspects of community for those who seek it, and as the same time provide, affordable, sustainable, healthful living, working and recreational spaces and environments.

Shelter really isn't enough for all people. Shelter is by definition impermanent, whilst dwellings should, with the help of sympathetic and creative input from architects and builders, offer aesthetic appeal and technological improvements to ensure that they are more sustainable in all that the term implies. We should strive for more than shelter, even while recognising beauty in simple and natural found and built forms which are 'native' (vernaculus) in different societies. Le Corbusier called the inhabitants of deserts and African mud huts, *"men in tune with the fundamentals."* (quoted in Oliver, 1969) In more complex societies even recognising those fundamentals can pose a problem. Through enabling more connections to be made between ideas, and between sources of information and knowledge, between people and organisations and networks, this process can be encouraged. Books, the Internet and involvement in meetings and information exchange, in the street, and at community, national and international levels, are all a part of this process. The essence of the process is to reintroduce and re-birth dwellings that have souls, even a little magic. Maybe that is central to what Wines has called the 'environmental revolution' – a revolution which may still prove as radical in its effects as its previous agricultural and industrial counterparts.

For me, I have managed to find a bit of that magic, a bit of that revolution, alive and well in the lives of the people represented in this book. They share a common respect for, and an appreciation of, the environment. If we and they cannot be at one with the environment, we cannot be at one with ourselves. If we can, we are in a proper *bofœllesskab,* Danish, according to McCament and Durrett (1989) for *a living community.*

So, it seems appropriate that this now becomes your book. Remember that a housing *ex*-pert is someone from the outside. To be effective in the world of eco-dwellings, ex-perts must work *in*-partnership, *in*-the environment, and *in*-tune with all the elements of the people and the dwellings.

I hope that this book provides something for you, your family and friends to write the next chapter of.

Not an ending, but a beginning.

For all our futures

References

McCament, K. and Durrett, C. (1989) *Cohousing: a contemporary approach to housing ourselves.* Ten Speed Press.

Oliver, P. (1969) *Shelter and Society.* Frederick Praeger.

Schmitz-Günther, T. (English edition, 1999) *Living Spaces – Sustainable Building and Design.* Köneman.

Wines, J. (2000) *Green Archtitecture.* Taschen.

Alan